Staking Our Claim
The Fight for Better Housing in the 1970s

A Memoir
Patrick Morrissy

Copyright @2025 Patrick Morrissy

Written by Patrick Morrissy

All rights reserved. No part of this book may be reproduced by any mechanical, photographic, or electronic process, or in the form of a phonographic recording; nor may it be stored in a retrieval system, transmitted, or otherwise be copied for public or private use—other than for "fair use" as brief quotations embodied in articles and reviews—without prior written permission of the author/publisher.

The conversations in the book all come from the author's recollections—they are not written to represent word-for-word transcripts. Rather, the author has retold them in a way that evokes the feeling and meaning of what was said, and in all instances, the essence of the dialogue is accurate.

Published by
Chestnut Street, LLC
Carbondale, Colorado

ISBN: 979-8-218-64245-7

All profits from the sale of this book are donated to Shelterforce.

Qualis Socius
Talis Domus

The motto of the Saint Francis Club:
As the Members So Goes the Club

✦ ✦ ✦

*". . . that sense of fulfillment and reward
that you can only get
when you work to try to build a better world
for your fellow man . . .
you have that deep sense of achievement . . ."*

~ Walter Reuther, 1967

To Rita Morrissy 1920–1995

Mom, you taught me so much more than you know.

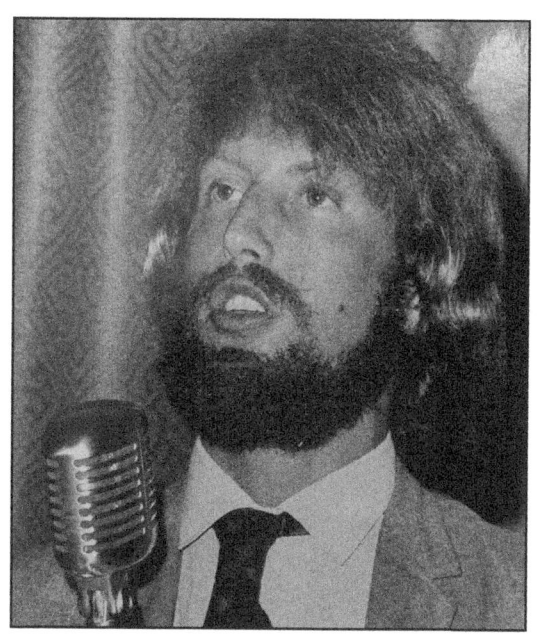

To Ronnie Atlas 1942–1979

You started this whole thing and were taken from us way too soon.

Table of Contents

Introduction:
A Very Fine House — East Orange, New Jersey, 1975 ... 1

Part I: A Long Time Comin'
Chapter 1: There and Back Again.................................. 13
Chapter 2: Changing Times... 23
Chapter 3: Finding Our Groove....................................... 39
Chapter 4: Things Unwinding... 47
Chapter 5: Time to Split for the Coast........................... 51
Chapter 6: A New Direction.. 61

Part II: The Scene is Set (1970–74)
Chapter 7: A Solemn Pact 79
Chapter 8: Welcome to the Oranges............................. 107
Chapter 9: Our Toughest Organizer.............................. 127
Chapter 10: This Old House... 155
Chapter 11: Community, Nonviolence, Resistance... 171
Chapter 12: Settling In 181
Chapter 13: The Battering of East Orange................... 189

Part III: Keep On Keepin' On (1975–76)
Chapter 14: Connecting Nationally 205
Chapter 15: The House Fills Up.................................... 225
Chapter 16: Showdown in East Orange 241
Chapter 17: I Should've Seen It Coming 253
Chapter 18: Ain't No Stoppin' Us Now....................... 271

Part IV: *Stayin' Alive, Stayin' Alive* (1977)
   Chapter 19: No Easy Answers 297
   Chapter 20: Blow Up Your TV 305
   Chapter 21: A New Role and Big Dreams 315
   Chapter 22: Two Steps Forward 335
   Chapter 23: Beware the Wrecking Ball 347

Part V: Taking Our Shot (1978)
   Chapter 24: The Dems Come Calling 357
   Chapter 25: Rage Against the Machine 369
   Chapter 26: Lightning in a Bottle 385
   Chapter 27: The Fight's Not Over 397

Part VI: Unfinished Business (1979)
   Chapter 28: A National Tenants Union 409
   Chapter 29: All Things Must Pass 413
   Chapter 30: Unfinished Business 419
   Chapter 31: Really Shitty News 423
   Chapter 32: Tenant Resource Center
       and a Leadership Battle 427
   Chapter 33: Goodbye, 31 Chestnut 435

The Next Few Years 443

Acknowledgements 449
Selected Bibliography 451
About the Author 453

Preface

It was the fall of 1972 and I was a bit at loose ends when I sat with a new group of people my age. In time we would make a political pact and commit ourselves to the work of uniting ordinary folks, both the poor and the middle class, to build people power and fight back against the forces that were driving up rents and looting our cities. I made that pact with Ronnie Atlas, his brother John, Phyllis Salowe and the rest of their group in Orange, New Jersey.

We were in our twenties and committed to a bond of community, determined to live our values of cooperation and equality. Through collective action, we hoped to create a society that honors those values. We placed a high value on being *political*. We were part of a *Movement*. That was my group. You'll meet them soon.

We were a branch of the New Left, who understood that fighting for bread and butter issues—concerns that the poor, the working class, and the middle class have in common—would build a powerful coalition and a just and equal society.

Our story includes a big house where most of us lived. I was renovating that beautiful old wreck and learning the renovation trades.

This all takes place in East Orange and Orange, New Jersey, two small cities next to Newark, linked in a common struggle. The sibling cities were next in line to suffer Newark's indignities. Seeing those neighborhoods start to deteriorate spurred me on. I know the value of a good neighborhood. They are places that can shape people's lives. People in turn, shape those neighborhoods. And I know what it's like to lose a neighborhood.

The 1970s shaped the next fifty years of my adult life. It was a time of joy, excitement and discovery. I was filled with optimism and hope even as the dark clouds of corporate power and cultural backlash were merging on the horizon. Music was embedded in our politics. Dylan, Joan Baez, Marvin Gaye. They provided the soundtrack.

This book originated in conversations with two amazing coworkers—Wayne Meyer and Kelli Copeland. We worked together, years after the events in these pages took place, helping to restore the neighborhoods of Orange and East Orange. Kelli was curious about the *political 70s* when she was a kid. Wayne always connected the work that our group started with the evolving community development world in New Jersey. Kelli and Wayne told me numerous times, "You should write a book."

This book is written for them and my close community of New Jersey friends who have fought for social justice and built community with me for the past fifty years, and for my children, Campbell, Tim and Claire and for all our children, in the hope that they will achieve the loving society that we all tried to contribute to.

I have a special love for the people who dedicate themselves to the fight for better housing and to keep urban neighborhoods as great places to raise our kids.

I hope you enjoy it.

Pat Morrissy
March, 2025

A Very Fine House —
East Orange, New Jersey, 1975

The thirteen-room Victorian seemed to slowly inhale and then exhale, the only sign that the folks on the upper floors were even there. Mary and Woody were snuggled up behind a closed bedroom door. Mary's boys were probably asleep. Marianne usually slipped away mid-evening to her plant-filled bedroom, the one with its own private porch. She was likely reading or preparing for a morning court appearance. Phyllis and Stu were on the third floor blanketed on their couch, lit by the glow of the TV.

I sat alone in the front parlor-turned-office. It was one of six rooms on the sprawling first floor. WNEW played low on my paint splattered transistor radio, the one with a coat hanger where the antenna used to be. A still-warm joint sat in the ashtray, and my chair was pushed back from the sturdy standard issue oak clerk's desk, the one I got for twenty-five bucks at Atlas Used Furniture down on McCarter Highway. This was my late-night solitary ritual of planning, scheduling, strategizing, sometimes sketching or designing—pushing ahead the projects that currently filled my days, fed my soul, and paid the bills. The *Whole Earth Catalog* had distracted me from my usual routine.

I was twenty-seven when I arrived in my new city, just eighteen months earlier, and connected with this group of politically dedicated, fun-loving, East Coast folks. We lived communally and worked collectively. I was helping Phyllis build the budding tenants association in this rapidly changing city of East Orange, on Newark's western border.

I was renovating the big Victorian that we all lived in. We were hoping we could sustain *Shelterforce*, the national activist publication we'd just launched, and I was consulting on a proposed neighborhood rehabilitation project in Englewood. It was a lot but I was energized, especially about rebuilding this worn and abused 1890s house.

The hefty *Whole Earth Catalog*, whose cover advertised *Access to Tools*, swallowed me like Jonah. Its irresistible vision of self-reliance, small is beautiful, and liberation from consumerism was my new catechism. I read about how to seal the joints between triangular panels when building a geodesic dome, which I wanted to do someday, maybe in the Pacific Northwest like my college buddy Vince Lyons. I thought about how just last week, I'd created my own Windex by adding a small amount of antifreeze to a discarded spray bottle filled with tap water. Strike a blow against the *Consumer Republic*.

Cat Stevens reached out from my radio. The familiar lyrics of his classic ballad *Father and Son* pulled me down a darker street, the street where my dad lived. The lyrics echoed my own dilemma—unable to explain to my dad that I was following my own path not rejecting him. Like the song, I was ordered to listen and I had to go away.

I swept away visions of my six-hundred-miles-away family, without a thought of whether things would ever change. I was building a life and a community here. It was unlikely my two worlds would ever meet. I stacked the *Catalog* back under my other guidebooks and admired my growing collection. *Death and Life of Great American Cities* by Jane Jacobs, Baba Ram Das's *Be Here Now*, *The Timeless Way of Building* by Christopher Alexander, *After the Planners* by Robert Goodman, along with the big yellow Reader's Digest *Homeowner's Guide to Home Repairs* that my mom sent me for Christmas. A worthy library for an urban pioneer in new territory.

Yeah, I thought, *East Orange is changing—that's part of what I like about it. Yes, the house needs a lot of work. A whole lot.* But that was the idea, right? I'd found what I was looking for. A renovation project. A community and a place to belong to and a valuable role in The Movement.

I switched off the radio and then the lights. I double checked the front door lock and headed upstairs. A year earlier I'd set my mind to a plan: Buy a worn-out old house, fix it up, learn the trades, become an urban renovator, join this band of community organizers, and put down roots in the small twin cities of Orange and East Orange, New Jersey.

I always had a plan. When I was a kid, I'd lay in bed Friday nights balanced between planning my Saturday morning and willing myself to sleep so morning would come sooner. Saturday mornings I'd jump from bed the minute my eyes opened. Most kids wanted to sleep late. I wanted to get on with it—with whatever I'd been thinking about all week during school. Plans were not just what I would do, but how I saw myself. If my plan was to ride my bike to the Army Navy store more than a mile away to see how much a bayonet costs, I saw myself as a lone and secretive adventurer. I'd need to lie to my parents and ride on busy streets there and back.

I thrived in that Detroit neighborhood so many years ago. I yearned for that sense of belonging again. My feelings about the big, extended family I'd more recently left behind? Well that was more complicated. I'd call home occasionally, which pleased my mom. Some years I'd drop in around Christmas. But I wasn't going back. That much I knew.

First day of school.
That's me on the left with cousins Maureen and Tom.

PART I

A Long Time Comin'

Christmas 1952

By the 1950s, the economic boom that followed World War II had spread its prosperity widely, at least to Whites, and created a rapidly growing middle class. Blacks, who we referred to as Negroes, had just started to challenge the brutal Jim Crow segregation in the South. Cities were beginning to spawn suburbs. Shopping malls followed quickly behind.

One legacy of the New Deal and the war years that fueled the middle-class growth that my family was part of was a partnership between corporate America, labor unions, and the government. Working together to build a strong economy and to see that its benefits were widely distributed. We wistfully now view that as a form of "democratic capitalism."

In cities like Detroit, companies rapidly expanded to meet the pent up demand for cars, homes, and consumer goods. The consumers were the same union workers, making good wages, who made all those things. Meanwhile the government built highways that connected brand new suburbs and linked cities together and invested in public education and technological research.

After the war, the U.S. was a dominant player on the international stage. In the fifties, my uncle Howard fought in Korea as the U.S. sought to stop the spread of communism. About that time, the CIA supported the overthrow of Iran's Prime Minister when he nationalized the Anglo-Iranian Oil Company and the U.S. helped install a pro-western Shah of Iran. U.S. involvement in Korea and Iran would have very different consequences for our country going forward.

By 1960, when I was a high school freshman, the post-war economy had been charging forward for fifteen years. To my family and many Americans, the White House, with youthful John F. Kennedy and First Lady Jackie, was known as *Camelot*. The staid and uptight fifties of *Father Knows Best* was giving way to a modern, more hopeful and expansive time. The bold young president announced that the U.S. would land a man on the moon before the decade was out. He also announced the creation of a Peace Corps. The Anti-Communist witch hunts of the 50s were over, but Kennedy sent military "advisors" to Vietnam to combat the spread of communism there.

More kids were going to college, experiencing freedom and exposure to new ideas. Soon, a youth rebellion began to percolate, especially on the campuses. In 1963, when I was still double dating at drive-in movies, a small band of college radicals founded Students for a Democratic Society (SDS). Their manifesto, *The Port Huron Statement*, critiqued the alienation of modern life in America. It called for a more just and democratic society built around participatory democracy, economic justice, anti-militarism, and racial equality. SDS believed that change in American society would come through a student-led movement.

I thought racism and bigotry were just problems in the backward South. I was only peripherally aware of the nonviolent civil rights movement. Led by Dr. Martin Luther King Jr. and the Southern Christian Leadership, brave Black citizens and some northern White supporters were integrating lunch counters and Greyhound buses and registering Black voters. JFK and his brother Bobby, his attorney general, finally supported the fight against the segregationist South. Then the civil rights movement moved north to fight segregation and discrimination. On November 22, 1963, President Kennedy was assassinated in Dallas, Texas, and Vice President Lyndon Baines Johnson was sworn in.

Winning Civil Rights battles was slow going, and a growing "Black consciousness" began demanding more progress in the North too. Soon, militant groups challenged Martin Luther King's leadership and questioned the efficacy of non-violence.

Dr. King called on President Johnson to help end discrimination and segregation. Johnson managed to pass the Civil Rights Act of 1964, one of the most far-reaching civil rights laws in American history. He followed that up with a vast federal effort to create a Great Society and declared a "War on Poverty." But Johnson's action on civil rights came at a cost. The Texan did not have the support of Southern Democrats. His bill was the first step in a major party realignment. By 1968, Alabama governor George Wallace was running for president on the American Independent Party ticket. The staunch segregationist won five Southern states and 13.5% of the popular vote nationally.

Plenty of women worked in the war industries, but then they were relegated to a narrow group of job choices. Most women of the vast middle class, like my mom, were stay-at-home moms and housewives. With the creation of NOW, the National Organization for Women in 1965, a feminist consciousness began to grow and the feminist movement was born.

President Johnson authorized the first large-scale draft in 1965 and soon there were 184,000 U.S. troops in Vietnam. A year later, it was 385,000. An anti-war movement was growing among young people and liberals. The first signs of a split in the Democratic coalition appeared when hard-hat construction workers broke up protests and beat up the long-haired protesters.

By the mid-sixties, most of SDS was concentrated on ending the war, organizing student strikes on campuses and using more confrontational tactics designed to provoke a reaction from the police and authorities. They believed this strategy would expose the violent and oppressive nature of the state. The SDS splinter group, the Weather Underground (the Weathermen), engaged in bombings and violent conflicts with the police. Instead of gaining support, these divisive tactics widened the gap between working people and the New Left. In April 1967, Dr. King publicly denounced the Vietnam War.

During the long hot summer of 1967, more than 150 urban Black ghettos erupted in violence. Newark and Detroit saw the most death and destruction while White flight to the suburbs picked up steam.

In March of '68, with over five hundred thousand troops in Vietnam and no end of the war in sight, President Johnson decided against running for a second term. A return of hope arose when Bobby Kennedy threw his hat into the ring. He was seen as the one politician who could bring together Blacks, White liberals, and the White blue collar workers.

A mere month later, Martin Luther King was assassinated. Two months later, so was Bobby Kennedy.

In August at the Democratic Convention, while the Party's peace wing wrangled with the old time political bosses, Chicago police battled young protesters outside in the streets. A federally commissioned report called it a "police riot."

That fall, with promises to restore law and order and get American troops out of Vietnam, the silent majority elected Richard Nixon in 1968 over Minnesota liberal Vice President Hubert Humphrey.

In July of 1969, we watched an astronaut plant an American flag on the moon. In August, three days of Peace, Love and Music near Woodstock, New York, drew a youthful crowd of five hundred thousand. In November, I joined another half million in Washington to protest the war.

Inflation broke the spell of the post-war economic dream, and in 1971, Nixon imposed wage and price controls for ninety days. In a second phase of controls, he included limits on rent increases. Nixon had promised an end to the war; instead, he escalated it with bombing raids into neutral Cambodia. This led to a slew of protests and angry demonstrations. In April 1970, National Guard troops gunned down four students at a protest at Kent State University.

The art world moved outside of museums and galleries; street theater and public art would appear and then disappear. After years of securing approvals, the artist Christo, his wife Jeanne Claude, and a small army of young volunteers that included Jean Campbell, a Wellesley student home for the summer, strung a 1,250-foot wide orange fabric curtain across a river valley in Colorado. In just twenty-eight hours, a wind gust came down the valley, leaving the Rifle Valley Curtain in tatters.

George Wallace won the Democratic Primary in '72 in union-dominated Michigan, my home state. The cracks from the post-World War II coalition were widening. Achieving a Great Society wasn't going to be so easy.

Pony League all-stars with Bill Turner, 1959

CHAPTER 1

There and Back Again

I was midway through fifth grade when our family left Detroit. My dad had gotten a promotion, but it meant we'd have to move. He was the new Traffic Manager at a new Ford stamping plant in Chicago Heights, Illinois. Leaving Detroit was a big deal. At least for me.

My dad's parents emigrated straight from Ireland to Detroit, and my mom's grandparents had done the same from Germany. Aunts and uncles and a swarm of cousins all lived within a mile of us, on Detroit's northwest side. To Mom, leaving all this seemed unthinkable. But Dad told her the naked truth about corporate promotions, "The promotion you turn down is the last one they ever offer you." So off we went. My parents tried to convince me that I'd like it and that I'd make a lot of new friends. There was no way it could be as good a life as I had in Detroit. I was sure of that. But I was an obedient kid. I didn't complain.

Our family was like plenty of American households; my dad started working at Ford's when he was twenty. People in Detroit tended to call the Ford Motor Company "Ford's." With an apostrophe. Probably out of recognition that it belonged to Henry Ford. My dad worked on the assembly line in the upholstery department at the massive

River Rouge plant in Dearborn. He hadn't planned on being on the line long, so he took night classes, and within a couple years he was off the factory floor. He became a Rate Clerk and still worked at the Rouge complex, but now he wore a tie to work. My mom stayed home raising my brother and me and keeping a wonderfully comfortable house. It was all idyllic.

Our neighborhood was mostly one- and two-family brick homes built in the 1920s. Everyone was Irish or German with just a few Italians and one Jewish family on our block. My four grandparents all lived on that block, along with two aunts, an uncle, and two of my dad's cousins. I walked two blocks to St. Francis school, with my cousins Tom and Maureen who lived across the street. We had other cousins three blocks away. I biked around with a pack of friends and played football and basketball for our school. I was a happy kid.

Then my dad got the promotion and we were off to Chicago, leaving behind that cozy neighborhood. I was convinced that no place would ever feel like home the way that neighborhood did. In Illinois, my parents bought a brand new bi-level, one of five models in Longwood Farms, the newly minted tract subdivision at the edge of the gritty and time-worn city of Chicago Heights. A tiny maple tree in each front yard was a reminder that just a year ago, this land had been a cornfield.

I joined the fifth grade class mid-year in a basement classroom at Saint Agnes, a dark stone building from the 1800s that was downright dreary compared to my school in Detroit. But I made some friends; I won and lost marbles on the dusty playground at lunch time, and the next year I played on the basketball team. Then the parish boundaries changed and I started seventh grade at Saint Joseph's in the town of Homewood, a bus ride away, in a different direction. I still recall my first day on the blacktop playground after lunch, standing alone, feeling so conspicuous while groups of guys laughed and joked. One kid, I'll never forget, it was Dick Singler who finally came over and introduced himself. I eventually made a lot of friends; I was adaptable, but something deeper was missing, something I'd left behind in Detroit. A sense of belonging. Here I felt like a nomadic visitor. We were no longer in a city. We lived at the edge of Chicago Heights and I went to school two towns away past farm fields dotted with a few new subdivisions. Downtown Chicago was thirty-five miles away.

Then I caught a break. Bill Turner moved in next door. We were the same age and quickly became fast friends, though I went to Catholic school and he went to public. At the beginning of that summer, Bill brought me along to his Little League practice hoping to convince the coach to add me to the team. Coach said he had a full roster, but after looking me over he told me to step into the batter's box. He was giving me *one* chance. I choked up a little on the bat, like my dad taught me. On the first pitch, I foul tipped. Luckily I got real wood on the second pitch and hit it deep to the gap in right center. I went home with a red Cardinals tee shirt and cap. It was the first of many seasons of summer ball that Bill and I would play together. Our friendship became my anchor.

The Catholic church was a key part of our family life, especially for my dad, a borderline zealot. Two of his brothers were priests. He'd washed out of seminary after two years, something he always seemed to be compensating for. My maternal grandmother said she heard that he was asked to leave because he was too fanatical. I went to

Catholic schools, Mass every Sunday, and became an altar boy. I sold raffle tickets, worked on paper drives, saved money for *Pagan Babies*, and went to confession sorting my venial sins from the mortal ones. Fortunately, no amount of venial sins added up to a mortal sin that would damn me to hell if I died before going to confession. I get shivers when I think back on that guilt-ridden boy scouring his memory of the past week and recalling all the things he'd done and confessing some of them as sins. It was perverse. I never confessed my shoplifting. That wouldn't doom me to hell and I didn't want the priest to order me to pay restitution.

When I was thirteen, a newly ordained priest became our assistant pastor. I liked Father O'Mara instantly. One day after Mass, he asked me if I played hockey. I told him I loved to skate but it was rare to get to play hockey at the public outdoor rink. He said Father Hills, the pastor, gave him the go ahead to use the vacant lot across from the grade school, and he was getting some parish dads to build a rink with boards and lights. Father O'Mara loved hockey. This was Chicago; we'd have ice for at least three months every winter. I told him I wanted to help build the rink and by winter, we were playing at night with boards built from used lumber and some old lights on poles. Father O'Mara, who was probably twenty-seven at the time, was a great hockey player and taught us all how to play like a team. I played every night I could.

It was during eighth grade that I made a shocking decision; I wanted to leave home and go to a seminary. Study to become a priest. I planned to start the next year. Looking back it feels like such a confused decision. I've never been able to answer why I did it. To please my parents? To get away from my dad? Because Father O'Mara was my role model? My dad was supportive, thrilled even, but it was a crazy mistake. I was miserable and had become a "discipline problem." My parents came to pick me up in the spring, and I announced that I wouldn't be coming back. My dad didn't say anything, just shook his head. He knew my mind was made up. We all went to meet with Father Jacobi, the priest in charge, who agreed it was best. Dad hardly said a word on the three-hour car ride home. I imagined him thinking about when he was in seminary and was asked to leave.

My parents insisted that I needed the discipline that priests were known for and enrolled me in an all boys Catholic high school. I gave in and commuted an hour by bus and train to Chicago's south side. Mendel Catholic was a first-rate football power in the famed Chicago Catholic League, but unfortunately it was second-rate academically.

I made some friends, mostly the guys who took the same train from the south suburbs. Then in the spring, hoping to become part of what mattered at Mendel, I showed up for spring football practice. At the end of the month, Coach Magee released the fall roster. There was my name. A third string tackle. Magee was also my geometry teacher, and I knew from my test scores that my final grade would be an 88. Then my report card arrived. Geometry: 93. Football mattered at Mendel.

That summer, I worked full-time at the Dog 'n Suds drive-in. Root beer and hot dogs, eat in your car, carhops, minimum wage, ninety cents an hour. As I sweated over two deep fryers, the thought of summer football practice in mid-August seemed even worse. *What was I doing?* I hated football, and those South Chicago thugs on the team. I wasn't showing up for summer practice.

That meant telling Dad. He just shook his head with a look of disgust that froze my heart. He nagged me about quitting, spitting out the word. He didn't bring up the seminary decision, but I knew he'd branded me a quitter. I wanted to tell him how much I hated the bully culture of the football team, but I knew he'd just add sissy to his list. I was six feet tall, two hundred pounds, but felt small and ashamed in the face of his disappointment, like I wasn't man enough. It was a moment I never forgot. Over the years, I would carry his voice in my head, a script I played again and again. I was determined to prove him wrong.

The summer wound down and I quickly found a job for the school year. Every day after school and all day Saturday, working for Ildefonso Stanovich, the Polish janitor, sweeping and cleaning the parish grade school. Ilde was even more demanding than my father, but I quickly showed him I could sweep and mop with the best of them. I turned most of my earnings over to Mom, but I was independent and not home that much. Working bought me some respect from my dad.

Maybe he'll let me buy a car, I thought. But that wasn't going to happen. I envied my best friend next door. Bill had a motor scooter, and as soon as he turned sixteen he had a car and he didn't have to work after school or on Saturdays.

Bill and I developed that thing that I'm sure is common between teenage best friends. Kind of a shared consciousness. Which people are cool and why, which are not. Opinions about cars and practically a shared language. What's funny or not. Lots of stuff about girls. We favored our own version of low-cut Converse All Stars. At the end of the school year we'd prowl the locker rooms looking for left behind hightops and cut them down. Our bond was way more than the fine points of cool. We shared a jointly developed point of view, a shared critique of the world.

My cool buddy and I worked summer jobs together for the next few summers and double dated most weekends.

We had one difference. Bill was at home in the suburbs. Before Longwood Farms he lived in nearby Park Forest, a planned community built for veterans returning from World War II. Bill attended public grade school and then the newly built and highly regarded Homewood-Flossmoor High. He was part of the same social group for years, while I ping ponged from place to place. He and I were close but I never shared with him how out of place I felt.

At Mendel, I had no academic motivation and no particular interest in college until Father Gavin, the senior class advisor, read me the riot act. So I told him I liked the University of Detroit. He was pleased that I'd picked a good Jesuit school. I applied, got accepted and figured I'd study business, back in the city of my youth.

At U-D, I found a new home among the tight-knit community of guys in the Saint Francis Club. The Club was a student cooperative that provided cheap meals to about seventy members in a building across from campus. Two older ladies did the cooking and the members did all the rest—washing dishes, pots and pans, setting tables, building maintenance, and cleaning. This group of college guys ran the Club and managed its affairs. With seventy members, three meals a day cost just fourteen bucks a week. I pledged and soon I was a member.

We elected officers; not just president, vice-president, and treasurer, but a purchasing agent and a custodian. Everyone had rotating volunteer responsibilities. We managed a budget of fifty thousand dollars a year. Shared responsibility built solidarity. The Latin motto on our crest read: *Qualis Socius Talis Domus*, which we claimed, translates to: *As the Members So Goes the Club*. I learned what it took to have a strong organization—broad participation, shared responsibility, shared decision making, cooperation. The club was like a family. Some of those members became my brothers, and a few still are today.

My social life took off and I aspired to be a BMOC, a big man on campus, like some of the older guys in the Club. I got elected to the student senate and later became the student government treasurer. I had a big circle of friends and felt like I belonged. I was elected social chairman of the Club; I organized "mixers" with sororities and scheduled parties in low-rent church halls with kegs of beer and a cheap band. A legendary event was the Club's Irish-German tug of war, the weekend before St. Patrick's Day. The event always ended in a donnybrook where we ripped off the opponent's tee shirts as souvenirs. Then we all retired to the Golden Twenties for pitchers of green beer. Junior year my two close friends were competing team captains. Dick LaFond led us Irishmen and Charlie Merz, my Chicago buddy, commanded the Germans.

Life was good. I lived off campus with LaFond, upstairs from Bob Yost, a crusty but loveable old widower who treated us like a pair of delinquent grandkids. When he heard us open the front door, he'd step out and snort "Whatta you two pot-lickers been up to?"

We'd ask him to join us on the front steps for a beer and he'd share his old man stories. Bob grumbled that if I left my motorcycle out it'd get stolen. Then he grumbled when he made room for it in his garage.

I had found my groove just a mile from where I lived as a kid. My mom was thrilled that I was able to visit her mother during the school year, who was now widowed and lived alone on the old block. Of all the people on both sides of our big extended Detroit family, my mom's mom was my favorite. I was her first grandchild and it was clear, at least to me, that I was her special favorite. In her eyes I could do no wrong; she was so proud of me attending college and majoring in accounting. She'd tell me how impressed her friends were when she told them that in the summers I worked in the accounting department at an auto plant.

"I tell them it's not the assembly line, he works in the *accounting* department."

My mom was less thrilled about my remaining in the city. I cringed at the resignation in her voice when I told her each spring that I'd be staying in Detroit.

I was an earnest grad student.

CHAPTER 2

Changing Times

The sixties as a period of rebellion and social change would finally find me on the Catholic college campus in America's heartland. I was in high school when Bob Dylan broke on the scene, when the Students for a Democratic Society gathered in Port Huron and when Martin Luther King brought a Poor People's March to Washington. None of that would resonate for me until about three years later.

I'll never forget a long talk over draft beer with Vince Lyons at the Venice, a favorite watering hole near campus. Vince, like me, was going to graduate in a year. The serious, skinny student from Cleveland had majored in architecture, a six year co-op program. I admired Vince and the rest of the guys studying architecture. They had one foot in the world of art, culture, and design that linked them to a realm distinct from the rest of us who were heading into mundane careers of business, industry, teaching, or law.

I asked Vince how he planned to start his design career. He said he was more interested in urban planning and that he'd already formed a consulting group with three other guys, and they already had a couple of projects in Detroit. I was stunned and fascinated. I got us two more drafts and Vince explained it all, beginning with how cities like Detroit were changing. This young urban consultant knew I grew up in Detroit, so he laid out the whole unfolding scenario for me, starting with racial segregation and White flight to Detroit's suburbs, major expressways, tract subdivisions, and shopping malls. Vince had a vision for cities of the future and he made the case loud and clear that unless we planned and advocated for that vision, the future of cities like Detroit wouldn't be pretty. Vince spoke a language I wanted to learn. I wanted to do what he was doing and that wasn't our last conversation. Suddenly I was in a hurry to know what Vince knew. My interest in a business career evaporated while my social and political awareness grew.

With senior year approaching, I looked back at all those accounting and business courses. It had all seemed so useful three years ago. *But I actually learned so little*, I thought. Fortunately I had a bunch of elective credits left, so I took sociology courses and in an urban issues seminar, we explored what was happening in Detroit's decaying inner city and its booming and sprawling suburbs. I drank coffee in the Student Union with philosophy majors and drank beer at the Golden Twenties with architects and artsy types. My new girlfriend Scubi was a singer, and we hung out with her crowd of musicians. The sixties were in full bloom on both coasts and as close as Ann Arbor, but it was just dawning on our campus. As I headed toward graduation with a degree in accounting, I was trying on a new identity. I was on an adventure. Motown and Dylan and Joan Baez were my companions.

Music would become integral to the journey that I was on. Baby Boomers first broke free with rock and roll. But Bob Dylan's poetic lyrics and his rough, almost harsh singing style had a raw honesty that spoke for our individual and collective struggle to make sense of our society that we felt was making a mess of the world. I got a buddy to lend me his old guitar and teach me a few chords. Maybe it's true of every generation, but *our music* was something we owned that our parents and their generation didn't. That winter, I applied to the Peace Corps.

Three months later my Assignment Letter arrived. A two-year stint in Monrovia, the capital city of Liberia. I had to look it up in the *World Book*. I was disappointed the posting was a job in the municipal Water Department, helping establish a modern billing system. The accounting world was determined to follow me to Africa. I imagined myself in a remote village somewhere, helping people get clean water or build a school, not in an office in downtown Monrovia.

Of course, living in Africa was already *way* outside my comfort zone. I'd never even been on a plane. If I really wanted to break with my past and strike out on my own, the opportunity was staring me in the face. I got fingerprinted at the local police department and my unique identifiers were sent off to the government. I had no Plan B.

Two weeks later, another letter arrived, this one from the General Accounting Office, the auditing arm of Congress. Some weeks earlier at a student career fair, I'd applied for a summer job on a whim and checked the box for San Francisco. The letter said to report to the GAO's West Coast office once I graduated. It wasn't Monrovia, but then again, I'd never been west of Saint Louis.

The rest of Plan B fell into place. At U-D, I was accepted into an interdisciplinary Master's program and awarded a teaching assistantship: free tuition and two hundred bucks a month for teaching four sessions a week of Introduction to Accounting to freshmen business majors. My accounting degree opened an important door.

Maybe San Francisco was adventurous enough.

I dutifully sat through the endless mid-April graduation ceremony—caps and gowns, folding chairs. It was important to my parents, so I couldn't possibly have skipped it. We were seated alphabetically by subject major.

When the philosophy majors were called, Murphy, who sat to my left, leaned over and joked, "Good luck finding a job."

I chuckled, and I suppose Murphy thought I agreed with him, but to myself I thought, *Good luck, Murphy. Balancing debits on the left and credits on the right until you retire. Accounting's already in my rear view mirror.*

Our commencement speaker was Adolf A. Berle Jr., a key advisor to FDR during the New Deal. I wish now that I'd taken notes. The Detroit Free Press reported that Berle spoke about Black Power and said that it's "time for its proponents to say what they want it for—what they propose to do with it if they get it." Along with Berle, U-D conferred an honorary degree on Robert H. Weaver, who'd recently been appointed by President Johnson to head up the first Department of Housing and Urban Development (HUD). Weaver was Black. I wondered if he and Berle had discussed Black Power. Weaver and I received degrees from U-D the same day. I had no idea that I'd end up spending my career in housing and urban development work.

After graduation, there was a family party at my grandma's house on the old block where I'd grown up. The big dining room table was set and in the center was a steaming baked ham and German potato salad and plenty of side dishes. There were two cases of Stroh's in the basement fridge.

Part I: A Long Time Comin'

When the dishes were done and all the Stroh's had been drunk, I said thanks and goodnight to my grandma. She laid her head against my chest and gave me a tight, long hug. Then she held me at arms length and looked straight into my eyes.

"You've earned something that nobody can ever take away from you."

I hugged her tight and felt ashamed that I'd wanted to skip my graduation. It wasn't about me. It was about our family.

A week later, I was aboard the first plane ride of my life. For the four-hour flight to San Francisco, I brought along Ayn Rand's thousand page *Atlas Shrugged*. I bought it right after I finished *Fountainhead*, the story of an uncompromising and innovative architect, Howard Roark. I identified with the bold and talented designer who refused to conform to society's expectations. His design work was an extension of his authentic self, his personal integrity. I saw my own life in those terms. That story inspired me and supported me as I sought to break free.

Atlas Shrugged turned out to be an altogether different story. The main character John Galt was a rugged individualist capitalist out to preserve his fortune from a society that wanted to ensure that everyone could have a decent life. The book was engaging but eventually I saw it for what it was: a simplistic defense of unbridled capitalism. Ayn Rand had lost her appeal. I now saw her as the enemy.

I landed in San Francisco. I found a bus headed downtown and stepped out into my new life. I found a rooming house and booked a room for two weeks. When I pulled out my checkbook, the landlady sighed and shook her head.

"I can't take a check, honey. I've been burned more than

once." I had never traveled. I never thought about not being able to cash a check. I was learning. I had an idea, "How about holding on to my 35mm camera as collateral until my check clears?" She hesitated but I didn't look like the type who would rip her off. I had my room.

I spent two weeks in her rooming house and then found a cheap apartment with a shared bathroom down the hall just walking distance from *Haight Ashbury.* San Francisco in 1967 was a far cry from parochial Detroit. The Haight was the epicenter of hippie culture, overflowing with head shops, record stores, good drugs, bad drugs, cool turned on people, and more than a few lost runaways. The Jefferson Airplane lived in a big house at the edge of Golden Gate Park, not far from my apartment. The whole scene blew my mind.

The GAO work was about what I expected. I trailed along with an audit team, preparing financial schedules, examining documents, and recording information for the auditors. I wondered what Murphy was doing, along with all those "unemployed" philosophy majors. My pay was more than decent and the city was a gas. I took an evening course at University of San Francisco and went to coffee houses in North Beach, where I listened to poetry I didn't understand and just grooved on the vibe. I met a few girls and beat away the loneliness. I hitched down the coast to Esalen Institute and Big Sur. I went to The Fillmore. I heard Janis Joplin for free in the Panhandle park, and I hung around City Lights Bookstore. My after-work life in this vibrant place was punctuated with pot and sex. It was a lot for a kid who'd never been out of the Midwest. It was a far cry from Detroit. I ate it up.

It was late July when one of the auditors asked me what I knew about the race riot in Detroit. I remembered my parents talking about one in the forties, but I had no idea what they were. At lunch I went to a news stand that sold papers from all over the country. The guy told me the Free Press hadn't arrived the last couple of days, that he heard they weren't publishing because of the riot. I called home and Mom said the Michigan National Guard and federal troops were patrolling the streets downtown around 12th Street. She said there were fires and looting but she didn't have any details.

"There's a lot of talk," she said, "about 'why those people are destroying their own neighborhood.'" She told me how she responded to such comments. "If I was treated like the Negroes are treated, I'd probably start a riot too." I was proud to hear her say that.

Detroit's terror erupted when police violently raided a "blind pig," an illegal after hours joint. By the time it was all over, there were forty-three deaths and over four hundred buildings destroyed. Two weeks earlier, twenty-six had been killed in Newark when a riot erupted after cops beat a Black cab driver. More than a hundred cities saw sustained violence in that *long hot summer*. I worried what Detroit would be like when I returned. The violence in northern cities signaled a change for the civil rights movement. It no longer just focused on the blatant racism of the South.

Back at U-D, my interdisciplinary studies required that I have a faculty advisor from the social sciences. I approached the taciturn sociology professor from my senior year.

He was reluctant but didn't want to discourage me so he said, "Yeah sure I'll do it, but I don't have a lot of time to spend with you. You'll mostly be on your own."

I was fine with a do-it-yourself Master's Degree.

Teaching Freshman Accounting was harder than expected. I had to cram each evening before the next morning's classes. But being a TA brought an unlikely bonus. One of my office mates was Steve Tomczyk who, like me, had grown up in Detroit. We got to talking about the city; we really didn't know the city beyond our immediate neighborhoods. Steve's insular neighborhood was 90% Polish. Neither of us knew Black Detroit at all. We figured we should, especially after the summer's violence.

Steve had a friend who worked in a daycare center in the inner city, so we went to visit her at work. It was a start. She asked if we wanted to accompany her while she stopped in to see a few families after work. We tagged along and were welcomed into Black people's humble living rooms while their child's teacher talked with them. I had never sat in a Black family's living room before. What was remarkable was how *unremarkable* it felt.

I knew nothing about Detroit's art and design history. My first revelation was visiting the stunning Detroit Industry Murals by Diego Rivera at the Institute of Arts downtown. Then the Cranbrook School campus north of the city, designed by Eliel Saarinen in the 1920s. Detroit had so much for us to learn.

My courses ranged from Urban Economics to the History of Architecture and to U-D's inaugural offering of Afro-American History. I enrolled in an urban problems seminar. It was the height of the civil rights movement. Saving cities was on the federal government's agenda. I was studying the urban environment and Detroit was my classroom.

The Radical Priest

Scubi and I were back together after a summer apart. She was as curious about what was happening in Detroit as I was. She was even more passionate about the gross racial inequality that now seemed so evident and appalling after the summer's violence. We wanted to do something.

A bulletin board posting in the Student Union was meant for us: A church youth program in the heart of Detroit needed volunteers. I called the number and reached Church of the Messiah. The church secretary put me through to Father Tom Jackson, the assistant pastor. Tom explained they didn't have a youth program as such, but he was open to suggestions. Scubi was a social work major, so I figured she'd come up with something. We agreed to meet the following Saturday.

We liked this inner city priest immediately—his openness and humor, his passion. Tom thanked us for volunteering and surprised us when he said that six boys were waiting for us in the parish hall. The boys were ages eight to twelve, all of them Black. We asked them their names, what they liked to do, where they went to school. Were they Tigers fans?

Then Scubi said, "Why don't we go to Belle Isle. We can fit you all in the back of my Jeep. How's that sound?"

A couple of them spoke up, saying that sounded good, but another couple looked at the others, kind of mystified.

With some hesitation, James, one of the younger boys said, "What's Belle Isle?"

Tyrone, an older boy, mocked him. "Boy, you don't know where Belle Isle is? Where you from anyhow?"

Scubi stepped in. "Tyrone, younger boys don't necessarily know everything you know. The same way you don't know everything that adults do." Then she turned to the chastened eight-year-old. "James, Belle Isle is a beautiful park on an island in the middle of the Detroit River. We can drive there—over a bridge." Scubi was a natural talking to kids.

James smiled at the thought of going to an island but still looked perplexed. I wondered if he knew where the Detroit River was. It was a little shocking that this boy who lived probably no more than eight or ten blocks from the bridge wasn't aware of Belle Isle Park.

The boys piled in the back of Scubi's long-body Jeep, and we made a day of it at Belle Isle. When we got back, Father Tom was full of questions for the boys and then sent them on their way home and turned to us. His whole face smiled, and we smiled back. Then he gave us the first of what would be about a million hugs. Guys hugging was strange back then, but I loved it immediately and what it communicated.

Tom asked, "Do you two have time to come over and meet my wife, Judy? We live just three blocks away. I'm sure there's cold beer in the fridge."

When we got there, Judy was busy painting. She was putting the last bright touches on their classic 1920s brick two-story with a wide covered front porch. It was a block of mostly recent, Black homeowners. Judy was happy to put down her brush. We drank beer and wine on the porch and watched the neighborhood go by, our conversation flowing. Then we cooked dinner together. Scubi and I never wanted to leave.

Every Saturday we introduced the kids to their city. One Saturday we took them to my new favorite place, the famed *Detroit Industry* murals by Diego Rivera at the Institute of Arts. They were blown away by the size of the frescoes and their vivid imagery. I brought them close up to a few panels depicting the Ford Rouge Plant assembly line and told them that my dad worked on that assembly line.

"Which one's your dad?" asked one of the boys.

Scubi smirked at me when I pointed to a guy wearing a brimmed Irish cap.

We hung out at Tom and Judy's on plenty of Saturday evenings—evenings full of earnest discussions and just as many laughs. A growing friendship over dinner and drinks. Scubi and I were planning on getting married at the end of that summer. We imagined living like them, maybe in this neighborhood, joining this integrated urban community.

Tom's example finally helped me put religion in its rightful place. It was the place of purpose. A place of moral action in the world. A place of personal exploration about living an ethical life. A place of celebration, community, and lifting up. Tom was only three years older than me and had a baby face. Without his black shirt and clerical collar, he looked like a college kid. To me he seemed wise. He'd keyed into such a purposeful path for himself. I began looking to him for guidance to find my own path.

Tom had a surprising past. His father owned a steel fabricating company just north of Detroit and left Tom a modest trust fund. The young minister spent his high school years at Culver Military Academy in Indiana, a storied institution from the 1800s with a college style campus on a big lake. Tom shared some pictures in his full dress uniform. He had been the Captain of Cadets, and in the pictures he was leading this pack of high school "soldiers" marching in full military regalia. It was militaristic, an image that was hard to reconcile with the inner city priest who cared so deeply about peace and the lives of the urban poor. But I could see in Tom the assuredness and command certainty that must have come with being the Captain of Cadets.

Through Tom and Judy, Scubi and I saw what our lives

could be after college. Lives of purpose, the excitement of creating something new. Lives that were deeply connected to moral values that we'd learned as kids but were just finding their expression

The Radical Professor

These days, the group of graduate courses that I'd stitched together would be known as Urban Studies. I wanted to engage my urban environment, so I scoured the course catalog and chose Urban Economics, History of Architecture, an Urban Problems seminar and Afro-American History, a brand new offering. My "advisor" was true to his word; he was too busy to spend time with me, and after a five minute discussion, he signed off on my first semester.

In my second semester, one of my professors, Dr. Michael Whitty stopped me after class and invited me for coffee. That was a first for me. Over coffee he asked me what I thought about the previous summer's violence. I told him what my mom said and that I agreed with her. He liked that. He said he needed someone to occasionally sit in for him on the University President's Task Force on Minority Recruitment, and he wanted me to be that someone.

"What do I know about minority recruitment?" I said.

"You'll learn," Doctor Whitty said, and told me to get a meeting with Mr. Frank Ditto, the director of the *East Side Voice of Independent Detroit,* an inner city community organization.

So that's what I did. I called Information, got the number, and gave a call. Frank Ditto's secretary checked his schedule and gave me a time and I wrote down the address.

Ditto was the moving force behind a dozen "Black Pride" projects, and he ran a black-uniformed corps of 120

Black youths who patrolled the ghetto, escorting people through the crime-ridden streets and protecting threatened store owners—both Black and White. Frank Ditto was looking after a neighborhood that White Detroit had turned its back on. I got the idea that this community organizer wasn't fond of White people. I was nervous about our interview.

I showed up at the low rent storefront on a street with some burned-out shops probably from the past summer's riots. I was dressed in a nice button down shirt and a trench coat. I'd never been in an office like this. Black power posters, pictures of Black Panthers, and flyers with community events were pasted on the wall. A beautiful woman with a big afro welcomed me and quickly informed me that unfortunately Mr. Ditto wasn't available but she pointed to a couple of unsmiling guys sitting nearby—one in a Dashiki and the other in a black leather coat chewing on a toothpick, both of them wearing dark sunglasses.

She smiled and said, "These gentlemen would be happy to meet with you."

Still not smiling, they nodded and stood and with another nod, indicating I should follow them. They opened a door and headed down to the basement. I was hesitant but I followed. The pace of my urban studies had definitely taken a turn.

One of them indicated with a hand gesture which folding chair I should occupy at the lone bare table and they sat down across from me. I told them about the minority recruitment idea, and that I was interested in their ideas on how U-D could make it successful.

"First of all," said one, leaning across the table, "why would some young brother or sister want to come up to Six Mile to some all White college?"

I felt like they were just trying to intimidate me, and the only thing I could think to say was what I thought was true, that it was a good school and obviously a college degree was a good thing to have. The discussion continued but the tenor didn't improve. My notebook sat unopened in front of me when I stood up and thanked them for their time. Not waiting for a response, I headed for the stairs. I thanked the gal at the front desk.

"I hope they were helpful," she said, still smiling.

I nodded and smiled back. "Oh yeah."

When I did attend my first meeting of the President's Task Force, I had some real inner city intel to add to the discussion, mostly about the vast gulf that inner city Blacks felt between them and our White campus on Six Mile. It would be a challenging cultural bridge to construct.

It was February when Dr. Whitty suggested I call Mr. Hosea Williams at the Southern Christian Leadership Conference in Atlanta and find out what I could do to help organize for Dr. King's upcoming visit to Detroit in May. By now I felt more confident. When Mr. Williams got on the other end of the line, I would have been plenty nervous if I'd been aware that Mr. Williams was third in command behind Dr. King and Reverend Ralph Abernathy.

The civil rights leader's southern warmth immediately put me at ease. He told me Reverend C. L. Franklin, pastor at New Bethel Baptist Church in Detroit, was coordinating Dr. King's visit and that he'd surely find something for me to do.

Signing off he said, "Thank you, brother. Every one of us is valuable in this struggle. God bless you."

Hosea Williams just called me brother.

As his message washed over me, I felt officially recruited to the struggle. I would answer his call.

Reverend Franklin was just as welcoming. "I'm so happy to get this call from you, my friend. Dr. King's visit isn't until early May. Do you mind calling me back about mid-April? There will be plenty to do starting then."

I never did meet Reverend Franklin. When I'd read about him in the papers, I'd recall his deep embracing voice and the personal warmth he conveyed in our short phone call. Dr. Whitty asked if I was familiar with Dr. Franklin's daughter, Aretha.

"No shit," I said, "he's Aretha Franklin's dad?"

Whitty shook his head. "Yeah, she grew up singing in his church." The radical professor said if I wanted to get to know Detroit, I should listen to her latest record.

April 4th, 1968 was a Thursday evening, and I was in the church hall waiting for Tom. He hurried in, distressed.

"Martin Luther King's been shot and killed. I don't know any details."

I looked at Tom and we grabbed each other. My mind whirled. This was the worst possible turn of events. I imagined the anger and hopelessness, the fear and deep despair that would follow. Surely the Black ghettos would erupt again. I wondered if Tom and I were in danger— White faces in a mostly Black neighborhood.

I thought back to Hosea Williams and how completely disheartened he must've been. I recalled his words to me. *Everyone of us is valuable in this struggle. God bless you.*

That night, the idea of returning to school in the fall and sitting in a classroom felt so totally irrelevant. Like I'd be turning my back on Mr. Hosea Williams. A War on Poverty was mobilizing. I planned to enlist.

By now, Tom and Judy were our dearest friends. Tom was my confidant and guide as I digested all I'd learned in the last eight months.

In May, the Poor People's March came to Detroit on its way to Washington. Hosea Williams spoke and called the city "a dungeon of shame." Detroit's liberal mayor, Jerry Cavanaugh, welcomed the protesters and declared that the City of Detroit believed in their quest for freedom and equality.

Two short months after Dr. King's death, Bobby Kennedy was assassinated. Public life was getting much more tense, threatening even. Everything was unraveling. Then just when Scubi and I were wondering how we might have Tom officiate at our Catholic church wedding coming up in August, Tom suddenly announced that he'd interviewed for an assistant pastorship in New Jersey, and he'd accepted the offer. He and Judy would be moving soon.

We were punched in the gut. We had just signed on to this mission. Scubi and I felt abandoned and immediately adrift. Our next steps? Well they'd just evaporated. *Shit.*

I'd already dropped out of my graduate program and told the Accounting Department I wasn't coming back. Someone else probably already had my Teaching Assistantship. But we were in love and getting married in a few months. Scubi found work as a waitress and I got a job with my brother Mike unloading ships on the Detroit River. The fall seemed a long way off. After our honeymoon, we'd figure something out.

CHAPTER 3

Finding Our Groove

Three weeks before our wedding, Scubi and I drove out to Englewood, New Jersey, to hang out with Tom and Judy. They'd bought a nice old house a few blocks from the church and were busy remodeling—fresh paint and bright fabrics. It was an airy and comfortable place, probably built in the 1920s. We settled into one of the extra bedrooms. Tom was now the Assistant Pastor at St. Paul's Episcopal church, a mainline institution of Englewood's WASP community. The young minister from Detroit who was willing to openly challenge his own church to live up to its Christian ideals was a magnet for young folks and social gospel types. Tom and Judy's life in this racially integrated small city so close to New York City really appealed to us. Again, we could see ourselves in their movie.

The East Coast felt exotic to a couple of young midwesterners and New York City's gravitational pull was irresistible. I wasn't going back to Detroit. My parents didn't like Scubi. I watched them cringe when she'd burst in the front door and run up and hug my dad sitting in his chair watching TV. She'd laugh out loud while she told him about what we'd been doing that day. Then she'd go right into the kitchen and put her arm around my mom, who was peeling potatoes, and ask what she could do to help with dinner. Then she'd open the fridge and answer her own question before my mom could say anything. "I can make a salad." My parents felt invaded. And then there was her name.

"Susan is such a nice name," my mom would say. "Why does she insist on calling herself Scubi?"

I'd shrug and explain it was a family nickname. Her sister Margaret was called Muggsi.

My dad made it clear he took a dim view of my life choices—not just the wild wife I'd chosen, but leaving behind a business career, my anti-establishment politics, almost everything. His disappointment hurt, I wanted to stay out of range, make my way on my own terms. I was determined to prove him wrong.

In New Jersey, Scubi and I answered help wanted ads and quickly found work. At my interview with the director of the Neighborhood Youth Corps in Hackensack, I leaned into my inner city youth work in Detroit to impress him, hoping he'd overlook that I had no social work background. But he was more interested in my accounting background. He showed me the budget reports to the Feds and asked if I thought I could handle filing those every month.

"I hate doing those damn things," he said. It looked pretty simple to me so I looked at it for another thirty seconds.

"Yeah, I can see why you hate these with all the other responsibilities you must have. I can definitely do this every month." He hired me on the spot.

I love that accounting degree.

A day later I called the director back and told him I was draft eligible and that I might be able to get a "teaching" deferment if we could convince my Draft Board that my work helping dropouts get their high school diplomas was equivalent to teaching. I applied to my Draft Board and drafted a letter of support from him and dropped it off to his secretary.

Scubi, with her Social Work degree, got hired at the Settlement House in Englewood's all Black Fourth Ward.

Then, the wedding day came. In the church in South Euclid, a suburb east of Cleveland. Tom didn't officiate but he was on the altar and dressed in full priest vestments. Coming up the aisle, we spotted him, his palms together in prayer mode, a deferential distance from the priest who was standing dead center. Scubi and I gave Tom a sly wave. His face lit up and he bowed his head in our direction.

Living near Tom and Judy and working with young kids felt a lot like the adventure we'd started a year earlier. The foursome was back together.

Then a letter from my Draft Board arrived. I clenched my teeth as I opened the envelope. A one-page form. I was classified 2-A, a one-year deferment. What a relief. Maybe the War would end or I'd get my deferment extended. Only men under twenty-six were being drafted, so I had two years and nine months to go. A year's reprieve seemed like a long time. For a year I was safe.

Scubi and I soon met Esther and Davis Ross and Martin Clarke, three of Tom's close followers, at Saint Paul's. Davis and Esther were warm and generous, a few years older than us, with three young kids. Meeting people who seemed so "established" yet who had an earnest, no-nonsense moral commitment to social justice was eye opening. It wasn't just young people with long hair alienated from the mainstream who made up this movement we'd joined.

Martin Clarke was as different from the rest of us as

could be. He was Black and bearded with a deep, melodious voice with just a hint of his family's roots in Bermuda. Martin was married and the father of three immensely talented sons, who were budding actors and performers, but he lived the life of the freelance independent spirit. He designed and built theater sets, created magazine and newspaper ads, and traveled everywhere by foot, bus, and subway. His African shoulder bag held pens, pencils, brushes, usually a library book, and his constant companion, the sketch book. Hoping that some of Martin would wear off on me, I bought a shoulder bag and my first sketch book.

When I told Martin I wanted to make a stained-glass window as a wedding present for my friends Terry and Ann and that I needed a design, he said, "Buy me a beer and I'll see what I can come up with." He asked about Terry and Ann. That was easy.

"They're adventurous, creative, free spirits."

We sat at the bar and two beers later he'd sketched it out, ripped the page from his sketchbook, and handed me a finished design—an abstract with sharp angles and all straight lines. With a little concentration I realized it spelled out the word LIFE. Martin said that color variation was key to making the design work. A week later, we visited a glass importer in a loft building in Soho, and Martin helped me pick out deeply colored sheets of European glass. From his sketch I made a full-size template and I began cutting the imported glass. It's still a thrill for me to see the window hanging in the living room of the octagonal house that Terry built in Petoskey, Michigan.

St. Paul's was an interesting mix of wealthier WASPs, educated middle-class liberals, and a small Black population, a legacy of England's empire in the Caribbean. The congregation had two distinct groups. While the Yale educated pastor Dave Gillespie kept the wealthy donors happy and raised huge amounts to restore the hundred-year-old organ, our group, centered around Tom, formed an anti-war, social action contingent bent on making the gospel of Jesus mean something in the face of war mongering, racial unrest, and persistent poverty.

Martin, Esther, Scubi, and I brought an idea to Tom. We wanted to form a teen drop-in center at the church, open to all teens not just from the parish. An unused storage room under the church sanctuary with its own entrance seemed ideal. Tom encouraged us to approach Gillespie and get him to put up some funds for some minor renovation, a pool table, maybe a fridge. We made our pitch, including that we'd all be volunteering to staff the center. Gillespie quickly agreed and we immediately got to work fixing up the space.

Scubi spread the word among kids she worked with. The Escape Hatch was open every Friday and Saturday evening from seven to eleven. It attracted a wide range of teens—White kids from the area around the church and Black teens from the Fourth Ward.

Youth work at the church expanded with weekend youth retreats. Then a family therapist staffed weekly teen rap sessions with another psychologist, and I was soon a paid "trainee," learning to guide discussions with teens on sensitive personal topics. Gillespie was happy to support it all.

The liberal pastor was less excited about our stand on the moral issues of the war, civil rights, and poverty. He chafed when we occasionally disrupted the solemn flow of Sunday service with a call for prayers for the "Black Panthers who'd been murdered by the Chicago police" or "the innocent Vietnamese villagers napalmed by U.S. war planes." We knew we were testing the limits of St. Paul's tolerance for activist social gospel.

A Fortuitous Meeting

I liked my work with the Neighborhood Youth Corps and it fulfilled my sense of purpose, but I was becoming convinced that the anti-poverty programs wouldn't come close to ending poverty in my lifetime.

My second month on the job on a Friday afternoon, we had an all-staff meeting of the entire Bergen County Community Action Program. The meeting felt pointless. There were people from Headstart, Legal Services, Youth Corps, Meals on Wheels, the three Neighborhood Centers, the Job Training and Placement program and all the administrative staff, but there was no give and take between all these staff and the directors.

It was getting late, near quitting time, when Jack Lyle, the executive director, asked if there were any questions. John Lyle had the stiff bearing of the tug boat captain that he used to be, and he wasn't interested in much dialogue. I knew everyone was anxious to go home, but I'd been stewing during most of this uninspired gathering. I wanted to say something but was apprehensive. I'd only been working there a month, but I couldn't stop myself from raising my hand. I asked "Big Jack" if he thought our organization was achieving the federal mandate of "maximum feasible participation of the poor."

He frowned slightly and shook his head, but then he smiled and without missing a beat he delivered a lengthy and detailed non-answer. He didn't want any follow-up questions and he didn't get any. Meeting adjourned.

On my way out the door, a tall bearded guy my age approached me.

"Hey, we've gotta talk." He introduced himself as Ronnie Atlas and that he worked for the Legal Services program, upstairs from me. I had no idea I just met my new best friend.

Staff was filing out, heading to their cars and we did the same.

"I liked how you took it straight to Big Jack Lyle with that question," he said.

"Thanks," I said, trying not to beam with too much pride. "I happen to believe the War on Poverty could really make a difference in peoples' lives. But this CAP program doesn't feel like that."

We had lunch together the next day and as often as our schedules allowed. Besides lunch, Ronnie and I didn't spend that much time together. We had wives and separate groups of friends, very separate lives, but I always made time if Ronnie stuck his head in and asked if I was available for lunch. Our acquaintanceship soon turned to deep friendship. Over lunches we talked about our private lives, how we were sometimes frustrated in our marriages, and worried out loud about how we were unsure how to deal with that. It was an incredible opening between the two of us, all this intimate conversation. We explored feelings of uncertainty, even inadequacy. It brought us very close.

Ronnie asked a lot about my work with the high school dropouts. His interest felt like such a compliment. He seemed surprised, even fascinated, by the intensity of the teen rap sessions I told him about at St. Paul's. It was all so unfamiliar to him. The open and revealing discussions. The expressed feelings. Exposing usually hidden emotions. He wanted to know more and develop some of that in himself. That's what our discussions began to do and it deepened our connection. My relationship with Ronnie became an anchor, an important place where I could be myself. He became a role model.

Ronnie didn't talk about his accomplishments. He had a demanding caseload and was constantly in court. He was part of the Fort Lee campaign to pass the state's first rent control ordinance and worked alongside Martin Aranow to establish the New Jersey Tenants Organization. He spent evenings advising tenant groups all over northern New Jersey. I only found this out much later.

In November of 1969, we traveled with our wives to the big anti-War march in DC and stayed with Ronnie's brother, John, and his wife Deena. I liked John immediately; he had a great sense of humor. Like his big brother he was a lawyer working for the poor. We three were a good trio.

The march was the massive Student Mobilization Against the War. The morning of the march, we told John and Deena we'd meet them at the foot of the Washington monument, where the march ended. When we got there we met up with the other five hundred thousand people marching to end the war. It was mind blowing.

Meanwhile, things had fallen back into place for Scubi and me. We had a community of like-minded friends, I had a new best friend, and we both liked our jobs. Scubi had found her role working with Black teens at the Settlement House and was well regarded. She thrived on being noticed and thought well of. Those low days in the spring of '68 when our dream life in Detroit had unraveled were dim memories now. Little did we know what was coming next.

CHAPTER 4

Things Unwinding

Tom Jackson, my other role model, was on thin ice and didn't know it. The radical priest from inner-city Detroit was undaunted in delivery of his spiritual gospel. *Jesus meant for us to lift up the poor. What was the purpose of religion if not that?* As churches go, St. Paul's was a wealthy parish and considered liberal, but its group of conservative parishioners made their views known to the pastor. Dave Gillespie kept all this in balance, but now Tom was upsetting that balance, and due to his cocksureness bordering on arrogance, he constantly challenged the pastor's commitment to the true gospel of Jesus. I admired Tom's guts, but I wondered why he didn't steer a slightly more accommodating course.

Finally it was too much for the pastor, who found himself upstaged by his bearded assistant. After less than two years at St. Paul's, Tom was fired.

We were outraged but I knew Tom wasn't blameless. He wouldn't, or couldn't, moderate his arrogance and his uncompromising stances. A group of us protested to the parish Vestry but that was a waste of time. They were in the pastor's pocket. I doubt they even thought twice about Gillespie's decision to let Tom go.

Tom and Judy retreated to their place in the Catskills, but it wasn't long before Tom accepted a job as Campus Minister at University of Ohio and we had to say goodbye to Tom and Judy. Again.

Our group had lost our spiritual leader, and our strong sense of cohesion began to unravel. Looking back, I see now how young and impetuous Tom was. I had been drawn to him in part because he was so gutsy, so outspoken, but he didn't have the patience that comes with maturity to really lead a congregation. He talked a lot about Jesus telling truth to power and suffering because of it. I think he saw himself that way. His firing was inevitable and the cracks in my role model began to show. I'm surprised he lasted two years.

With Tom's firing, I felt another thing too, and maybe for the final time. Religion had no place for me. This time it was church politics—moneyed parishioners and the dominant pastor with his WASP pedigree. It was their church and they simply tolerated people like us. But only up to a point. This would be my last try at organized religion; I was quite sure of that. If I wanted to be part of something that inspired people to create a more peaceful and egalitarian world, then I needed to look elsewhere. Meanwhile, another shake-up was just around the corner.

I still enjoyed my work with the Youth Corps and loved those wayward kids. Getting some of them back on their feet was a great feeling, but the whole anti-poverty system no longer felt that meaningful. Community Action agencies were like a tiny band-aid, or worse. They were a delusion. These programs weren't going to make a dent in the ingrained poverty and inequality that was endemic to the richest country in the world.

I despised the "liberal" Board of Directors, people I

didn't even know. I imagined them at cocktail parties patting each other on the back, so proud of tackling poverty head-on. And the top management, I was certain they had no passion for the task of waging a war against poverty and were probably all politically connected hacks. They had comfy jobs spending federal money to help the poor. Why upset the system? The way I saw it, none of them were interested in empowering people. If you weren't interested in empowering the poor then you're just perpetuating the system.

The poor needed a voice and they needed to organize for collective power. I thought of Dr. King and the Poor People's Campaign. He had rallied Black people to challenge the economic, political, and social system that kept them impoverished. King didn't organize a movement so that the poor would be treated like patients who needed professional help. Battling poverty with social work had come to feel like a perverse joke.

In college, I read *The Other America* by Michael Harrington. The socialist author documented that an incredible one in four households lived on less than three thousand dollars a year. The poor were mostly invisible in urban ghettos and hidden in rural areas, places where middle-class folks rarely went. Harrington knew it would be a battle to get the government to address poverty at a scale as big as the problem itself. It would require a political movement that demanded America live up to its ideals, a battle that would challenge the powerful interests who benefited from the current economic system. Entrenched power would not give in easily.

Harrington was right, and I felt like I'd been hustled. I believed in the War on Poverty but the solutions were fake—mostly a bunch of modest programs that pretty much left the poor right where they were, still at the bottom of the economic heap. I wanted out. I hated feeling like I was part of the problem. I quit my job and I felt good about it. Liberated. No longer part of a dishonest system. I barely gave a thought about losing my draft deferment.

Within a week I was working for a two-man landscaping business. I packed a lunch every evening, got up early every morning, and rode my motorcycle to work. Hard work in the sun felt satisfying. I finally developed some muscles. My hands grew tough and calloused and I had plenty of time to think about my future. I was working with my hands, doing good honest work. It all felt right.

But the words of Eldridge Cleaver, leader of the Black Panther Party, managed to haunt me. "If you're not part of the solution, you're part of the problem." Planting trees and laying sod and pushing a wheelbarrow wasn't exactly being part of the solution. I needed to figure things out.

CHAPTER 5

Time to Split for the Coast

Married life wore on Scubi and me. We'd married too young and our emotional immaturity was catching up with us. We always had so much enthusiasm and energy for each other's ideas and projects. We enjoyed working together and learning crafts like stained glass. Now we were aggravated and discontent. We squabbled over senseless things.

Scubi loved to tell me about her day. She'd recount what some kids had done in the after school program. I knew their names from so many previous accounts. She talked constantly about Moose, her co-worker, a handsome Black guy our age, who'd grown up in Englewood's Fourth Ward. I think she idolized Moose because he was Black and grew up poor. I was getting tired of hearing those stories and her over-dramatized telling of tales that weren't that interesting. I'd feel trapped, so I'd start making dinner. I wanted to scream out, "Scubi, shut up! Don't you ever stop your phony chatter? Do you really think this is of any interest to me?" But I kept that to myself.

One night we were in the kitchen. I was cleaning up after dinner when she said, "Do you even listen to me anymore? I'm talking about stuff that matters to me and you have nothing to say. Not a comment. Not a question.

Meanwhile you expect me to listen to your latest, uh, whatever fucking thing, with the wonderful Ronnie Atlas. Maybe you two should get married."

I bit my lip and she noticed my barely suppressed laugh.

"Go ahead and laugh you fucking self-centered, self-important piece of shit."

I stopped cleaning the dishes and looked at her across the kitchen eating some peaches. "Oh, Scubi just shut up for a while, would you?" I turned back to the sink when a bowl of peaches flew by my head and smashed against the cabinet. My wife was nothing if not dramatic.

The next couple days were pretty dicey. I knew we needed to talk, to try and get at what was going on. As good as we seemed at helping others sort out emotional stuff, we couldn't do it ourselves. After work I brought home a chilled bottle of rosé and set out two jelly jars.

"We need to talk about our relationship," I said as I poured her some wine. We sat at the kitchen table and I laid out the sadness I felt at what we'd lost. Scubi recounted the things that brought us together. When the rosé was empty I opened a bottle of red. We were so relieved to have broken the ice. We slid into bed and made love like the old days.

The next day I suggested we needed a change of scenery. So we talked about traveling. We barely had any money but we decided to quit work and hitchhike across Canada and down to Mexico. It seemed a little crazy but what did we have to lose?

So we quit our jobs, I sold my motorcycle, we paid the landlord two months' rent, and we hit the road with full backpacks and about three hundred bucks.

We were light on our feet with that fresh anticipation that comes with the first step of an adventure. We hiked over to the Palisades Parkway with our packs and a cardboard sign that read MONTREAL. At the top of the ramp we planned to catch all the northbound traffic. We stood with our sign and thumbs out for about forty minutes. A clean-cut couple hitchhiking, that was supposed to be the trick to getting quick rides. This might be tougher than we thought. To amuse Scubi, I flipped the sign over and carefully printed MEXICO. The third car stopped.

"You know Mexico's in the other direction, right?"

We piled in. We were on our way, feelin' groovy.

Outside Montreal on the Trans Canada Highway, a massive logging truck pulled over. We ran to it and scrambled up into the high cab. The taciturn leather-faced driver with a wool cap greeted us tersely in French, his only language. There wouldn't be much conversation. A couple hours into the unpopulated forests of western Quebec, the driver suddenly and without explanation hit the brakes and pulled over. There was nothing but the great Canadian outdoors for miles in any direction. I gave him a threatening stare.

His face lit up and he pointed across the small lake.

"*L'orignal. L'orignal,*" he said, miming with his fingers, some antlers and then snapping a photograph.

I grabbed my camera. A moose was in the shallows at the opposite shore. Click. It would only be a dark speck on the snapshot but I gave the driver a thumbs up, smiled, and said, "Merci."

He smiled and nodded back.

We were on the road making memories. We'd gotten our groove back, living life as an adventure. That's what brought us together. This trip was just what we needed.

Hitching rides and crashing in strangers' apartments across Canada and down to San Francisco was a Kurt

Vonnegut dream. We'd arrive in a city and ask about places where young people hung out. In every city there was a district—with coffee houses, macrobiotic cafes, head shops, bars with live music, and plenty of people our age. Our backpacks signaled that we were *on the road* and people made conversation immediately. Suddenly, we were making new friends over a draft beer or a mug of herbal tea. We'd soon have a place to crash—a floor, a sofa, a futon, sometimes a bed and a hot shower and usually breakfast before we took off the next day or the day after. Even sleepy Winnipeg was like this, a midwestern city with a turned on youth culture.

Our days and nights were full of new experiences, new people. We could have made time to talk about where our relationship was at, but we didn't. I feared that I just didn't know how to make a relationship work, didn't know how to love. But out on the road, together, those thoughts were far away.

After two days in Winnipeg with new friends we'd likely never see again, we took a westbound city bus to the edge town. We jumped off the bus, anxious to log some miles westward across the endless plains of western Canada. Our mood plummeted. Stretched out along the highway, was a line of at least fifty hitchhikers. We walked about a quarter mile to the end of the queue and put down our packs and waited. As the sun baked us and the dust off the Manitoba plains powdered our faces and arms, our lighthearted mood dissipated. Not many of those plains dwellers were stopping to help vagabond youth live out their dreams.

Defeated, we grabbed a bus back into town and found the Greyhound station and its dreary waiting room full of poor people, Indians, and old folks all waiting to go

Part I: A Long Time Comin'

somewhere. We had twelve hours to kill on those hard benches and then a long bus ride. The mood reminded us that back home, we weren't getting along all that well.

After some fitful sleep, then black coffee and a couple donuts, we dragged our asses onto the bus and watched the Manitoba and Saskatchewan wheat fields roll by. We stretched our legs during bathroom breaks in Moose Jaw and Swift Current and Medicine Hat, names that on the map conjured up cowboys, ranchers, and Indians. In reality they were hot and dusty, faceless places. Eight hundred miles and fourteen hours later, we were relieved to get off in Calgary, where we hoped our hitching prospects would be better.

Just outside Calgary, a friendly couple our age in a VW camper picked us up. They were a pair of professional travelers. Their van was comfy and hip and well equipped. They'd been on the road for weeks, all the way east to Halifax and now heading back westward. We camped together a couple nights near Lake Louise and before they turned south, they gave us their address in Bellingham, Washington.

Were we back on track, Scubi and I? It was hard to know. The truth is, we knew that things weren't right, that it was the thrill of being on the road that bonded us. We talked a lot about how we'd lost the love that originally linked us and we never replaced it with something more solid. We knew that once we were off the road and making a normal life together that the same distance and resentments would take over. We headed north to Jasper National Park and the Athabasca glacier, and in the August chill at the foot of that monstrous piece of frozen geologic history, we decided to end our marriage.

It was liberating. We suddenly felt freer. A touch of

sadness bonded us in a way that was unexpected, and we continued our journey as friends and lovers for another five weeks.

We were headed to Vancouver hoping to meet up with our college friends Dick and Lois LaFond before heading down the Pacific coast. Our new friends with the tricked out van would be home in Bellingham in a couple weeks, so we'd take them up on their offer of a visit.

In Dick and Lois's old Dodge van we headed up the British Columbia coast where the lush rainforest meets the craggy shoreline of the deep blue Pacific. Our adventurous college pals heard about a beautiful place to camp. We backpacked in for hours. It was a hard uphill hike through old growth forests, but the feeling when we arrived was overwhelming: shimmering turquoise Garibaldi Lake with a glacier at the far end. And we were the only ones there. For a night at least, this would be our own private retreat.

August nights up there were bitter cold and in the morning the edges of the lake had a thin film of ice. We were still drinking coffee and talking about our incredible luck at having the place to ourselves when the sun melted the icy shoreline. It was about then that we heard the groan of a single engine plane and watched in awe as a seaplane made a water landing near the glacier. We were outraged. We looked at each other and in unison stuck out our middle fingers. *Fuck those rich people! We had to lug our backpacks uphill all day to get here.*

A different route down the mountain crossed flowery Alpine meadows with a view of the Black Tusk, an ancient eroded volcano whose rigid lava core is all that's left. The whole place was magic.

In Vancouver, we said adiós to our old college friends

and headed south back into the U.S. and a three-day reunion with our camping friends in Bellingham. The lush Pacific Northwest and our new found "freedom" made us care free. We were just lovers on an adventure. We headed south along the Oregon and northern California coast to San Francisco to crash with another college buddy, Terry Carolan.

By then we ran out of dough and Terry told us we could make money selling the *Berkeley Barb* underground newspaper to tourists on the street. We made a few bucks and were able to hang out for ten days but we had to scratch Mexico from the itinerary. We snagged a "drive-away" to Connecticut and drove hard across the country. In Kansas City, we located Mike Bestor, a guy from the St. Francis Club who had gotten assigned there as a VISTA to work in a public housing project. Then we drove right past Detroit and Cleveland, our home towns.

Back in New Jersey with a stroke of incredible luck, I found a good job and Scubi got recruited to work at a new teen drug intervention program in Englewood. We muddled along pretending that we hadn't decided to part ways.

We went to counseling, but we were just going through the motions, hoping I guess that someone or something would fix us. We never did say, out loud, and to each other, "We can do this. We can make this work." We finally pulled the plug and split up. It wasn't a trial separation.

Thank god my new job was completely engrossing because I was lonely and emotionally exhausted. And I didn't want to be alone with my thoughts. I sure didn't want to face my parents. It was months before I wrote home and told them we had split up and were getting a divorce. They didn't like Scubi much but I knew they'd see my divorce as another failure. Certainly my dad would. He was now on medical retirement and more miserable than before. I thought of my sister Marie still living at home and figured unfortunately she was now the only child for him to boss around. We were eight years apart and not close growing up. I wish now I'd reached out to her back then. My mom too. But I was trying to figure out my own life.

The first thing I needed was a place to live. For two months I lived with Vince McCarthy, a lawyer friend of Ronnie's, in upper Bergen County. We played guitar together and I learned some new songs. When Vince upgraded and bought a Martin, I treated myself and bought his Guild D-25, with its deep mellow sound and a handsome spruce top. Next I answered an ad and shared an apartment in Ridgefield Park with another guitar player.

Sometime during those first couple months, I went to the opening of the new youth drug intervention program. The crowd was full of people who worked with teens in Englewood and I knew most of them. I spotted Claudia Tokuyama who I'd met just once before. She was the picture of the hip urbane youth worker—a short Asian with long black hair, bell bottom jeans, a peasant blouse, a couple of necklaces, and half a dozen silver bracelets. Along with Scubi and a couple of former addicts, she was a staff counselor. I caught her eye and she looked right at me as I crossed the room toward her. We smiled, hugged, and chatted about the new center. Somehow she already knew that Scubi and I had split. We then spent the whole time moving among the crowd together, never leaving each other's side. She was new to Englewood so I introduced her to everyone I knew. Since it was a drug program there was no alcohol at the reception, so after we'd worked the crowd, I suggested we head to the bar down the street.

We sat at a small corner table and flirted over drinks. I was looking for an escape from my feelings of failure and my loneliness. Claudia had just what I was looking for. She was sexy and artsy. She even felt a little dangerous. Unfortunately I was bunking way up in northern Bergen County and she was at her parents house in Queens, so we spent a long time by her car kissing good night. I promised to call her the next day.

When I moved to Ridgefield Park, my new flame spent a lot of nights there. It was beyond awkward that she and Scubi worked together, but I was in love and it wasn't long before Claudia and I talked about living together. Claudia found us a rent-controlled sublet in Washington Heights in upper Manhattan. We bought a waterbed and some spider plants. Claudia had a cat. In Chinatown, I bought a wok, a Chinese cookbook, and some herbs and spices. We drank rosé from stemmed glasses and took bubble baths together.

Each evening and weekend as I crossed the George Washington Bridge, I slid into a world I'd never really known before, filled with love making and psychedelics, ethnic foods and urban adventures, art museums and small film houses, spring walks along streams rich with flowering mountain laurel. Claudia connected me to a carnal lust for life that forever liberated me. Meanwhile my other life, my new job in Englewood, was filled with purpose. I didn't know it then but that work marked the beginning of a five-decade pursuit: the struggle to save urban neighborhoods.

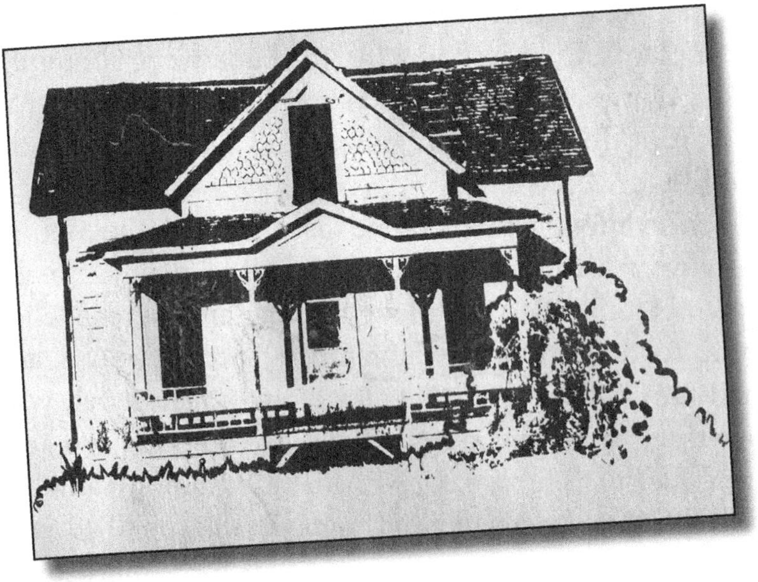

CHAPTER 6

A New Direction

The job I'd landed when Scubi and I were in marriage limbo was at the Englewood Redevelopment Agency, a federally funded Urban Renewal program. My business card read *Rehabilitation Loan Officer*. My Accounting degree paid off again. I worked in a neighborhood in Englewood's all-Black Fourth Ward. I arranged low-interest loans and construction grants for homeowners to fix up their houses. Quickly the world of urban revitalization opened up to me, and I was part of an emerging and hopeful trend: *Don't demolish old houses. Don't uproot established communities. Rehabilitate. Save old homes. Preserve neighborhoods.* I thought back on my discussions with Vince Lyons, who I'd heard was out in the Pacific Northwest and by now probably an urban planner. *I should look him up*, I thought.

I threw myself into the challenging work. I got to know a lot of the families in this all-Black neighborhood. It was exhilarating to contribute to their neighborhood's future. It didn't feel like *social work*. I harbored none of the doubts that I had at the anti-poverty agency. Most of the office staff was Black and they were a chatty group, so I learned all about Black people's everyday lives. It was eye-opening, this edge that solidly middle-class Blacks had when they talked about White society.

One day, one of my female coworkers said, "So I'm waiting for my car at the carwash and this *White* man is there. He looks at my car and turns to me. I think he's gonna say something about my Cadillac, my *ten-year-old Cadillac,* by the way. Well he says, nice as could be like, 'Can you tell me why your people follow that Muslim Farrakan?' Now mind you, I'm a Baptist. What does this man mean by asking what MY PEOPLE are doing? Can you believe that?"

I thought maybe the guy's question was more innocent than she imagined. But she and the rest of the staff clearly saw it only one way.

Occasionally someone would say to me, "Pat you don't think we hate *all* White people do you?" or "Pat, when I say that, you know I'm not talking about *you,* right?" It felt like a compliment that they didn't hold back when I was around, and I had a front row seat with a view into Black life.

My entry to a predominantly Black community was a new and reassuring experience and made it easier to imagine a society where equality reigned. On the one hand, I got to see how their daily concerns were no different than other middle-class people, but they were not part of the dominant culture and were so aware of being short changed because of their race.

One Friday morning, I got let in on a new slice of Black life. We were all working at our desks when Patricia, the Relocation Officer, jumped up waving her newspaper, "My number hit! Straight!"

The office filled with smiles and congratulations.

George, her older assistant added, "I hope you bet at least a buck, cuz you're buying lunch. I'll drive over to

Sylvia's. We'll introduce Pat to *real* soul food. Pat, you ever been to Sylvia's? In Harlem?"

Patricia waved me over to her desk, where her newspaper was spread open on top of someone's case file. Two pages of numbers—yesterday's stock quotes from the New York Stock Exchange, and at the bottom of the right hand page were the U.S. Treasury reports. She pointed to the last three digits of the US Treasury daily balance.

"See. Here's my number, 231. If you ever want to play, I place my bets next Friday for two weeks. Let me know, honey."

I asked Patricia how she picked her number.

"Here's how Black people do it, honey," and she told me a long story about a dream that involved her mother, and then she gave me a copy of her "dream book" with lists of three-digit numbers linked to all kinds of things—animals, occupations, relatives, situations, stuff in nature, cars, just about everything.

Patricia said, "Say you wake up and you had a dream about a circus or a river or a ghost; you just look it up in the dream book and you bet that number that day. I've already changed my number since mine just came in. It's not likely to come in for quite a while."

I resisted telling her how probability works.

I had a dream about the husband of Marlene, our gorgeous office secretary. He was a cop. When Patricia asked me again, I gave her twelve bucks for the next two weeks.

"Put it on 367," I said. "Straight not boxed."

I decided to go for the big bucks. I contributed over three hundred bucks a year to the mob for the next two years. My number never did come in.

• • •

The work of the Redevelopment Agency was bite-sized, as Urban Renewal projects go. It was limited to an eight-block area with the worst housing conditions in the all Black Fourth Ward. The streets were potholed, the curbs and sidewalks were cracked, and broken down. Four of the blocks were a rundown slum with deteriorated houses, all absentee-owned. Some were more like shacks. This was the Clearance Area. The Agency planned to acquire and demolish the entire four-block patch and relocate tenants to new subsidized apartments, then build a hundred new, affordable townhouses.

The adjacent four blocks where I worked were designated as a Rehabilitation Area. The old homes were larger, solidly built, and mostly owner-occupied. The majority of the homes needed work, and there were two or three that needed to be demolished. A small investment of public dollars and low interest federal loans could renew those four blocks, and the neighborhood would enjoy a long and stable future, which indeed is what happened.

There was a grim underside to a lot of the redevelopment that took place under the umbrella of "renewal." Across the country, older urban areas, mostly Black neighborhoods, were leveled using federal dollars. Stable Black communities were destroyed and people were uprooted. Those communities had little power to fight City Hall, and there were never alternative plans considered to improve conditions and maintain the stability of those poor neighborhoods. Just tear it down, make something new. Some neighborhoods fought back but few of them won those fights.

Projects like the rehabilitation of historic Society Hill in Philadelphia were the rare exception to the Tear Down and Build New paradigm. The Society Hill project became a model of urban renewal that was sensitive to the neighborhood's history and its character. Most of the eighteenth- and nineteenth-century townhouses were saved and rehabilitated. New townhouses that were built retained the same character as the original ones, and neighborhood parks and walkways were created. The restored community was touted as an unqualified success and won plenty of awards for the city planners, but in the end the project displaced a lot of the original working-class and low-income residents who'd lived there for generations. Saving urban neighborhoods for the people who lived there just wasn't on anyone's agenda.

In tiny Englewood, where the project was initiated by clergy and community leaders, preventing displacement was the number-one concern. Affordable replacement housing would be ready before buildings were demolished, and all of the new housing built on the site would be affordable.

In general, except in historic districts, the restoration of old houses had not caught on yet; Bob Vila, his sidekick, Norm, and "This Old House" wouldn't air on TV for another five years.

At the end of my first year, I got sent to a conference in Minneapolis, my first ever. I swapped work tales with other urban restorers. I took notes during workshops from experts who'd been at this work for a decade. Over coffee or a drink, people would look at my name tag and ask me about Englewood and what I did there.

"We're saving a couple of neighborhoods," I'd say. I reveled in my new identity. I was now a practitioner and here I was, exchanging ideas with urban revitalization professionals. I couldn't wait to get back to Englewood. On the flip side of the professional coin, I got a mailing from a guy named Chester Hartman in San Francisco, who was launching the Planner's Network, an association for radical planners, urbanists, academics and urban practitioners like me. I sent Hartman a letter and a check for fifteen bucks. Maybe a worthy professional career was coming together.

Confidants

When Scubi and I split, Ronnie told me about the new "no-fault" divorce law in New Jersey, and he agreed to file our papers for us whenever we were ready. My buddy wasn't surprised when he heard we'd finally pulled the plug. My doubts and struggles were well known to him. I remember telling him, "If only she'd just disappear. I wouldn't have to face up to the failure of getting divorced."

He would talk me down. "You're so fucking hard on yourself," he'd say. "Did you get that from your dad and all that Catholic upbringing? Ya know, my inner struggle is kinda the opposite. You see how my mother treats me, like I can do no wrong? She's always showing you those news clippings she saves. What I want is to curb my drive to always be better than other people, to be the most important, the one with the most newspaper clippings about him. I don't like that urge in me. That's my challenge."

I was now trying to reassure *him*. I saw what my good friend was struggling with. Ronnie valued his impressive counter-status; he wasn't traditionally successful but he was a highly regarded poverty lawyer. He was a draft counselor, definitely admired by lots of liberals and lefties. I knew that his attachment to that status is what he wanted to change, and I appreciated his willingness to confront it. That's not an easy attachment to give up.

Our conversations were always meaty, and we shared

stuff with remarkable ease. Maybe it was our different backgrounds that drew us together. I grew up in an Irish working-class neighborhood, attended Catholic schools right through college, while Ronnie was Jewish. His family was upper middle class. He'd traveled—been to Europe a couple times, and to Southeast Asia. My biggest trip was a family pilgrimage to Saint Anne de Beaupre cathedral in Quebec when I was six years old. He was the first Jew that I became friends with. Maybe I was the same for him.

Ronnie had split with his wife Marilyn. He told me about his new love, Joanne. One problem, Joanne was married and had two kids. I know he felt like she was the one and he seemed willing to give her the time and space to figure out what she would do. I was sure I wouldn't have been able to do that. The uncertainty would gnaw at me but he seemed resigned. I always thought that inside he had a kind of Buddhist nature. I wondered how long he'd hang in there.

We spent more and more time together. We played guitar and taught each other new songs and different fingerings. We traveled together—to Costa Rica, the Cayman Islands, other parts of the Caribbean—bumming around, low budget with our backpacks and guitars.

We talked endlessly about our work and politics, and the *politics* of our work—how the system is what creates poverty, not people's personal failings.

When Ronnie argued a welfare benefits case before the New Jersey Supreme Court, I sat in the chambers, in awe, learning. I was so proud of him. He could've done anything he wanted, and he'd chosen to do this. He was tall and handsome, gifted, and so accomplished. He was the co-founder of the New Jersey Tenant Organization. He'd toured around Vietnam and he spoke at anti-War teach-ins.

He ran a winning campaign for Joel Shain, his law school roommate for mayor of Orange. I couldn't imagine what running a political campaign was like. My friend's talents were so varied.

I remember in 1969 when he appeared in court with an upside down American flag sewn on the shoulder of his sport coat. The judge was pissed and called him up to the bench.

"What's the meaning of this display, Mr. Atlas? I hope you're not here in my courtroom to make some kind of political statement. You've got a client to represent."

Ronnie quietly pointed out that cops in the courtroom all had unauthorized flags on their shoulders; that the flag was not an approved symbol for police uniforms. He'd be happy to remove his if the judge required them to do the same.

The frustrated judge shook his head and told him to back away from the bench and get on with representing his client.

Maybe a Fresh Start

One day in '72, Ronnie and I met at a bar behind Englewood City Hall. It was a no-account place with a forgettable name, but the bartender was friendly and the drinks were cheap. I said hello to Scotty behind the bar and ordered a draft. Ronnie asked for a whiskey with one cube and just a splash of water.

I asked him, "Hey, did you send any slumlords up the river today?" Ronnie worked one day a week as the prosecutor for the Englewood Building Department.

"Not exactly, but I did get to mess with a couple of con-artists who'd been serving up lame excuses to the inspectors. The judge was pretty fed up, so I got him to lay on some heavy fines." He hunched his shoulders and clinked his glass against my beer mug. "Hey. *One small step for mankind.*"

As we walked to our cars, he said, "Hey, I almost forgot, why don't you join me Sunday? I'm going to Orange to meet with a bunch of folks who are pretty political. It's more of a bagel brunch than a meeting, but the discussions are always right on. I'm anxious for you to meet them. You'll like 'em. It's at John and Deena's place. It starts around 10:30. We can ride together if you come pick me up."

I knew that John had moved to Orange and was a Legal Services attorney. I looked forward to seeing him again.

"Sounds cool. I'll pick you up at ten," I said.

"Oh, and we might play touch football in the park after," he said.

I thought about our deep friendship as I headed to my car. Ronnie was really my last anchor. Other friends left and moved on. Except for Ronnie and Claudia, I was alone. My job was great, so full of interesting challenges, and I was learning the business of neighborhood revitalization, and city life with Claudia was exhilarating and irresistible, but I didn't have a "community." I worked in one place and lived across the river in another state. I felt nomadic. Like Chicago Heights when I was a teenager.

My subcompact was shoehorned between a couple of normal-sized gas guzzlers down the street from the bar. If my dad had seen my Japanese import, he'd have revoked my Detroit passport, but the fuel efficient '69 Toyota was perfect for a guy who trolled Manhattan streets every evening looking for a parking space.

I squeezed into the Toyota and lit up a Luckie as I girded myself to enter the scramble of six major highways dispensing thousands of cars, toothpaste-like, into the toll booths on the Jersey side of the massive George Washington Bridge. With winter approaching, the sun departed earlier with every cooler day, and as I joined my legion of commuters, low-hanging clouds seemed to shroud the massive bulk of Manhattan's skyline. My exit was right at the other end of the bridge, so I wouldn't have to join the crawl of the West Side Highway toward Midtown. That night, I welcomed the quiet time alone before entering the pull of Claudia's emotional vortex. I wanted to savor Ronnie's invite to join the group in Orange on Sunday and privately relish this promise of a fresh beginning.

He'd said, "You'll love this group."

I sure hope so, I thought. *I'm desperate for a fresh start.*

PART II

The Scene is Set

1970–74

SELECTIVE SERVICE SYSTEM
NOTICE OF CLASSIFICATION
This is to certify that
Patrick Joseph Morrissy
(First name) (Middle initial) (Last name)
Selective Service No.
11 115 45 297
is classified in Class 2-A
until October 1969
by Local Board unless otherwise checked below:
by Appeal Board
vote of 3 to 0
by President
6-20-69
(Date of mailing)
(Member, Executive Secretary, or clerk of local board)
(Registrant's signature)
SSS Form 110 (Rev. 5-25-67)
(Fold along this line)
BOYCOTT
LETTUCE
WIN WITH BEN
COUNCILMAN EAST WARD
OUT
NOW.
BOYCOTT
GRAPES
STOP
THE WAR
NOW

The early seventies were indistinct from the supercharged 1960s. The economic, social, and political landscape was still shifting. Civil rights, the Vietnam War, and poverty were still center stage and far from settled. The decade would be a testing ground of whether America would evolve to a more equal and peaceful place.

For me, the sixties ended in late '72 when Nixon was re-elected in a landslide. It was a bad year for Democrats that began when new Party rules opened up the delegate selection process. Delegates were no longer hand-picked by big city bosses and labor leaders; the Party opened its doors to a broad spectrum of grassroots voices—women, minorities, and young people. Despite the well-meaning intentions for more diversity, disunity was the short-term result.

At the Democratic Convention in Miami, Chicago Mayor Richard Daley's Illinois delegation wasn't seated because he hadn't followed the new rules. Instead, a delegation led by Jesse Jackson was recognized. Esteemed Massachusetts Congressman Tip O'Neill lost out in the delegate election to a nineteen-year-old McGovern supporter.

The big battle for delegates was between Senator George McGovern, the darling of the liberals, and Senator Hubert Humphrey, another liberal who'd been Lyndon Johnson's vice president and the Democratic nominee in '68 after Johnson decided not to run. Humphrey was the candidate of the Party establishment. A Black candidate, Congresswoman Shirley Chisholm, hoped to unify Black delegates to use as leverage on a second ballot. McGovern won the nomination on the first ballot.

Nixon won re-election in the fall with 60.1% of the vote. The only state McGovern won was Massachusetts. The Democratic Party was battling with itself. McGovern later famously quipped that he, "Opened the doors of the Democratic Party and twenty million people walked out."

We all hated Nixon, especially when he started his second term in 1973 and canceled a lot of Johnson's Great Society funding. When cities needed help the most, federal funding was cut and local tax bases shrunk. Cities in the northeast and midwest were becoming poorer and Blacker as Whites moved to the suburbs and manufacturing moved to the non-union South and Southwest.

Urban desperation was captured on TV when the sprawling, high rise Pruitt-Igoe public housing complex in St. Louis was demolished because it had become unlivable. The buildings were only twenty years old. Then our presidential nemesis placed a moratorium on all federal housing subsidies. There were a few protest rallies in big cities over Nixon's cuts, but most of the outcry was Op-ed columns and Letters to the Editor.

By 1972, unemployment pushed above 5% and was much higher in the poor cities. Inflation, driven by spending on the war and the Great Society programs, began driving up consumer prices. When Nixon's ninety-day wage and price controls were lifted, prices rose quickly. And then in 1973, a group of Arab countries, the Organization of Arab Oil Producing and Exporting Countries, imposed an oil embargo against countries that supported Israel during the Yom Kippur War. Oil prices quadrupled. There were long lines at gas stations and energy costs increased worldwide. The strong post-war economy was beginning to weaken. The oil

Part II: The Scene is Set (1970-74)

embargo created a move toward energy independence and a couple dozen nuclear power plants were constructed.

Meanwhile, big business and their ideological allies had quietly begun to organize politically. They'd been waiting for a time when they could rewrite the decades-old compact with government and labor that lifted the country out of the Depression. Milton Friedman and his disciples at the University of Chicago were the intellectual muscle behind a laissez faire economic policy that they claimed would untie the hands of innovators and corporations and unleash a rising economy that would "lift all boats." Capitalists like Joseph Coors and the Koch Brothers funded the Heritage Foundation and the Cato Institute, pro-business think tanks. Without fanfare, the CEOs of America's largest corporations created the Business Roundtable, preparing to take advantage of a weakening economy and claim a bigger share for themselves.

On the other end, renters were feeling the economic pinch of inflation. From 1960 to 1970, rents in the New York-northern New Jersey area rose twice as fast as the Consumer Price Index. In 1973, the CPI for New York and Northern New Jersey rose by 10.8%. With a rental vacancy rate of 2.6%, rents rose even faster.

Amidst all these economic and political shifts, environmentalism had its coming-out party in April of 1970 when millions of Americans participated in rallies, teach-ins, and activities across the country to celebrate the first Earth Day. Public awareness of air and water pollution increased, which put pressure on the government to act. Then Nixon shocked us when he announced the creation of the Environmental Protection Agency.

SDS and much of the New Left was now focused solely on ending the war. The 1973 Paris Peace Accords brought

75

an end to U.S. troop involvement in Vietnam, but air support and funding for South Vietnam continued, as did the anti-War protests, including the bombing of draft board offices. In 1973, the CIA played a secret role in the military coup that overthrew Salvador Allende, the democratically elected socialist president of Chile.

In 1972, the Equal Rights Amendment was finally approved by Congress and would require ratification by thirty-eight states by 1979 to become part of the Constitution. The following year, the Supreme Court legalized abortion when it decided *Roe v. Wade*.

In June of 1972, reporters Bob Woodward and Carl Bernstein began reporting about a break-in of Democratic Party headquarters in the Watergate Hotel. They revealed that the five men arrested had ties to the Committee for the Re-Election of the President (CREEP), but the story didn't catch fire until after Nixon's re-election.

By early 1974, both the House and Senate were investigating the Watergate break-in. Senator Sam Ervin and Congressman Peter Rodino quickly became familiar names to all of us as Nixon's impeachment took center stage. In August, we cheered when Nixon resigned.

Gerald Ford, Nixon's vice president, was kind of an unknown, but a week into his presidency, we hailed the new leader when he granted conditional amnesty to young men who refused the draft. A month later, we booed him when he pardoned Nixon of all wrongdoing related to Watergate.

Watergate made Americans trust the government even less, and the weakened economy reduced support for spending to fight poverty or combat urban decline. The Republican brand had clearly suffered, but there was a conservative force emerging that would soon be called the New Right. This group of conservative think tanks and seasoned political operatives with plenty of financial backing hoped to exploit this moment of distrust in government, a weak economy, and opposition to affirmative action and other racial remedies to attract working-class and middle-class people away from the Democrats.

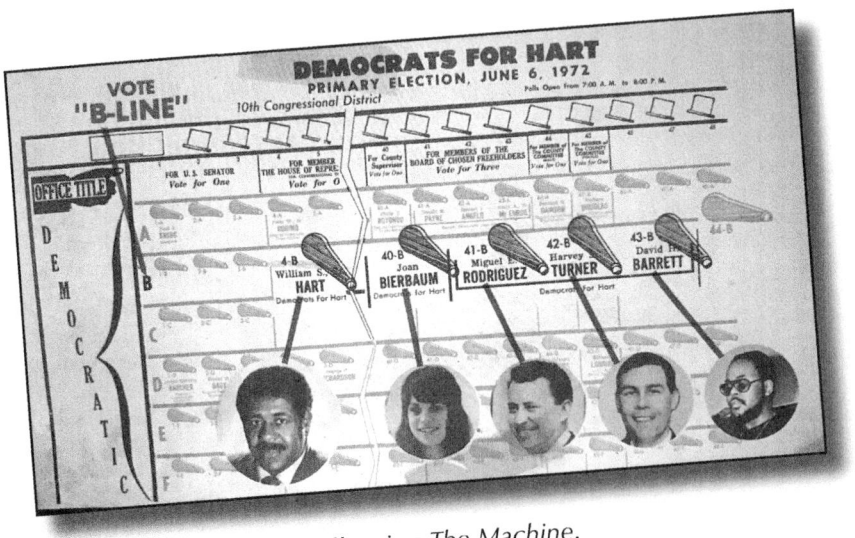

Challenging *The Machine*.
That's PACT's Joan Bierbaum, candidate for County Supervisor.

CHAPTER 7

A Solemn Pact

When Ronnie invited me to that "political" bagel brunch, he knew that I was at loose ends, looking for friends and comrades, a community to be part of again. I picked him up that Sunday morning and we headed to John and Deena's apartment in Orange. I liked John from the little time we'd spent in DC and was glad he was back in New Jersey.

"Tell me about the people in the group," I said. "Are they all intellectuals like John?"

"So you think John's an intellectual? Ha! He'll be happy to hear that. You're not nervous are you?"

"A little," I admitted.

"Listen," he said, "this group needs someone like you. Yeah, there's some intellectuals, but what *they* need is a guy from the Midwest. They're planning a camping trip. You probably own a tent, right?"

I laughed. "Sure. And a kerosene stove, a lantern, a bunch of stuff."

Ronnie smiled. "See, you're indispensable already."

Still feeling a bit shaky when we arrived, I took in the place, scoping out John and Deena's furnished-by-Goodwill apartment while scanning all the faces, most of them looking toward my tall handsome friend. I was glad to have Ronnie's imprimatur.

With an arm on my shoulder, he grinned and announced, "Hey, guys, this is my good buddy, Pat. The guy I told you about." He leaned back a little as if looking me over, "Don't be put off by his lumberjack look or the fact that he's from Detroit. He'll grow on you."

In people's eyes I sensed warmth and welcome. A few called out, "Hey Pat."

John pulled me into a big hug. "Welcome to PACT, brother Pat." And with his arm around me, he began introducing the group.

Nodding toward a guy in a button-down Oxford shirt, he said, "This is Marty, our college professor. Though right now he's teaching fifth grade to avoid the draft."

Definitely an intellectual, I thought. I imagined a tweed sport coat with leather elbow patches. I wondered if he smoked a pipe.

With a warm and open smile Marty asked, "Are you sure you're ready for a bunch of opinionated Jews?" He clearly meant it as a welcome but I was already feeling like the kid who got put into the advanced class by mistake.

"I'll just sit next to you, if that's okay."

Marty nodded.

John pointed to a woman sitting back in an overstuffed chair who responded with a big smile. "That's Marty's wife, Joan. She's our only scientist but also our social chair-*person*."

"You can sit by me," said Joan. "I don't pay attention to half of what these guys are saying."

Joan and Marty had already made me feel more at ease.

"Then there's Mark." John nodded toward the bearded, balding fireplug in an argyle sweater vest. "He's our resident therapist and in charge of political theory and using big words."

Mark smiled at me and shook his head, rolling his eyes about John's remark. I was curious about Mark, the Sigmund Freud look-alike. I soon learned that the fireplug therapist had been a boxer or once aspired to be one.

"You know my wife, Deena," John continued.

As I stopped to say hi to Deena, who I hadn't seen in two years, John moved on. "Meet Linda and Joanne, who had to skip Mass to hang out with a bunch of Jews and eat bagels and lox."

Linda Barucky and Joanne Corris seemed like polar opposites. Linda was thin and sat straight-backed, her hands folded in her lap and her lips pursed in a tight, midwestern smile at John's remark, while busty, artful Joanne tossed her head back and let out a hearty Sicilian laugh, her red lipstick shining.

"This is Phyllis," said John, leaning toward a woman who seemed startled that she'd been put on the spot.

She responded with barely a smile and a simple "Hello." Phyllis seemed tentative, like she was the one meeting this group for the first time.

John nodded again toward Phyllis. "Sometimes I think she's the only one here who listens when I speak, *and* she's the only one here who's gone from a picket line to a jail cell."

That made me wonder. Nothing about Phyllis spoke of a "hardened activist." She seemed quite the opposite, not reserved exactly but maybe just socially awkward.

John gave my shoulder a brotherly squeeze. "There's a few others in the group who aren't here today. Maybe they heard *you* were coming. I don't know."

I filled a coffee cup as Joanne Corris approached. I was about to say hello when all conversation stopped. A short, squat woman with an electric presence came through the door, suddenly filling the space—an explosion of frizzy hair and earrings, dressed in jeans and a peasant blouse, beads and bracelets. She radiated the room with her chubby face and huge smile, and electric presence. This was my first encounter with Marsha "Earth Mother."

With a theatrical roll of her eyes, she threw her arms up. I could almost hear the drum roll as she emphasized each word. "Guess — what — the — *fucking* — Gavones — did — this time!" She let out a sigh of disgust and reported in hilarious detail what her next-door neighbors, the Gavone family I guessed, had done. Yet another crazy, un-neighborly thing.

Everyone knew about her neighbors, the Gavones. The *fucking* Gavones. So I asked Joanne, "What's the deal with the Gavones?"

I was caught off guard when she flashed me a sweet and tender look and laid her hand on my shoulder. "You know, Pat," she hesitated and smiled broadly, "that's not their name. *Gavone* is Italian slang. It means, like, a lowlife, or an uncouth person."

I looked up toward the ceiling as we both laughed.

"Well, now you've met Marsha," she said. "I'm Joanne Corris. Well, my family name is Leone. My dad's here sometimes. You two will get along. His name's Peter. He's a short Sicilian with a big nose and a big heart and old-time blue-collar politics. This group of college grads, they all love him. I kid him that he's their working-class mascot. I can't wait for you to meet him. He's a union welder."

"Joanne, I'm afraid to ask, what's PACT?"

"Oh, there's no reason why you'd know *that*. I don't know who named our group. It stands for Political Action Coordinating Team — of the Oranges."

Part II: The Scene is Set (1970-74)

I was about to hear more about Joanne's family when Marsha called across the room, "Who's the new guy? Hey, new guy! What's your name?"

I didn't appreciate being put on the spot by Mama Cass. "*New guy* is fine," I said. "Just call me New Guy."

People laughed and she flashed a big grin.

"I like this new guy."

I was starting to feel at home.

Joanne was still laughing about Marsha when she said to me, "Wait til you meet our bigger-than-life, union militant and former Communist agitator, Whitey Goodfriend."

"That's his *real* name? *Whitey Goodfriend*?"

"Oh yeah and he's real—*really* real."

People settled in with their coffee and bagels. I sat on the floor next to my newfound interpreter Joanne, listening as folks talked about this and that. My head was spinning.

What an interesting group of folks. I could fit in with this group, I think. I hope!

Suddenly the discussion kicked into high gear. People were talking about the recent Primary Election in Essex and apparently Joan was on the ballot.

Joan said, "Don't forget, PACT had its own candidate on the ballot for Essex County Supervisor." She looked in my direction and said, "Me."

"That's right," someone said. "Joan could be running the County government now and we'd all have no-show jobs. She just needed about thirty thousand more votes."

"That's right," Joan said. "You guys let me down. I did my part. And now *you're* paying for it. You'll all have to earn an honest living."

People all laughed while John tried to focus the discussion.

"Listen," he said, "if we want to build a *movement*, it's

83

got to be around *bread-and-butter* issues." He paused for effect. "Things that directly affect people's lives, not some far off notions about making government more efficient or responsive or even more honest. *Pocketbook* concerns." John was a Legal Services lawyer and it became clear that he had a plan that he wanted PACT to get behind. He continued, "Like rising rents and landlords who don't make repairs or even do simple maintenance. All week long I represent tenants. These are the issues they're facing and they're not alone. All tenants—poor *and* middle class—are facing higher rents. Rents that are rising, way faster than wages."

John understood issues of class and race from his inner-city work in DC. Meaningful political action was his thing, and he could articulate a practical political analysis, one that was immediate and that we should act on. I began paying closer attention to John as he pitched the strategy of a citywide organization to represent all tenants.

He had been right earlier when he said that Phyllis paid attention when he spoke. Phyllis was hard for me to figure out. She liked to talk about people—who was up to what or who said what about someone else. I wasn't prepared to take her very seriously, but I could see that she brought her teacherly attention and discipline to this discussion. She was asking about how to organize a group like John was advocating.

Ronnie caught my eye, grinned, and nodded toward John, as if to say, *This is what I was talking about when I said you'll like this group.*

As the discussion and brunch gathering was ending, Joan Bierbaum was the first to come up to me. Smiling broadly, she asked, "What do you make of our little group here?"

By way of answering I asked, "Did you really run for—what was it? County Supervisor?"

"Yeah," she said. "I got this call from Whitey; wait til you meet *him*."

I told her I had already been warned.

"So Whitey says," Joan put on a serious look and dropped her voice to imitate him. "'So listen, Joan. Baraka is putting together a county wide ticket and their slate already has a Black, a Puerto Rican, an Irishman, and an Italian. They said they wanted a Catholic woman from Bloomfield, but I told them they need a Jewish woman to round out the ticket and I have just the right person. You *gotta* do this.' It was clear he had already suggested my name and that I was with PACT. He said, 'Opportunities like this don't come around every day. Your PACT group can get into an alliance with Baraka and the Black nationalists from Newark. That's like striking political gold. It's what your group is missing. The Black/White alliance.'"

Joan smiled and shook her head. "I'd never run for office before, but Whitey said 'You don't have to do anything. Nobody expects you to win or even to campaign. They're trying to win District Leader spots on that ticket and shake up the Party. They just need your name on the ticket.' So, I said I'd do it. What'd I have to lose?"

I loved that Joan would say yes to a wild, out-of-the-box idea like that. I soon saw a campaign flier for the ticket, complete with photos, and sure enough, there was the United Nations coalition.

The 1972 ill-fated campaign where Joan had been the candidate for County Supervisor was meant to be a significant challenge to Democratic County Chairman Harry Lerner, and it was birthed in several locations throughout Essex. There were pockets of opposition everywhere, but Lerner beat them back easily. The guy controlled all the county government patronage—jobs, contracts, appointments and more. It was easy to demand loyalty when you had that much largesse at your fingertips.

After brunch, Sam, Marsha's husband, and a few other guys joined us in Orange Park, where we met up with another group for some touch football. John was our quarterback. He ran the huddle and told us all what to do. Guys suggested other options, but we always ran John's plays.

After the game, both teams retired to Toast of the Town, the big bar room at the back end of a liquor store. It was the kind of well-worn place that went unchanged for generations. There was a long hefty wooden bar, some long tables, and a few round ones. The walls had the standard neon beer signs, and the clock behind the bar was fifteen minutes fast to ensure the place was empty before the legal closing time.

It was my kind of place. We ordered pizza and pitchers of beer. Then the post-game trash talk began.

Ronnie asked, "Has anybody wondered why John always plays quarterback and he calls all the plays?"

I added, "It was his ball we were playing with, right? He might go home if we don't run his plays."

John jumped right in. "Look, somebody suggest some plays."

Then someone said, "We do but somehow we always end up running yours."

"I can't help it if you guys don't have the guts to stick up for what you think. Anyhow, my team won today. That says something, right?"

And on it went, back and forth.

Ronnie leaned over and put his arm around my shoulder. I felt like I was already a part of this cool group.

On the ride home, Ronnie made it clear that PACT was not just politics and some touch football; there were parties, potluck dinners, camping trips, playing music. I confessed that maybe I'd found my new community. Ronnie tried to hide his pleasure. His recruitment had been so effortless. I kept coming to brunch and touch football and pizza and beer. Soon, I was invited to a spaghetti dinner at Sam and Marsha's, then a house party to which I brought Claudia. Before long, I was subsumed into the ranks. There was no secret handshake, but I thought back to when I'd pledged the St. Francis Club. The Club motto was *Qualis Socius Talis Domus*—As the Members So Goes the Club. I felt the possibility of that same sort of bond.

I was new to all this political organizing; I'd protested and worked with wayward teens and with poor homeowners to fix up their homes, but Ronnie and John understood *politics*—how to fight back politically. Ronnie was comfortable speaking to large groups and dealing with the press. He advised tenant leaders on how to bring people together and build organizations, get laws changed, and make the government accountable. John was obsessed with articulating how power is exercised in our society with political strategy to build power at the grassroots. I found it all irresistible.

Years after Ronnie went to the 1972 Democratic Convention in Miami, I heard how he'd gone with Joel Shain, who had just been elected mayor of Orange, with Ronnie running his campaign. Joel, a political newbie, convinced Harry Lerner, the Essex County Democratic Boss, to name him as an at-large Delegate. Then Joel somehow maneuvered himself to give a speech seconding the nomination of New Jersey Congressman Peter Rodino for Vice President. Ronnie wrote Joel's three-minute nominating speech.

Though Rodino was not yet the national figure he would become when he presided over the Watergate investigation,

Joel relished his visibility on behalf of the revered Essex County Congressman. Despite Joel's rousing delivery of Ronnie's nominating speech, only fifty-seven delegates (2%) voted for Rodino.

By 1972, Rodino, the son of Italian immigrants, represented the 10th District in the urban core of Essex for twenty-three years. Now the district was majority African American, and Black leaders had an eye on that seat. But Rodino was popular, had the backing of Boss Lerner, and held fast to a liberal agenda. It was that year that Rodino faced his first real Primary challenge when East Orange mayor Bill Hart, leading the anti-Lerner ticket, ran against him. Rodino prevailed over Hart and two other Black candidates, but Hart's candidacy represented a coming wave of Black political power in Essex.

Bill Hart fought his way into public office, becoming East Orange's first Black City Councilman in 1960. Nine years later, he was elected the first Black mayor of a New Jersey city. Hart knew how to work with the established political bosses and when it made sense to challenge them.

Joan Bierbaum had been on Hart's ticket, but PACT still wasn't even a blip on the electoral radar. That would come later when John's organizing vision, modeled on his older brother's, came to fruition.

The two brothers, now radical lawyers, had grown up in a comfortable, upper middle-class neighborhood of Teaneck, New Jersey. Their father, Manny, owned a string of shoe stores and the family had a live-in maid. I remember seeing a picture of John in college with a girlfriend. Maybe it was Deena. They were in a convertible with the top down at University of Miami, a party school known as Suntan U.

The photo of a college playboy was difficult for me to

square with the serious and intellectual guy I knew. When I asked John where he first got introduced to left politics, he told me about this one professor who inspired him intellectually and taught him about the *power elite*, the small group of individuals who hold disproportionate control over corporate business, the military, the political establishment, and the unequal society that flows from that.

After graduation, John followed Ronnie to Boston University Law School. He wanted a law degree, but he didn't feel law school was a good fit. He wasn't going to practice the type of law that most law students were preparing for. After law school, he got a VISTA assignment to a Washington DC slum, where he worked for the Cahns, a husband and wife pair of law professors who ran an urban legal clinic. John was assigned to work with a Black community group, battling to save their neighborhood from the Urban Renewal wrecking ball.

John told me that the Cahns proposed a radical vision: empower low-income citizens with legal tools to fight systemic injustice and transform the poor into active participants in their own liberation.

When John came back to New Jersey, he wanted to be like the Cahns. Ronnie was working in Orange City Hall and he told John about a position at Essex Legal Services. John was eager to follow in his brother's footsteps and organize tenants, so a job at Legal Services was the perfect starting point.

John hoped to replicate what the Cahns were doing in DC. He thought that if Legal Services were to live up to its promise of equal access to the law, then it should act as lawyers for the poor people's *movement*. In Orange, he didn't find a poor people's organization that was dealing with housing issues, so like Ronnie, who co-founded New

Jersey Tenants Organization, John set out to make one happen.

I'd now been to a handful of PACT meetings, some house parties, and a few potluck suppers. The political discussions were lively, drifting week to week from topics like the war, civil rights, Black power, Nixon. I loved it. The brunches had the feel of what I thought the European salons must have been like. Mark was known for historical and literary references, while Marty soberly delivered short unimpassioned lectures. Then Marsha would pipe in, "You're both full of shit," and she'd bring the discussion down to earth. Marsha saw it all differently. She was a diehard communitarian. *Put your efforts into building a beautiful community within this mess. Love each other. Spread peace. Help one another. Have fun. Get laid. Get high.* I would come to really love Marsha.

PACT's Trailblazers

I gradually picked up some of Orange's surprisingly rich political history. PACT had a spiritual and ideological predecessor from early in the civil rights era. It was a Black organization named Citizens for Representative Government (CRG). I came to hear about CRG because Mark talked reverentially about Ernie Thompson, the organizer behind the grassroots group's successes. Ernie sounded larger than life, a Black union organizer with the nickname "Big Train."

To PACT members, Ernie was a legend. He organized for the United Electrical, Radio and Machine Workers of America (the UE), a militant union affiliated with the relatively new, left-wing Congress of Industrial Organizations, the CIO. Eventually, Ernie, a leader of the National Negro Labor Council, was labeled a Communist and run out of the labor movement by the forces of McCarthyism.

Part II: The Scene is Set (1970-74)

Suddenly, Ernie found himself with time on his hands, living in what he called the "two-bit Jim Crow town" of Orange. I wish I'd met Ernie. He'd died just a year before I arrived in Orange. Many years later, I worked with his wife, Maggie, his daughter, Mindy, and granddaughter, Molly, in Orange.

It was 1958 when Ernie brought his talents to political action in Orange, and Black citizens became civil rights activists and fueled the fight for Black political representation. Back then, there were no Blacks on the City Council or the Board of Education, and none who worked in City Hall. A handful worked on the garbage trucks. There were no Black teachers or coaches in the high school. CRG quickly won a fight to desegregate a pair of elementary schools and got a Black educator appointed to the School Board. The all-White City Board of Commissioners was their next target.

Orange politics was tightly controlled by leaders from its two dominant ethnic groups: the Italians and the Irish. The Italians had the upper hand it seemed in local politics, though the Irish, through the Codey and Dodd families, represented Orange in the state General Assembly and Senate. Blacks and Jews were on the outside looking in.

Black-led CRG built an integrated alliance and desegregated the elementary schools, changed the City Charter, and elected the first Black members to the Board of Education and City Council, creating the first cracks in the White power structure. Young activists from the East Ward like Becky Doggett, who would go on to be a grassroots force in Essex County, learned coalition building from the talented union organizer.

After the school desegregation victory, CRG set out to dismantle the system that perpetuated White control of the City Board of Commissioners. It was an outmoded form of government that vested all city power in the hands of Commissioners elected city wide. This left Blacks with no representation. The mayor was chosen by the Commissioners.

Changing the City Charter could change that, but it meant mounting a successful petition drive and then mobilizing a majority of voters. After a hard-fought and bitter campaign, a Mayor and Council form of government was adopted in 1963. Benjamin Franklin Jones, a Black CRG member, was elected Councilman from the majority Black East Ward. Finally, a third of Orange's citizens had representation.

Ben Jones was re-elected in 1967, but that celebration was short-lived. A nasty fight over building a new high school raised anti-Black sentiment, and incredibly, in 1969, with CRG on the wane, the city's charter was changed again back to Commission form. But by then, Ben was a popular Councilman, and in 1970, he ran citywide for a spot on the Commission. So did Joel Shain. That spring, when PACT held a peace rally in Orange Park, they asked Ben to speak to their crowd of two hundred people. PACT endorsed Joel and Ben. That's when Joel recruited his college and law school buddy, Ronnie, to be his campaign manager.

With Joel and Ben Jones running with PACT's endorsement, and Ronnie running Joel's campaign, this created an opening for PACT to expand its political base. Decades later, I asked Joel to tell me about his long-shot election as Orange's mayor.

At Rutgers, the former mayor met Ronnie, who helped him get elected class president. Joel was in ROTC, so after law school, he was shipped off to Vietnam and returned home to Orange in 1970. He told me how Joel Freedman, the owner of Muriel's Dress Shop, called him to a meeting in the back of the dress shop with Leroy Jones, a Black community leader.

"Freedman said, 'We'd like to support you running for office, would you be interested?' I told them I didn't have any money. 'Don't worry, we'll raise all the money. Leroy will run your campaign.' I called Ron immediately. 'What do you think?' He said, 'I'm in. Let's get that billboard at the corner of Main and Day.' We spent most of our money on that billboard. It was Orange and Black, the Orange High School colors. Ron and Leroy ran the campaign."

Jones and Shain were elected to the five-member Commission, along with Harry Callahan, Carmine Capone, and John Trezza, all part of the old guard. The trio probably weren't happy sharing power with a Black and a young liberal Jew, but when it came time to select a mayor from among their ranks, the two Italians couldn't get the Irishman to support one of them for mayor. Joel was the compromise, and the lanky, personable, and ambitious newcomer became mayor.

Joel needed Ronnie to help him navigate the political minefield that he'd face running the city. That's how Ronnie became City Treasurer. Leroy Jones was appointed Deputy Director of Community Development. Ben Jones got to be in charge of Parks and Recreation. That's where he first earned his reputation as a guy who really delivered for the people in the neighborhoods.

Like Ernie and CRG, John was charting a course to grow "people power." I admired his vision and his unfounded optimism that PACT members wanted to go there with him. He was so earnest when he'd say, "If we want to build a movement, then we need to organize around *bread and butter* issues—things that make a difference in peoples' lives like rents and living conditions." At Essex Legal Services, he represented poor tenants in Orange, East Orange, and the other small cities and inner ring suburbs bordering Newark. His caseload was a constant flow of tenants facing eviction or fighting with landlords over repairs and maintenance.

John wanted all of us in PACT to see things through a "power lens."

"Housing should be a fundamental human right. It's not something that people can do without. It's not just another commodity, subject to the whims of the market. But without political power? Well, then the landlords, bankers, real estate developers, they'll make the rules. And we get screwed."

The local housing market was tight. The vacancy rate in New York and Northern New Jersey was 2.6%, and from 1960 to 1970, the Consumer Price Index (the inflation rate) rose by a third while rents rose by almost twice that.

John made another convincing and compelling strategic point. "This is an issue that unites the poor and middle class, unlike so many issues that divide us. That's important." He explained how New Jersey Tenants Organization didn't emerge from poor, inner-city tenants battling slumlords. It started among high-rise tenants facing large rent increases in middle-class Fort Lee.

John's vision was urban tenant organizations coalescing with the momentum created by NJTO's middle class and suburban base. What a powerful coalition.

He sketched out a model: City- and town-wide organizations with dues paying members and elected leaders. The groups represent the interests of tenants in their city or town. Sort of like labor unions.

I bought it. Completely.

John was articulating what I was thinking and feeling: that people should have control over their housing and communities.

Orange was still a city dominated by the clannish and clubby Irish and the conservative old world Italians, but with Joel as mayor and Ronnie in City Hall, maybe John and PACT could write the next chapter of politics in Orange.

Orange Tenants Association

On Sunday mornings, John continued to press his message. I admired how clear and confident he was: "We need to build grassroots organizations that can contend for power. Power over things that matter to poor and middle-class people. Building those organizations is what will make a difference. Nothing else. Not lawsuits. Not op-ed opinion pieces. Not candidates." He'd pause, "Well. Unless of course we run our own."

The first step was membership organizations of tenants, and John wanted PACT to help lead the organizing. Not everyone in PACT was willing to sign on. John was relentless but never confrontational. It wasn't his nature. He hoped, I guess, that the strength of his ideas would convince us. Marty Parker and Linda Barucky joined and helped to build a tenant association in Orange. Phyllis chipped in, but she saw a bigger role for herself in East Orange. The Newark school teacher was John's most important convert.

I found John's message of grassroots political power irresistible. It was what I was looking for when I quit the anti-poverty agency; I'd seen how social services that helped poor "clients" were vastly different from empowering people to speak for themselves and demand that government and society and the economy benefit them too. I now dismissed the *do good-ism* that liberal America cherished.

I was prepared to devote myself to building a movement with all the people who weren't getting a fair shake and stake our claim to a society where no one is left behind. A society where if you're willing to work, you can make a living and support a family and live in a community that's a good place to raise your kids. Growing up in Detroit, I thought most people were like us: that they lived in modest houses in decent neighborhoods, except of course, for the rich—they lived in a few swanky neighborhoods, but there weren't that many of them. It wasn't until maybe seventh grade that I saw what life was like on the other side of the tracks.

I remember approaching Comiskey Park one day. My dad was cruising for a cheap parking spot as my first White Sox baseball game was about to start. Black men in undershirts were trying to flag in patrons to park for a buck on the dusty patches in front of dingy, overcrowded houses, where mothers on kitchen chairs rocked little ones and stared out from crumbling front porches. It was my first view of a Negro slum. I remember feeling like a voyeur; people's destitute lives were on display for me to peep in on. I looked away, but I couldn't help gazing back again. The movement I was now a part of with John wouldn't allow that level of poverty. Not in a country this wealthy.

John was on a mission. His immediate goals were to pass a local rent control law *and* create a citywide tenants organization in the process, often strategizing with Ronnie. Joel Shain was now mayor and he was anxious to bring rent control to Orange.

With politics in Orange in flux, this could be the right

moment for tenants to get some help from their city leaders. The Irish and Italian pols had engineered a return to the archaic Commission form of government to cement their hold on city government, but then a Black and a Jew were elected. And they supported rent control.

John and Ronnie modeled a rent-leveling ordinance on the one that Ronnie penned for Fort Lee a year earlier. Joel was prepared to introduce it, and Ben supported it. What about the old guard? Could they get a third vote? Passing the rent ordinance would affect a lot of family budgets.

John focused on getting people engaged in the fight. A good political battle, especially when you win, could build an organization. People would become *political*. They would learn what it takes to move the levers of power—how to bring out their neighbors, speak at a public meeting, pressure elected officials, and speak to the press. That's what was needed: people with an issue campaign under their belt. Winning was way better than losing. Losses can be debilitating, but political experience was something invaluable, and you didn't have it until you'd been in a public fight. That's what John wanted.

It was important for John to connect to Black community activists. Alberta Mitchell surfaced at city council meetings, and along with Letters to the Editor, she demanded city action on poor housing conditions. For various reasons, John and Alberta didn't make a formal alliance at first, but the public impression was that they were on the same team. The Tenants Rights Team. Alberta spoke of an Orange tenants association as if a formal organization existed. It was more of a concept that all tenants in Orange wanted the same thing: fair rents and decent conditions. John subtly promoted the idea that he and Alberta were allies working closely together.

Soon, the Orange Tenants Association was founded, at least on paper. John recruited Marty Parker and Linda Barucky to act as board members, and the paper organization began to take shape in the weekly press. John was feeding press releases to the *Orange Transcript* while Alberta was calling the editor regularly. Understaffed weekly papers welcome press releases that are well written with people quoted. A public issue like rent control and apartment living conditions is solid news in a city of thirty thousand. They got lots of press.

One day, John asked if he could quote me.

"Sure," I said.

A few days later, Alberta Mitchell and Patrick Morrissy, the *volunteer accountant* for the Orange Tenants Association, were quoted in the *Orange Transcript*.

I could see John's strategy playing out as he worked the media. He was both giving voice to beleaguered tenants and projecting the image of a place for them to join with others and win real change in their living conditions. It helped that the civil rights movement had legitimized, even romanticized, organizing and protesting. I wondered if the OTA would become a viable vehicle for both the poor and middle class like John imagined. If so, that was exciting.

With the night of the Rent Control vote approaching, the fate of the rent ordinance was still unknown. It needed the vote of one more Commissioner. Articles in the *Orange Transcript* and the *Star Ledger* brought out tenants from around the city. Phyllis and I stood at the door to the Commissioners' meeting, handing out Orange Tenants Association flyers. If people hadn't known about the OTA before then, they did now. The process of getting the ordinance up for a vote was what began to gel a citywide tenants organization. I learned that for an ordinance to become law required two separate votes: passage on First Reading, and then at least thirty days later a Second Reading, with a public hearing, and then adoption.

The Ordinance got the necessary votes to be put up for Second Reading, but passage was still not guaranteed. We had a month to mobilize support, starting with the new names and phone numbers we'd collected at the First Reading. John made it clear that the landlords would be well represented at the public hearing.

We were now officially engaged in politics. This is what I'd been looking for.

The ordinance had a legal wrinkle that would allow opponents a way to delay passage. The state Supreme Court had not ruled on the constitutionality of local governments regulating rents. The 1972 Fort Lee Ordinance that Ronnie had authored had been upheld on appeal and was on its way to the state Supreme Court. John and Ronnie and Joel felt certain that it would be upheld, but the unresolved legal issue created cover for elected officials who hoped to dodge the issue.

For Second Reading, the Commission chambers were packed, with people standing three deep in the back. Again, Phyllis and I manned the entrance, handing out flyers. I loved greeting each person and explaining our flyer. Passion filled the air as tenants complained about rising rents and bad conditions. Landlords raised the scary specter of Orange becoming an abandoned slum because building owners couldn't make a profit. This blend of beautiful chaos was real democracy in action. People needed their government to take action. More than two dozen tenants experienced their first time at a mic, reminding elected officials that they'd been elected to protect the citizens of

Orange. I got goosebumps. Poor and middle-class tenants had come out, Black and White. John's vision was taking shape.

The Rent Leveling Ordinance passed. Landlords were now prohibited from raising rents more than the change in the Consumer Price Index. Tenants were jubilant. John and Alberta were interviewed by a news reporter, and both mentioned the underlying story, that a grassroots organization had taken shape. Tenants had come together to fight for their right not to be "rent gouged." John felt doubly victorious. OTA had a ways to go before it gelled as a solid organization, but it was no longer a *paper* organization. There was work to be done, and John imagined a role for everyone. We didn't all have to be an organizer; we could type or mimeograph leaflets. We could write a press release or be the volunteer accountant. The way John put us into action was impressive. He was the quarterback.

The *Orange Transcript* ran a front page picture of John at the microphone and named him "The Leveler." We enjoyed the double meaning. The OTA was leveling the political playing field for people who usually had no influence. Four or five PACT members had played a role, getting our feet wet and learning how to navigate in the political arena. Phyllis was taking notes. She was now a tenant in East Orange and had already started advising tenants who needed help with their landlords.

The Oranges felt like a good fit for me. I was desperate for a political community, and I liked all the people in PACT. The urban neighborhoods and the shopping districts felt familiar to a guy who'd grown up in Detroit, but I'd never planned on becoming a tenant organizer. Though once I got a taste, it filled something essential for me: I was now part of building grassroots power, fighting alongside people for control over something so essential as housing. A community coming together—Blacks and Whites, the poor and the middle class, working to ensure that in this powerful rich economy that no community was left behind. I saw from just a handful of group discussions and two city council meetings that this strategy of grassroots organizing had real promise. What was germinating in urban Essex County was the real thing. I planned to become a part of it.

Englewood

Meanwhile, in the City of Englewood, I was knee-deep in the work of neighborhood rehabilitation. Englewood was a fascinating small city. It had been biracial as long as anyone could remember. About one-third of its twenty-five thousand residents were Black. The mansions on the hill toward the Palisades above the Hudson River were originally occupied by New York financiers. Their Black servants lived on the flat land down the hill on the other side of the railroad tracks that ferried the big shots to Wall Street.

Englewood was a divided city. The East Hill of the First and Second Wards contained big houses that got decidedly bigger as they reached the crown of the hill, with views of the George Washington Bridge and New York City. Across the tracks was the Third Ward, mostly blue collar and White, and the all-Black Fourth Ward.

Even in the early seventies, most Black people still lived in the Fourth Ward, though the Third Ward was becoming integrated as more Black middle-class families found their way to Englewood. The city had good public schools, and its connection to New York attracted a lot of creative people.

The city had an active civic culture. People were involved in PTAs and served on all kinds of committees and in volunteer posts. The effort to deal with the down-and-out neighborhood in the Fourth Ward grew out of that culture. When I'd taken the job, I had been unaware that the project had started at the grassroots level with clergy and community leaders. I now spent every working day in that neighborhood, working for the organization they'd created: The Englewood Redevelopment Agency.

In the late sixties, a group of elected officials, clergy, and Black community leaders crafted a vision of clearing out the slum housing. They wanted to build new high-quality subsidized apartments, help homeowners fix their homes, and rebuild the streets, curbs, and sidewalks. Community leaders smartly insisted that affordable replacement housing be built before people were displaced from the clearance area. The history of Urban Renewal projects is littered with the stories of people displaced who somehow never managed to reoccupy the new replacement housing.

The nonprofit Greater Englewood Housing Corporation (GEHC) was established, and two sites were chosen for the new housing: one in the Fourth Ward and the other at the far edge of the Second Ward south of Interstate 80. The project was nearly upended when a lawsuit was brought by a Second Ward homeowners' organization, the First Association of Citizens and Taxpayers (FACT). FACT challenged the property subdivision and zoning variances and raised fears about crime and property values. Attorneys for the city rushed into court and battled the meritless suit all the way up the state Supreme Court. In June of 1970, the justices decided against FACT and upheld GEHC in every instance.

The City Council designated the eight-block area as the

Humphrey—William Street Urban Renewal Area and applied for the federal money. The city was awarded a federal Urban Renewal grant for six million dollars.

I loved helping to lift up that neighborhood, especially getting to know each of the homeowners. I typically scheduled our first meeting in their home. At the kitchen or dining room table, I'd explain the program: If you fix up your house, there are outright grants of $3500 that most of them qualified for. That caught their attention. And there were 3% federal loans, a rate far below conventional home improvement loans.

One day, Paul called me into his office to say that he wanted to pick up the pace of the rehabilitation project, and he planned to hire an additional person. His plan was to hire a loan officer and to put me in charge of the program, overseeing the new loan officer and Harold, the construction manager. He added that he had more assignments for me in addition to the rehab program.

I interviewed six-foot-six Fulton Hines. He had a lending background, but I noticed that his first employer immediately after college was listed as The Harlem Wizards.

"Did you *play* for the Wizards?" I asked.

"I sure did. Eight years. But the travel schedule got too much. I wanted to start a family and get on with my career. But let me tell you, except for the nonstop travel, it was exciting."

It wasn't long before I asked Harold, the crusty construction manager, if I could accompany him on his inspections. I asked endless questions about his work write-ups and cost estimates that we kept in each property folder. The real work of fixing up these houses was way more interesting than deciphering title searches, reading credit reports, and putting together loan packages. I wished I had that construction knowledge, but it was impossible to really get it second-hand by tagging along on inspections and asking questions.

There was a small, two-bedroom house, maybe about a thousand square feet, in the rehab area that was scheduled to be demolished. It was in bad shape and wasn't much of a house, even when it was new.

I asked Charlie, our acquisition officer, if I could see his property file. I reviewed the photos and the property details on the appraisals. The acquisition price was ten thousand dollars.

Maybe I should buy it and fix it up on weekends.

The more I pondered the idea, the more I realized that what I really wanted was to learn the rehab trade, to become a renovator. I got Harold to inspect the house with me, and together we worked up a rehab estimate. It was definitely doable, especially if I did most of the work. I decided to approach the director with my plan.

I used a fiscal approach with Paul about how the Agency could recoup its acquisition costs and not have to pay for demolition. Paul liked my enthusiasm, but the optics of the Agency taking a property by eminent domain and then selling it to someone on staff looked suspect, regardless of the appraisals or the cost savings. It simply looked bad and Paul couldn't take that risk.

I asked Charlie if the owner might accept a private offer.

"Probably," he said. "The guy's anxious to sell. He's pushing us for a quick closing."

Charlie gave me the guy's phone number. When I called him, he said he didn't care where his ten grand came from, but that a closing was scheduled in just two weeks.

"Just don't screw up my deal with your agency if you can't come up with the dough in time."

There was no way I could get ten thousand dollars in two weeks, and I knew the guy would raise hell if I delayed his closing. The deal slipped through my fingers, but the idea still burned in my gut. I had already dreamed about taking that old, worn out house and making it new again—swinging a hammer, hanging windows and doors, updating the kitchen and the bath, plastering, painting, refinishing the old floors.

John had a completely different itch. He was trying to clearly articulate how our work related to the larger fight against growing corporate dominance. I listened intently and tended to always agree with his latest insights. I'd read the articles he recommended; the academic journal articles were obscure and suffered from a constipated academic style, but I always tried to understand the concepts. But I wasn't a theorist, and I wasn't satisfied with just ideas. I was oriented toward doing. That's what attracted me to the work of neighborhood rehabilitation. It was the inheritance of my Irish Catholic upbringing: hard work and moral action. It fit my own sense of personal mission, though my exact role was evolving. On my way, I had John and Ronnie as my political mentors. Within PACT, I still felt a little like an outsider. They were all from New Jersey and lived close to their parents and saw them frequently. Whereas I'd moved six hundred miles away from my family.

LEFT
EXIT 47 A
280 EAST
The Oranges
Newark
EXIT ONLY
80 EAST
Paterson
New York City

CHAPTER 8

Welcome to the Oranges

Interstate 80 cuts eastward through the farmland and exurbs of northern New Jersey on its way to the George Washington Bridge, and then on to New England. Before it does that, there's a freeway extension, I-280, that takes you to lower Manhattan. But first it slices through some urban neighborhoods and then across the Meadowlands, then snakes its way through Jersey City to the Holland Tunnel and lower Manhattan. The I-280 exit is marked The Oranges and Newark, referring to the four municipalities at Newark's western border: the cities of Orange and East Orange, the Town of West Orange, and the Village of South Orange.

The four Oranges were once part of the Township of Orange but three broke away in the 1860s, mostly over taxation and spending issues. For a century, each city cherished its distinct identity, but by the 1970s, the rest of the world saw just a singular divide: *urban* East Orange and Orange and *suburban* South Orange and West Orange. Construction of the interstate tore through Orange and East Orange, eliminating entire blocks of businesses and homes and separating neighborhoods from the bustling Main Street that linked the sister cities.

By the 1970s, Orange and East Orange were on a slippery slope of change that would accelerate with each passing year. Rapid suburbanization, White flight, and business disinvestment fueled that change. It was a familiar pattern in cities of the Northeast and across the Midwest. After a few years, it felt like a race to the bottom.

When I arrived, Orange and East Orange were well integrated. The 1970 census counted the Black population of Orange at 36% and East Orange at 53, with Blacks mostly concentrated in certain areas. In Orange, the Black area was the East Ward that stretched along the border with East Orange. In East Orange, it was the Fourth Ward on the Newark border.

Growing up in Detroit, city neighborhoods were my home, my playground, my comfort zone. If I'd visited East Orange in the mid-fifties I'd have immediately registered its distinct character—dense and city-like but with a genteel, even suburban, feel. There were neighborhoods of large houses with servants and neighborhoods of modest three-bedroom homes. There were apartment districts with large apartments that had doormen, while other streets had smaller buildings and smaller apartments. Parks and public spaces were beautifully kept, and the tree-lined streets were lit at night by gas lamps. It was the home of Upsala College's beautiful campus. It had no industry. Central Avenue was known as Little Fifth Avenue. You could shop at Best and Company and B. Altman. It was an up-scale little city on the commuter train line to New York.

In 1945, East Orange was ranked the twentieth best place to live in the country among cities of a similar size. This city of sixty-seven thousand people that bordered Newark was named the "Cleanest City in America" three

Part II: The Scene is Set (1970-74)

times before 1970. During the fifties and sixties, fifty insurance companies moved to East Orange to a new office district along Harrison and Evergreen Streets. This was a city of stature, a place with lots of self confidence.

A 1955 brochure entitled "Where the City Blends with Suburban Living" touted East Orange's economic engine as, "a modern insurance center with 24 home, branch and regional offices that employ 1500, and a fashionable downtown where shoppers spend $359,000 daily." Twenty years later, the city created a business development authority to deal with the large quantity of vacant office space.

I learned that East Orange was a city with a deep sense of civic pride, and that its Black population, who had been there for at least a couple generations, cherished that pride, even as Whites abandoned the city. Black citizens of East Orange had a history to be proud of. Back in 1905, Black parents protested a move to create segregated schools and established their own brand of "freedom schools" in local churches.

Things began to change in the late fifties, when the Garden State Parkway, a multi-lane limited access highway that runs the full length of the state, sliced through the city and isolated a quarter of the city along the Newark border. It was ten years later that Interstate 280 bisected the city east and west, cutting out a swath of houses and businesses between its commercial corridors on Central Avenue and Main Street. The small compact city, with its tree-lined neighborhoods, was badly scarred and its confidence shaken.

Signs of slippage were evident. Sunday attendance in the White churches—Catholic, Episcopalian, and Presbyterian—declined, as did the money in the collection baskets. Meanwhile, those stately old church buildings needed more and more repairs. A prestigious Jewish synagogue moved out to South Orange. Catholic school enrollment began to dwindle. Clothing and department stores moved westward to the new malls. Popular restaurants closed, some moving to the suburbs. There were now vacant stores on the once-bustling Main Street and Central Avenue.

In 1968, hoping to reinvigorate the business district, city leaders applied to the federal government to redevelop the area of Main Street adjacent to the Brick Church commuter rail station. The Brick Church Urban Renewal Area was designated as blighted, and a plan emerged to attract business that had been lost to the suburbs with their new shopping malls.

Suburbanization and racial change following the 1967 Newark rebellion accelerated the population turnover. Social networks in neighborhoods, churches, and schools are the glue that holds good towns together, and in East Orange, those social networks were fraying. A decline in social cohesion is a subtle, barely noticeable quality. It's not like an abandoned building or a business that leaves town, but it's equally damning to a community.

East Orange was proud that it was *not Newark*, its immediate neighbor to the east. It saw itself as classier, suburban even. But things were changing and city leaders feared it could become like Newark. They were determined not to let that happen. I'm sure that back then, they had no real appreciation of how severely the forces of suburbanization, White flight, and disinvestment would impact their city. Maybe nobody at that pivotal moment in time understood the level of urban devastation that would be wrought by market forces reacting to the potent social changes underway. I was as clueless as anyone, optimistically preparing to put down roots in a *changing* neighborhood, determined to make a stand.

Meanwhile, the Black middle class from the region saw East Orange as a proud Black community, and they moved there rather than to nearby White suburbs. But the Black emigres from Newark were not middle class like the Blacks that had been in East Orange for years; they were poor and generally less educated. East Orange was becoming poorer and Blacker.

East Orange elected Bill Hart as its first Black mayor in 1969. Hart and a racially integrated city council struggled to maintain East Orange as a good place to raise a family. The community's leadership was determined not to let the forces of racial change and disinvestment destabilize their comfortable community.

Their first response to that threat was to craft a comprehensive program to stabilize conditions in the area bordering Newark, which had been cut off by the Garden State Parkway. They applied for federal funding and received 4.2 million dollars from the Model Cities Program to combat juvenile delinquency, housing disrepair, unemployment, low educational achievement, and neighborhood deterioration. The officials believed that a strong dose of citizen participation in this effort might bring that community together and ensure a stable neighborhood.

In '72 and '73, when I started coming around, East Orange looked a little tarnished but its storied past was still evident. I learned it had been developed as an enclave for Newark's industrialists escaping the soot and grime and their own immigrant employees. Additionally, with three stations on the Erie Lackawanna commuter train line, it became home to finance, law, and insurance professionals that worked in Newark or Manhattan.

With higher incomes than its blue collar neighbors, East Orange turned over quickly after the Newark riots, when the rush of White flight cascaded westward along the interstate toward the sprawling suburbs and the even greener exurbs of the Garden State. Racial turnover picked up steam. Soon, businesses followed their White customers to the westerly suburbs. The Fourth Ward, sandwiched between the Newark border and the Parkway, underwent the most dramatic change. By the time of the 1970 census, it was 92% Black. The Parkway was like a broad river with few bridges. The neighborhood on the east side of the "river" was so disconnected from the other 80% of the city that it felt like part of Newark. It's where the wave of abandonment of houses and apartment buildings started, a trend that would eventually drag down a lot of East Orange's neighborhoods.

By the early seventies, tenants across the city were unhappy. Rents were rising faster than the general cost of living. Conditions and maintenance, especially in the smaller, older buildings, was getting worse. Tenants complained to City Hall about no heat or hot water. It wasn't just the tenants who were unhappy; civic leaders and elected officials were frustrated by the city's inability to enforce Property Maintenance Codes and deal with this new breed of apartment house owners. Many of the new landlords were inexperienced. Some were crooks. Property Maintenance inspectors claimed to be overworked, but tenants with landlord complaints doubted that and thought most of the inspectors were lazy and usually more sympathetic to the landlords, or else they were on the take. Everyone was frustrated by the spreading deterioration and really at a loss about how to reverse it.

The Fight for Community Control

Construction of the Parkway left a vacant 8.2-acre site east of the Parkway exit. The site was owned by the Garden State Parkway Authority. The mayor pushed the Parkway Authority to deed the site to the city and planned to develop it with new affordable housing. Frustrated with the private sector, city officials were excited to work with the United Auto Workers union and their nonprofit housing corporation to build federally subsidized apartments.

But a community coalition from the Model Cities neighborhood rose up in protest, demanding that the development be locally controlled by Black people. They complained that the UAW was demanding an abatement from local property taxes, essentially a subsidy borne by all the city's residents. The coalition demanded that the development not be rental but co-ops. They wanted occupants to have an equity stake in ownership.

The UAW was an experienced nonprofit developer. The union's housing corporation would get the project done on time and on budget and manage the apartments well. But the coalition's homegrown plan was so attractive to Black leadership. They were anxious to take control of the city that Whites no longer cared about. The alternative plan called for ownership instead of rental with the development paying full taxes. The fact that it came up from the neighborhood made it a strong symbol. The community was determining its own future in the face of the massive forces of change that were undermining urban neighborhoods everywhere. As a concept it was irresistible, but putting a project that size in the hands of a "community controlled" developer was a big risk. City leaders were mixed on what to do.

The neighborhood coalition formed a corporation and called itself the Fourth Ward Urban Renewal Corporation.

To the surprise of city officials, 4WURC raised four hundred thousand in equity and put forth a solid development proposal for 247 apartments in two- and three-story townhouse buildings. The ownership model was a limited-equity co-op whereby the units would remain affordable to future buyers *and* the owners could gain limited equity. The development was to be called Kuzuri Kijiji, Swahili for *beautiful community*. The project would not seek a property tax abatement from the city; it would pay full property taxes just like any other housing complex. It was a beautiful dream.

City officials were in a bind. Housing development and construction was a complicated business. The city would be left holding the bag if the project went sideways. But the neighborhood coalition was relentless and city officials wanted to honor what the community wanted, but this was one small part of the community making the demands. Supporters of 4WURC were vocal, and their vision of Black community control and property ownership instead of rental struck a chord in a city that was suffering. White Councilman Harold Karns, who lived in and represented the mostly Black neighborhood and was no friend of Mayor Hart, fought hard on behalf of 4WURC.

City officials granted the contract to 4WURC. And in 1973, the cooperative housing complex opened to much fanfare. It was touted as a model for the future. To me that sounded right. East Orange needed more cooperatively owned housing. All cities did.

Meanwhile, over at the Model Cities program, things were going sideways. The Fourth Ward neighborhood needed decisive intervention if it wasn't going to be lost to blight, but public officials and community leaders were wrangling and publicly slinging accusations back and forth. The conflicts were never over programs or projects; there was unanimous agreement on every new idea that came along, like home repair grants to homeowners, and a small tool library. The battles were about who got to make those decisions and especially who got hired for the many Model Cities jobs.

Citizen participation and empowering the poor were powerful watchwords back then. There was no disagreement that the community, the people, the citizens should determine the direction of the neighborhood but citizen participation got complicated when the question of *which citizens* came up. Who really represents *the community*?

There were disputed Advisory Board elections and angry accusations that Mayor Hart was hiring his friends and political loyalists. Hart threatened to use his power to replace all the elected Advisory Board members. Despite the public bitterness, there was a general feeling that the program initiatives were making a difference. There was hope that the neighborhood preservation effort might succeed and the blocks on the Newark side of the Parkway might not succumb to forces that were toppling some of Newark's neighborhoods. But the Fourth Ward was not going to be saved by bite-sized efforts like five-hundred-dollar home repair grants and a small tool library, no matter how popular they were.

Then suddenly, Nixon cut all Model Cities funding. Most of the East Orange Model Cities staff was laid off. The sleazy liar marketed the cuts as part of his New Federalism doctrine, a system of federal revenue sharing that devolved decision-making about spending down to the state and city level. That all sounded good, but there was little doubt that New Federalism meant a big cut in the federal commitment to cities and to the poor.

Most of the Fourth Ward neighborhood programs were shut down. Kuzuri Kijiji was the solitary signal of community progress. Predictably, with no funding for services and without a vigorous citizen participation effort, the poor, Black, and isolated neighborhood on the Newark border declined. It was a discouraging foretelling of a fate that might overtake the entire city. The Chamber of Commerce and the East Orange Clergy Association pressed the case with city leaders. So much more needed to be done if they were going to win this war. But there was no federal funding.

By 1973, the budding East Orange Tenants Association was propelled by Phyllis's leadership. It was a group that brought Black and White tenants together. Tenant associations were organized in scores of buildings as conditions for tenants deteriorated, and they were demanding action.

East Orange was changing as it became more racially integrated, but to a newcomer like me, the changes weren't alarming. Frankly, I had little appreciation for the inexorable power of the market forces, fueled by racial angst, that were bearing down on East Orange. Back then it didn't seem that obvious. Eventually I would see that Orange and East Orange were entering a period of destabilization and suffering, though I didn't know that it would last for decades.

Unlike East Orange, the smaller city of Orange was blue collar to the bone, with the small exception of the upscale Seven Oaks area that borders South Orange. The center of the city between the commercial strips on Main Street and Central Avenue was a jobs mecca. The Rheingold Brewery alone employed seven hundred unionized workers. The sprawling Orange Memorial Hospital and Orthopedic Hospital on ten acres employed several hundred. The

Valley, which straddled the Orange/West Orange border, was once known as "the hat-making capital of the world," employing hundreds of European immigrants. The hat manufacturers departed in the 1920s and '30s, but Monroe Calculating Company built out four acres in 1940 and employed a couple hundred workers. Small and mid-sized light industrial firms occupied the former hat factories.

Folks from Orange wax nostalgic about the period after World War II, especially the fifties and early sixties. As I got to know more people from Orange through the years, I came to appreciate how selective some of those memories were. Most Whites, especially the working-class Italians, liked to talk about those days when "we all got along."

It was common to hear stories like, "I remember Mrs. Williams; she treated me like one of her sons. 'Here, Tony,' she'd say, 'take another piece of fried chicken home with you.'" Meanwhile, there was a parallel reality. Tony played basketball at the big YMCA on Main Street, an imposing brick building, while Mrs. William's son was at the "Colored Y," a small repurposed frame building that was torn down when the expressway was built.

It was the late sixties when the east/west interstate highway sliced through East Orange and Orange, leaving both cities badly scarred. Neighborhoods south of the massive freeway and its six service lanes were now disconnected from bustling Main Street that ran through both cities. The highway not only disrupted the stability of the two cities but it fueled westward flight to the suburbs. The two small cities were changing fast. The population of Orange in 1960 was 23% Black. By 1970, it was 36%.

• • •

Claudia and I rang in 1973 at Joanne Bodner's house. John and Deena were there and Ronnie too, though he and Joanne were not a public thing yet. It was incredible to us that Nixon would be sworn in soon to a second term. In spite of Tricky Dick's landslide victory, we were confident that our movement was ascendent. After all, our peace movement was bringing an end to the War. No draftees were called to duty in '72, and by year end, the last U.S. ground troops were withdrawn from Vietnam. We were feeling buoyant.

There were lots of reasons to believe that perhaps we viewed the future through rose-colored glasses, because the events of 1972 were definitely mixed. But for us, the Orange City Commission had passed rent control. And I found my community. Maybe 1973 would be our year.

The Housing Unit

John wanted Legal Services attorneys to help build a poor people's movement. To do that he'd have to get some control over the lawyers assigned to do housing work. He wanted a separate unit where attorneys weren't just swallowed up and overrun by individual cases and they could actually be attorneys for a growing movement. He knew that otherwise, good attorneys would just get burned out, and that for most tenants nothing would change. He set out to build a separate housing unit that he would lead.

The radical housing lawyer wanted to improve services to the clients by empowering them to build a strong tenant movement. He saw the unit as "a beacon of empowerment aimed at strengthening the tenant movement, securing media sympathy, and swaying the judiciary and political figures."

But John needed to sell the housing unit idea to Bob

Doris, the director who might not be willing to back such a full-throated embrace of movement building. John promoted it as simply a way to more efficiently represent clients with their housing problems and suggested that Sam Farrington, a very experienced housing lawyer, be John's co-director. John's uncertain boss harbored reservations about the plan, but he tentatively approved it.

Doris agreed to hire some additional attorneys. John and Sam would train them. John made it clear to each new attorney that they would represent individual clients *and* support community organizing. The unit would operate by consensus and they would function as a collective, truly unusual for a law office.

PACT had given birth to two new citywide tenants organizations, but the groups had no paid staff, just volunteers untrained in the law and with little knowledge about how city and town councils functioned. So the Housing Unit's mission became training and educating the grassroots leaders. The unit focused on the burgeoning tenant groups in Orange, East Orange, and then throughout Essex County, including Newark. Each citywide tenant leader had a direct line to one or more lawyers, who armed them with legal and organizing advice so they could unite their apartment buildings. The Housing Unit was the single most important resource we had available to assist our organizing efforts.

Joan Pransky was the first new hire to the Housing Unit, and she was a real find. Excited to be with a crew of motivated and serious legal troublemakers, she shared an office with the equally committed Patricia Thornton. Joan took direction from John about where to direct her legal energies—to groups of tenants willing to self organize—but she was under Sam's tutelage when it came to her case preparation and her courtroom work.

Joan recalls that, "Sam was far more serious and critical than John. We met weekly and he'd critique me. After my first trial, he said, 'Perry Mason, you ain't.' But he didn't dampen my spirits." Joan described Sam as a taskmaster. Pat Thornton, unlike Joan, who saw her work within a long overdue class struggle, Pat was fueled by the cold anger common among Black attorneys. Joan said fondly of Sam, "He really believed in justice and thought all would work out if we just did our jobs perfectly. Sam was also really loyal, so when Pat and I battled with the judges, he was always there for us and often came down to the courthouse to speak to the judges when we got a little out there."

Joan and Pat Thornton went around Newark, East Orange, and Orange, meeting with tenants at buildings on rent strike and going to court with them to seek rent reductions or representing tenants against retaliation for their organizing.

Joan loved her work and was still living in New York, so between her work day at the office or in court and attending night time meetings, she often ate at the East Orange Diner in her own booth with a file of documents. The place drew an odd collection of old timers and loners, many of them occupants of the Marlborough Hotel, a big and once-elegant 1800s lodging home just a block and a half away. They'd shuffle over in their slippers, pajamas, or house coats for dinner. Long after dark, Joan drove back across the dark and desolate Meadowlands and through the Lincoln tunnel to her Upper West Side apartment, her mind full of all the people who inhabited her new lawyer world—the brave and stalwart tenants she was developing strong bonds with, the uncaring landlords and their sleazy lawyers she battled with, and the jaded and biased judges she appeared before. As new and unsure of her legal skills as she was, this was a world and a battlefield she relished. It was made for her and she was just getting started.

Joan was passionate and a brawler, never afraid to take on a bad landlord, a sleazy opposing attorney, or a two-faced politician. She loved her clients, deeply respected them, and they in turn were loyal to her and loved her back. She was a perfect addition to John's Housing Unit and our growing political movement.

Don't Wait for Lefty

John's Housing Unit reflected our view of how to create change and build a better society. The democracy we believed in was wide open and participatory. At the heart of our organizing, beyond seeking justice and fair treatment of people, was the idea that democracy was about people affecting the decisions that impacted their lives. We encouraged people to speak up, make their voices heard in the public space of ideas and in the halls of decision making. That could be messy sometimes, and it often was, but it went to the heart of what we believed: Everyone has the capacity to be a leader, but if they never experience speaking up in public, they'll never begin to realize that. They won't act on their own instincts.

A friend told me about a play that I'd like. Back then I had little interest in theater, but this play had a political message. It was called *Waiting for Lefty*, a 1930s drama about labor strife and a union organizer.

I saw the play in a basement theater space in the Village. When the dim lights came up on a bare stage, we saw a fat labor boss trying to dissuade workers from going on strike. He talks about Roosevelt and how this strike will undercut what the president's trying to accomplish for working people. The union boss shouts down a man who tries to interrupt, "Shut your trap, you damn Red!"

The crowd of workers is unconvinced by the union boss's appeal to their loyalty to Roosevelt, but they're hesitant to take a strike vote without knowing what Lefty thinks. He's the chairman of the worker's committee and he hasn't shown up yet. One worker after another tells a tale of economic desperation that brought him to this moment where a strike was the only answer. A guy keeps going in and out, reporting back, *No sign of Lefty yet.*

The fat man continues to denounce those who propose a strike as Reds. The agitated workers look around nervously for direction. Still no sign of Lefty.

Some workers were pleading for a strike vote. "Don't wait for Lefty," one militant says, "he may never show. Every minute that—" The audience is surprised when a man runs down the center aisle from the back of the theater. "Boys, they just found Lefty. Out behind the car barns with a bullet in his head!"

The militant cries out, "We'll die for what is right! Put fruit trees where our ashes lay." He looks out at the audience and pleads, "Well what's the answer?"

The audience, carried away, joined the cast, shouting, "Strike! Strike! Strike!"

It was heavy handed and preachy, nothing subtle, but I loved it. I believed the message. *Don't wait for some leader to tell you what to do. Be a leader. Decide for yourself.* That's what our group was about. We intended to be leaders and help others become leaders too.

• • •

My life was full and getting fuller. I was spending more

time in the Oranges, drawn by the social and intellectual life and the grassroots politics. The PACT group began to replace what I'd lost when Tom and Judy left St. Paul's. One night I brought Claudia with me to a spaghetti dinner at Sam and Marsha's. Marsha latched onto Claudia and dragged her into the kitchen. They were kindred souls. Claudia felt immediately accepted.

It wasn't just my new friends in the Oranges that filled my life. Urban revitalization and rehabbing old homes was now in my blood, and I looked forward every morning to my work in the badly worn but welcoming neighborhood in Englewood. The work was an irresistible mix of the technical, the cultural, the historic, and a spiritual sense of renewal and rebirth. I was originating federal loans, so I had to learn to read title reports, a foreign language to me. A wonderful guy from the title company, twenty years my senior, took me under his wing. And I absorbed the day-to-day life of a Black neighborhood.

I don't know why this particular story sticks in my memory. Elderly but spry Mrs. Davis was sweeping the kitchen when I rang her bell. We sat at her kitchen table and she told me stories about the people whose houses she used to clean and about her husband—"God love him"—who'd been a janitor and how they struggled and saved to buy their house. And the troubles they had getting a bank loan even though he had a steady job at a decent wage. How he used to fix everything around the house, kept it in good repair. She almost cried when I told her she was eligible for a $3,500 grant to make repairs. She'd just planted flowers along her front walk and as I left she insisted that I accept a potted coleus for my apartment.

On the national stage, the nightmare of four more years

of Nixon had just begun. It hit especially hard that he beat McGovern so thoroughly, winning forty-nine states and 61% of the popular vote.

Tricky Dick took advantage of his electoral mandate, and one of his first official acts was to declare an immediate moratorium on all federal housing subsidy programs. All across the country, affordable housing projects that were on the drawing board or in the pipeline were stopped in their tracks. Nixon claimed, without proof, that there was widespread waste and corruption. He promised a new system of federal revenue sharing that localities could use to create affordable housing.

What horseshit! I thought. It was just a ruse. The federal government was backing away from its commitment to making housing affordable.

Nobody in PACT was surprised by Nixon's actions. Cuts in housing subsidies were no surprise. That was his agenda all along and the promise of something better was just pure bullshit, just like his promise to end the war in Vietnam. Someone quoted the Nixon poster, *Would you buy a used car from this man?*

Nixon's moratorium would totally sabotage the slum clearance plan in Englewood. How could the Redevelopment Agency displace all those tenants without new replacement housing? I attended a hastily called meeting with Marvin Gladstone, the Agency's legal counsel. Ninety-some ramshackle rental properties were being acquired by the Agency with the promise of relocating the tenants into new subsidized housing. Two new projects with 270 affordable apartments were already designed and approved, and the city had beaten back the NIMBY lawsuit. Funding applications for both projects and the hundred affordable townhouses to be built on the clearance site were in DC, waiting for HUD approval. Almost four hundred affordable apartments and townhouses for Englewood had vanished with a swipe of Nixon's pen.

Attorney Gladstone suggested that we shouldn't take the newspaper headlines of an *absolute* moratorium too literally. With the right connections in DC, we might be able to dislodge the Englewood funding. Talk of dealing with "Washington insiders" fascinated me; of course I was appalled by the concept that not all laws are applied equally, but the idea of an end run around Nixon's edict was appealing. Gladstone said he wanted to reach out to the well connected DC law firm of Arnold and Porter.

"Their hourly rates will be quite high and we may not be successful, but it's our best chance."

A few months later, Englewood's well connected DC lawyers got the funding flowing in spite of the nationwide moratorium. In East Orange, there was no such good news. The Model Cities money for the Fourth Ward was gone for good.

Bertha Collier gathering signatures for a stronger rent control law.

CHAPTER 9

Our Toughest Organizer

Phyllis Salowe was a mystery. When John introduced us at that first PACT meeting, she seemed shy but John said that she's the one who paid most attention when he talked about organizing tenants. She seemed more like a wallflower than an organizer. Then I heard that she had been jailed following the Newark teachers' strikes. She was a mystery.

This Newark elementary school teacher and repeat offender lived in Newark for three years before moving to East Orange in early '72. She'd known since her sophomore year at Boston University that Newark was where her inner city teaching career would begin. She was less certain about where to live and anxious about whether she'd find a social life. Before graduation, in the spring of '69 she'd locked up a teaching contract. In her junior and senior years, she had been a Newark substitute teacher for six to seven weeks between the end of BU's spring semester and the start of summer vacation for Newark's students and teachers.

Phyllis told me what a sweet deal substituting was. Newark paid better than most suburban districts and she was *connected*.

"These two old women who worked in school headquarters, they were friends of my aunt. They were responsible for filling the substitute positions each day. It was an hour drive from Bradley Beach to Newark, so I had to leave home about the same time that they'd start calling. I'd pull over to a payphone on the Parkway and call their office, just to see which school I should report to. I never missed a day."

I thought about how in my family, what she was talking about was viewed as *cutting in line*. I was taught that "You're no better than anyone else, you wait your turn." I thought, *Isn't this what's wrong with the system? There's insiders and outsiders.* The insiders are all self-dealing and scratching each other's backs. The outsiders are playing by the rules, waiting in lines and coming up short. It flew in the face of both my upbringing and my newfound egalitarian vision.

Phyllis admired people who were connected, like Harold Hodes. She wanted one day to be one of those people—a connector, a person of influence who could make things happen for others. A power broker even. But Phyllis was no ambitious insider; quite the opposite. It's unlikely, in those beginning days, that she believed she would become a power broker for the disenfranchised.

As a substitute, she was assigned to a different class almost every day, but she treated those kids like her own. She knew that every day in the classroom was important if those students were going to make it out of the ghetto some day. Plenty of substitutes treated a day in an all-Black school as a bad day of babysitting, handing out worksheets or giving reading assignments while they read the paper or filed their nails. Phyllis, still a student herself, checked the regular teacher's lesson plan and actively engaged *her* students. She imagined having her own classroom and planning out a year of instruction and learning. She knew that if she had a whole school year, she could make a real difference for those children.

Soon enough, this fresh young teacher with connections and experience as a substitute was teaching full time. It was just two years after the 1967 riot/rebellion. Newark's White exodus and headlong decline wasn't at full throttle yet, but Whites were on edge about the future of their neighborhoods, and realtors set up blockbusting operations where they spread fear among White families and scared them into selling quick.

The South Ward where Phyllis hoped to live had been a tight Jewish middle-class community for decades, but starting in the early sixties, it began slowly dispensing its White population to the suburbs. She wanted to buck that trend and was prepared to embrace this place that people felt so negatively about. She'd be one of its dedicated public school teachers. She'd live there and be a part of the city's life.

Phyllis got into a high rise, one that was still considered desirable, on Elizabeth Avenue, overlooking the big and bountiful Weequahic Park. Harold Hodes, who she first knew as a lifeguard from her home town of Bradley Beach, lived there. Harold had been a teacher at the school where she'd be teaching, but he was now the chief of staff for Newark Mayor Addonizio. The former lifeguard, now in a seat of power, made sure that Phyllis wasn't stuck at the bottom of the waiting list for this well above average apartment house. When the next vacancy opened up, she moved in. Again, "connected." The well maintained building was integrated, had a pool, and was full of young professionals, including a group of stewardesses who flew out of Newark Airport. Wynona Lipman, a famed Black woman with a PhD who'd studied at the Sorbonne in Paris, lived there. Lipman would soon be the first Black woman elected to the New Jersey Senate. Phyllis was where she wanted to be. Socially a little awkward and insecure, she imagined that the pool and all those stewardesses meant an available social life just outside her door, and she was joining the ranks of freshly minted teachers determined to make a difference in the lives of inner city kids.

Phyllis grew up "down the Shore," which is *north-Jersey-speak* for the oceanfront towns that line the state's Atlantic coastline. Her hometown of Bradley Beach with only four thousand people swelled with tourists every summer. She described her parents as "working-class Democrats, but they didn't vote in primaries, not wanting people to know their political affiliation."

I thought about that. In my neighborhood growing up, I guess just about everyone was a Democrat, except Mr. Proctor, the opinionated widower across the street.

Every summer, to help make ends meet, Phyllis, her brother, Alan, and their parents moved into a building at the rear of their property and rented out their home for two months to summer vacationers. Phyllis would never forget the humiliation of seeing some rich girl living in her room, playing her piano. Her dad owned a tavern in town and her mom was a legal secretary.

Like most of us, Phyllis had her political awakening at college. At BU, she protested the War and participated in a "sanctuary operation" protecting an AWOL soldier. She was dismissive of her involvement though.

"I just wanted to be accepted by the group that I thought was popular."

I can see now there was some truth to that statement,

Part II: The Scene is Set (1970-74)

wanting to be popular. We've all been there, but this image of the socially insecure student belied something deeper. She had such intense drive and a natural sense of organization and a deep ethical code that she brought to everything she did. I would later witness how elected officials underestimated her considerable competence and drive. For a long while, I couldn't reconcile this constantly self-doubting and insecure woman with the person who achieved so much in the public arena.

I asked Phyllis about her earliest involvement in activism or protest.

"My high school boyfriend and I made these bright plastic flowers and were selling them on the boardwalk in Bradley Beach. Cops stopped us and asked to see our permit, which of course, we didn't have one. They said we could just pack up our stuff and they wouldn't issue a ticket for violating the town ordinance. My boyfriend started packing up but I refused. So the cops wrote me a summons. Before my court date, I went to the City Council and told the council members their law was unjust. Of course, they didn't change the law, but that was my first public fight."

Phyllis loved teaching and spent her evenings planning her lessons and exciting activities to engage her elementary schoolers who loved her. After the Christmas-New Year's break, labor negotiations between the board of education, and the Newark Teachers Union were stalled and rumors of a strike, a violation of state law, began to circulate. Phyllis attended all the union meetings downtown at the Robert Treat Hotel and was tapped to be a *school captain* to coordinate picket activities if a strike was called.

Within two weeks, negotiations had ground to a halt and the union called a strike. Phyllis walked the picket line outside her school and at the end of each day checked in downtown at the Robert Treat. The strike, primarily around education issues and a modest pay increase, had broad community support and was settled in three weeks. The strike resulted in some meaningful improvement in education and a one-year contract for the teachers, but many months later, when the arrested teachers were sentenced and prohibited from striking again, the meaning of the strike had been lost.

A year later, a second strike lasted eleven bitter weeks, but this time the teachers had no community support and were seen as just striking for higher pay. It was 1972 when the striking teachers received hefty sentences. Phyllis and a bunch of fellow teachers spent fifteen days in jail. Carol Graves, the union president, was sentenced to six months.

Phyllis was three years out of college and already a somewhat jaded veteran activist with an arrest record. She was teaching in a stimulating environment with a progressive principal and engaged colleagues. But school politics were now racially charged and she hated her living situation. Maintenance at that desirable apartment house declined and the pool was closed. A group of stewardesses had not guaranteed a social life, and anyhow by then they'd all moved out. Her apartment was roach-infested, so she stayed with her aunt until her lease was up. She had few friends in Newark. All her college friends lived in New York and she had no love life to speak of. Her boyfriend since sixth grade was at law school in DC and she'd spent the last two years helping him get out of the National Guard, which he'd joined to avoid Vietnam, but he never acted like he was her boyfriend. She felt lonely and abandoned.

Newark was changing fast. The pace of its downward

slide was freefall. The newly elected Black mayor, Ken Gibson, said, "Wherever American cities are headed, Newark will get there first." A strange thing for a newly elected mayor to say but it was actually a cry for federal help. Gibson was well aware that cities, especially ones with Black majorities, were near the bottom of the federal government's Christmas list.

Displaced and discouraged, Phyllis was looking for a new place to land. Her friend and fellow teacher Anna Blume lived in a nice low-rise building in East Orange at the corner of Arlington and Chestnut Street, just a block east of the boarded up house at 31 Chestnut. By June of 1972, Phyllis moved into a sunny first-floor apartment with plenty of windows in the neighboring building on Chestnut.

Organizing East Orange Tenants

One day, Anna was hosting a PACT Sunday brunch and invited Phyllis. Anna must have sensed Phyllis's anxiety, so when she introduced her to the group she made it known that Phyllis had just completed two weeks in the Essex County lock up for her union activities. The group treated her like a celebrity. That's when she met John and Deena, Mark and Ruth Seglin, Marsha, and the incomparable Whitey Goodfriend. The Bierbaums she already knew and Marty was a fellow teacher. In spite of the strong reception, she was uncertain about her acceptance.

Phyllis soon formed a tenant association in her building and began to do in East Orange what John was trying to ignite in Orange: create a citywide tenants organization. Life was changing for tenants in East Orange; landlords were cutting back on maintenance, repairs, and services and renters were feeling the effects. Poorer Black tenants, most of them from Newark's hollowed out Central Ward, moved into the smaller, older apartment buildings. I learned those buildings generally had owners who were new to landlording, who expected quick and steady cash flow. Banks were no longer lending on those old smaller buildings, and those amateur buyers probably weren't bankable even in a suburban location, so it was likely that the previous owner held their mortgage. Owners who'd held those buildings for a long time and had a stable tenancy had little choice but to take back a mortgage if they wanted to sell.

Tenants in those buildings faced a host of problems. Occasionally no heat or hot water, generally poor maintenance, plumbing leaks, broken door locks and much more—and they called Phyllis for advice. Phyllis had no legal training, but with John and Ronnie as her coaches, she was catching up quickly. Most tenants who called had already complained to City Hall but their problems persisted. Some of them came out to City Council meetings and told their sad stories publicly. They often went away from a Council meeting thinking that now their landlord would be forced to do right by them. Maybe their councilman would take notes and call Property Maintenance the next day. Maybe an inspector would come to the building. Maybe something would get done about their complaint. But maybe not.

Black community leaders tapped into the spirit of the civil rights movement. These tenant leaders who stepped up were part of that group of empowered Black citizens determined to take control of their communities. But it wasn't a united front. Block associations were forming to make sure that neighborhoods remained good places to raise children, but mostly it was only homeowners.

Tenants typically weren't connected to their homeowner neighbors. Tenants focused mostly on conditions just within their buildings.

Plenty of tenants were hesitant to complain and assert their rights, afraid they'd be harassed and evicted. But New Jersey law now protected them. Protection against retaliation was the most basic of tenant rights. If landlords could retaliate and evict complaining tenants, then tenants would never complain and they certainly wouldn't organize. But NJTO had lobbied for and won an "anti retaliatory eviction" law in 1970.

The very first tenant who reached out to Phyllis was Florence Stevenson, a short and energetic tenant from 111 Halsted Street. This unafraid Black woman was a people magnet and seemed to know everyone up and down Halsted, a street lined with mid-sized apartment buildings. She certainly knew someone from each building. Phyllis and Florence began meeting with groups in most of those buildings.

That's how Phyllis met Bertha Collier, the leader at 148 Halsted, whose landlord wasn't providing heat. Bertha called a quick meeting of her neighbors and invited Phyllis. A good sized group was gathered in Bertha's apartment when Phyllis arrived. She advised them how to legally withhold rent and use their rent dollars to buy oil and get the steam boiler working again. She helped them find the oil dealer who normally serviced the building. The tenants established an oil delivery account and they paid cash. Bertha was feeling the power of someone who'd stood up for herself and prevailed. She was grateful to Phyllis for teaching her that.

Plenty of would-be tenant leaders responded to Phyllis's empowering advice. They loved that she wasn't afraid to take on this new breed of uncaring shoddy landlords. Phyllis told them she was starting an organization of East Orange tenants and she expected them to join, that a strong organization was the only way they'd get a fair shake. Florence Stevenson, Bertha Collier, and other fledgling tenant leaders responded to Phyllis's message that if poor and powerless people stuck together they would get justice. Phyllis was pumped up by their gratitude and their enthusiasm. It drove her forward.

Soon, Phyllis was meeting with tenants in two buildings each weekday evening, Monday through Thursday, week in and week out. On her break at school she would call John's office every day from a payphone. Then she'd call the tenant leader back and pass on the legal advice from John. She insisted that every building form a tenant association and get as many tenants as possible to join. Her message was that this was the only way to negotiate with these nasty landlords. The landlords relied on the fact that the tenants wouldn't act in concert. Most buildings had one, two, or three women (it was almost always women) who would take the lead and call meetings, invite neighbors into their apartments, draft letters to the landlord, and generally lead the tenants committee.

While John was talking about enacting rent control throughout Essex County, Phyllis wondered when she'd have enough people behind her to win a strong rent control law. Her stack of index cards with tenant leader names and numbers was growing. Now that she'd started organizing tenants in her new city, she didn't want other towns to get out ahead of her.

The answer came surprisingly soon. Councilman Bill Thomas led the headlong charge for rent control in East Orange. Thomas was tall, young, and flamboyant, with

Part II: The Scene is Set (1970-74)

experience down South registering Black voters in the early sixties.

When he brought the issue up, he announced, "Six other communities have already enacted and put ordinances into effect. East Orange tenants deserve protection against rent gouging." He planned to introduce a rent ordinance at the next Council meeting. That was December of 1972 and, in addition to Orange, rent leveling had already been adopted in nearby West Orange and Irvington.

Not everyone on the East Orange City Council was ready to pass an ordinance limiting rent increases. Most of them just hadn't made their intentions clear yet. Mayor Hart wasn't saying publicly one way or the other. When the crusading councilman brought the issue up for discussion, Hart's city attorney, Julius Fielo, impeccably dressed with the looks and charm of an Italian film star, addressed the council and advised that it would be premature and unwise to pre-empt the Supreme Court, which hadn't yet ruled on the Fort Lee case. Fielo, himself a seasoned and connected political infighter, always seemed eminently reasonable and above the political fray, but he was clearly the mayor's spokesman on this. Mayor Hart wanted to go slow.

Phyllis felt the opposite. Her new city was already lagging behind other municipalities in Essex. She worked the phone, calling upon her list of tenant leaders to come out to the council meeting. Tenant leaders she'd helped answered the call. I told her I'd be there.

By my guess, none of these new citizen activists had ever addressed a city council before. Phyllis told them it's the only way their story would get heard, the only way they would get justice. And they all did it, one after another, with stories of rent increases, poor services, no heat, no hot water, no repairs. For those Black women, the fresh memory and legacy of Martin Luther King was like a sacred bond, an obligation to stand up for what's right and fair. Like Dr. King did and all the brave Black people before them who stood up, who suffered for taking a stand. They felt they owed something to that legacy and were proud to now be a part of it. Phyllis recalled that in almost every apartment she visited there'd be a picture of Dr. King and usually one of President Jack Kennedy as well. To those women, the civil rights movement wasn't history; it was here and now and playing out in the way that Black people were being treated by these shady landlords.

Phyllis made sure John was at the council meeting. John was at his lawyerly best when he assured the council they were on the right side of the law by approving this ordinance, and that the Superior Court had already ruled on the landlords' appeal of the Fort Lee Ordinance, and that the Court stated in clear, strong language that the Fort Lee law was constitutional.

He said, "What that means is that the Fort Lee Ordinance will be upheld by the Supreme Court."

Then John held up some file folders and claimed he had evidence that landlords were rushing to raise rents, by unconscionable amounts, in anticipation of the Supreme Court's ruling. He paused and looked at the Council Members. "The time for the council to act is now."

I thought that was a bold move. I wondered what was in those folders. I was pretty sure it wasn't proof of landlords jacking up rents. The band of tenants in the audience clapped hard and so did I. It was thrilling.

Phyllis capped off the tenants' testimony when she went back up to the mic simply to say that, "East Orange tenants need relief now!" Her small group of tenants in the audience clapped loud and hard. Phyllis was pumped up. This was the opening skirmish of what might be a long battle. The council voted to introduce the ordinance, but that was just First Reading. The final vote would come a month later and the landlords would no doubt be out in force. The school teacher and part-time organizer was concerned her leadership would be tested before she had a chance to really get organized. She'd need help. John and Ronnie would be getting a lot of calls from Phyllis.

At the next PACT Sunday brunch, the East Orange Council meeting was recounted and dissected. John praised Phyllis's leadership, sort of implying, *What's preventing the rest of you from becoming organizers?*

Phyllis waved off the praise. "We'll see. We haven't won anything yet." She was still a mystery to me. Her leadership wasn't based on charisma or charm or wit or smooth talking. None of those. And she was no orator. But I did begin to cue in to her grit and determination, and I got an inkling that she'd be successful, at least at rousing people to follow her and take a stand.

Rent Leveling Showdown

A major political battle was heating up. The Rent Leveling Ordinance was on the agenda for the mid-February council meeting and the mayor hadn't shown his hand yet. He may have been waiting to see if Phyllis and her quickly assembled group of pissed off tenants could muscle a majority of the council. The landlords weren't formally organized yet, but their message was unified and succinct: The westward exodus from Newark's all-Black Central Ward was changing East Orange and the only way to avoid becoming a slum was to assure continued investment in upkeep, maintenance, and property improvements by landlords. And rent control would have the opposite effect.

At every opportunity, the landlords equated rent control with the devastation and abandonment of the South Bronx, where blocks and blocks of buildings were now abandoned. They always called it rent *control,* tying it to New York City's archaic and strict policy of no rent increases, where long-term tenants paid the same rent for decades. They understood the difference, of course. They just didn't want any limits on what they could charge.

That threat of abandonment was troubling to a city experiencing decline, but Phyllis and John argued that like the first ordinance in Fort Lee, they were asking for rent *leveling,* simply limiting annual rent increases to a modest and fair amount. Not the rigid form of rent control in New York where rents remained unchanged for years and years. They made clear that, under rent *leveling,* landlords could apply for *hardship increases* to raise rents higher if they weren't making a fair profit. They could apply for capital improvement increases to update apartments. That this ordinance was meant to keep rent increases in line with changes in the cost of living and to prevent landlords from taking unfair advantage in a tight rental market.

Tenants were a substantial majority in this city where only a quarter of the households owned homes. Council members were anxious to endear themselves to all those voters. Mayor Hart spent years in the political trenches. He wasn't one to react quickly. He was known to play his hand in a measured way.

The February 1973 council meeting was a raucous affair, but in the end, the East Orange City Council passed a law limiting rent increases to the annual change in the Consumer Price Index. It was a time of high inflation with

Part II: The Scene is Set (1970-74)

the CPI for New York and Northern New Jersey rising 10.8% that year. A glaring defect in the ordinance was the 25% allowable increase when a tenant moved out. Phyllis publicly slammed the council for rewarding landlords who would now force tenants out.

The new law was supposed to take effect immediately, but after a month City Hall hadn't done a thing to implement the ordinance. Phyllis figured the council and the mayor were now in agreement on slowing down implementation of the new law, so she went public. She first called Ronnie, her mentor and media master, and then she blasted the city's lawmakers in the press. "The City Council is playing games for failing to put the law into effect after they passed a weak, watered-down version. It's an absolute outrage."

Phyllis thought that calling out the council would light a fire under them but it had the opposite effect. A majority gave in to Mayor Hart's hesitation about the ordinance. The council president announced they were waiting until the Supreme Court acted on the Fort Lee case. Phyllis was outraged and so were a few of the council members.

Phyllis took the council's reversal personally and she decided to up the ante. She'd personalize the battle. So she denounced Hart, telling the press he was, "Insensitive to the serious housing problems facing East Orange residents." Then Councilman Harold Karns, not an ally of the mayor, doubled down.

Karns jumped in, claiming that, "Hart is in the pocket of the Democrats that run the county machine, the big contributors, and supporters of Harry Lerner," the Essex Democratic Chairman. Karns called Lermer "Hart's political patron." I laughed when I read Karns's claim. Just six months earlier, Hart led the reform Democrat ticket that tried to overthrow Lerner. I was struck by how an elected official could say something so untrue and illogical and never be called out on it.

But maybe there was some truth to Karns's claim because I got my next insight into local politics when I learned that after Hart's challenge, Lerner named him a delegate to the National Democratic Convention from the 10th Congressional District. I began to understand how party bosses like Lerner held onto their power. They kept challengers within the fold. As Don Corleone would famously say, "Keep your friends close. Keep your enemies closer."

Phyllis girded for a public battle to get the rent ordinance implemented. She called a city-wide meeting of tenants and lined up John and Martin Aranow, the NJTO president, to speak to the crowd. She placed an announcement in the weekly paper with her home phone number for more information and started getting calls from tenants, telling of their complaints. It was a cold February evening, but over a hundred disgruntled tenants showed up in the Clifford Scott High School cafeteria, looking for direction. Most of the leaders that Phyllis worked with were there and plenty of tenants from other buildings. Tenants from some of the nicer buildings reported they had fifteen to 20% rent increases and cut backs in services and maintenance. Others reported deplorable conditions, no repairs, rising rents, and decreasing maintenance.

Phyllis called the meeting to order and introduced NJTO president Marty Aranow, who brought the confident air of the businessman he was. Marty had gotten involved four years earlier when the landlord of his high-rent, high rise with a view of Manhattan sent out notices of a 20% rent increase. He reached out to tenants in the other Fort Lee high rises on the palisades along the Hudson River. That's how New Jersey's modern rent leveling movement was born. While lobbying for the Fort Lee City Council to pass an ordinance limiting rent increases, he reached out to Ronnie for help. After the Fort Lee ordinance was adopted, the New Jersey Tenants Organization was formed, and the two of them began traveling around the state to tenant meetings. Just like the one Phyllis called that night.

Aranow assured the tenants that if they stuck together and created a strong organization, they'd win protections against those outrageous rent increases and get the standards of maintenance they deserved. Phyllis introduced John as the volunteer attorney for East Orange Tenants Association. I'm sure he felt a thrill as he looked at that crowd. Phyllis brought together his *dream coalition*—Blacks and Whites, the poor and the middle class, in one organization, linked around the same bread and butter issue: decent quality housing that's affordable. His vision was taking shape. Ronnie would be impressed.

John took time to tell the assembled tenants about their rights under the law and how to get what they deserved for the rent they paid.

"The law is on your side," he said. "But you can't count on the courts." There were some good tenant protection laws in place. But a lot of judges were pro-landlord and hostile to tenants. He then repeated Marty's exhortation. "What's the only real way to guarantee your rights? A strong membership organization in your buildings." He made it clear that if landlords weren't keeping up with maintenance and repairs, they needed to have a majority of the tenants working together in a functioning organization. *And* they needed to band together in a citywide group.

It was not only a good turnout but the fed-up tenants

who came out wanted to take action. They were fired up by the speakers and exhilarated by seeing so many people from around the city at the meeting. A lot of them hung around and talked with John and Phyllis and Aranow. They exchanged landlord stories and their phone numbers with people from other buildings who they'd just met. By the time people cleared out of the cafeteria, a citywide tenant group was in the making.

The next PACT meeting was upbeat. Their focus on tenant organizing had already yielded tangible results. Rent control was enacted in two cities and two citywide tenant organizations were in the making. Amazing, I thought. I was excited. There was still lots of hard work ahead, way more than anyone knew at the time, but for now we were celebrating our successes. That's when John moved the goal posts and pushed a bigger agenda.

"Organizing tenants is not the *goal*," he declared as we were basking in our success. "Our *goal* is to build a mass popular political movement to challenge corporate power." There was some discussion but nobody knew how to get their arms around what it would mean to create a mass political movement. I sure didn't. That's when John decided he needed to write a Manifesto.

As if John's call for building a mass political movement wasn't enough, the idea of running district leaders was also on the agenda. It seemed to me that if the goal was to build grassroots organizations, then PACT should capitalize on the recent rent ordinance victories and get more people involved. The danger was that we might lose the momentum that had been gained from getting folks involved in a political fight. A winning one at that. But suddenly the group was off in another direction, and it was the young mayor Joel Shain who diverted them.

Part II: The Scene is Set (1970-74)

Electoral Politics

Joel Shain was young, ambitious and unafraid to mix it up with the established Democratic bosses. He was already at odds with Nick Franco, the Orange Democratic Chairman, and the brash young mayor was plotting to take over control of the municipal party organization. As mayor, he figured he had plenty of loyalists who would run as district leaders against Franco's people. He called upon PACT to help fill out his slate across every precinct.

If that move wasn't bold enough for a thirty-year-old who'd won just one municipal election, he declared himself a candidate for Chairman of the Essex Democratic Party to oust the powerful boss, Harry Lerner. Shain had balls. That was for sure.

There were scattered pockets of opposition to Lerner throughout the county. It was strongest in the suburbs and among activist Blacks. To convince people to get on board with what must have seemed like tilting at windmills, Joel recounted how he'd been called to a meeting in Newark Mayor Ken Gibson's office with Steve Adubato, Democratic Boss of Newark's North Ward, and East Ward Councilman Lou Turco.

Joel recalled, "Adubato said to me 'We want you to run for County Chairman. To get rid of Harry Lerner, we need a Jew to run against a Jew.'" With the backing of Gibson, Adubato and Turco plus all the anti-Lerner suburban reformers, Adubato made a credible case for Joel's shot at toppling Lerner.

So Shain became the candidate to replace Lerner, and if he was going to be credible, he needed to at least control the delegation representing Orange. PACT was brought into the fray along with others who Joel and Ronnie recruited. It was an amalgam of anti-machine reformers, liberal activists like PACT, and independent Black community leaders like Leroy Webster, a union carpenter and board member of Valley Settlement House who ran as district leaders. The formal title for district leaders is members of the County Democratic Committee. Elected district leaders then elect the party officers who hold the real power. In a solid Democratic county like Essex, all that power rests in the hands of the County Chairman. District leaders are elected every year, one man and one woman from each district sometimes called a precinct.

Following the Primary, Joel remembers the Party Reorganization Meeting, the gathering of all the newly elected district leaders to choose the party officers for the new term. "I knew that if we didn't win the vote for a secret ballot, it was hopeless. There were too many people afraid to *publicly* oppose Lerner. We lost that vote, so I decided to withdraw. Lerner wanted the show-of-hands vote to go ahead and his people blocked my way to the stage. I had to physically push my way onto the stage and grab the mic from Frank McQuade to announce I was withdrawing."

The drama was over. Lerner had beaten back yet another challenge to his dominance. Joel didn't win control of the Orange Democratic Party and not a single PACT district leader was elected. The diversion from the tenant organizing mission was complete, at least in Orange. Meanwhile Phyllis stayed the course.

At a PACT meeting after the district leader debacle, someone asked, "So, what'd we learn from our district leader fight?"

"The Machine knows how to get out the vote when they need to. We underestimated them."

"What the machine knows is how to stuff the ballot box," someone else added. "Where'd they get some of those people from? Showed up just when the polls were about to close. I talked to a few of them. They had no idea what they were doing."

"You're wrong about that," someone said in response. "They knew *exactly* what they were doing. Following instructions."

This was PACT's only electoral skirmish and it was a blistering defeat.

Marty Bierbaum, the teacher and one of the defeated PACT candidates, offered a calm and considered reflection. "Look, some of the people we were up against, they depend on government, financially, or someone in their extended family does. Whereas we're not in it for the personal benefit. We're not dependent on government for our well-being. We want to make government better, more efficient, and honest. They have a different stake in this than we do. They're not going to give that up without a fight." Marty, I'd learn, had the detached, studied, and observant perspective of the urban social scientist he'd soon become. A good balance to the hotter passions in the group.

A few stared into their coffee cups or looked up at the ceiling as Mark riffed on Marty's comment with a monologue on the fate of the working class and the struggling poor. Then he added, "It's like Hobbes famously said, life is nasty, brutish and short." I didn't even know who Hobbes was. I had a lot to learn, I guess.

As John pivoted the discussion and took charge, I wondered about this interest in reforming the Democratic Party. I grew up Irish, Catholic, and Democrat. I embraced the Irish part, but the church and the Democrats? I was pretty much done with them. John spun the district leader diversion in a positive direction.

"Listen," he said, "it was good we got involved. We

made our presence felt. We need to have one foot in the Democratic Party. But the other foot should always be firmly planted in our grassroots organizing."

I was skeptical but it was a refrain that I'd hear from John a lot and one that I would slowly come to agree with. Nonetheless, I loved my new PACT group.

If only my love life was finding a groove like I felt with this community. Claudia and I had the most romantic year imaginable, but I eventually felt trapped, like I was responsible for keeping her feeling constantly loved. She seemed to love me every second of every day. I didn't feel the same and was suffocating having that responsibility. And I didn't know how to talk about it without it sounding like a rejection. It was reminiscent of what happened with Scubi. The longer I put off telling her the more trapped I felt. When I finally told her I was leaving, she was devastated. I had no place to go immediately, and for days she begged me not to move out.

I found a studio apartment down on West 89th, and one day when she was at work, I moved out, leaving behind a tender and sorrowful letter. It was such a sad and miserable ending to a young love affair. Claudia was sexy and funny and a true romantic. She made me feel sexy and helped me become a better lover, opening me up to the romance of life. I knew I'd never forget her.

I found plenty of ways to stay busy and hide from feeling that I was pathetically incompetent at maintaining a loving relationship. I played music with Ronnie and took some yoga classes and signed up for classes in Transcendental Meditation.

There was a brownstone being renovated across from my new apartment. I spotted some big heavy paneled pocket doors at the curb, so I stopped over and talked

Part II: The Scene is Set (1970-74)

to the cute woman my age who was overseeing the construction. She told me her name was Bobbi Helpern, and they didn't need the doors and hoped someone would pick them up. They were gorgeous. Eight feet tall, oak on one side and cherry on the other. I dragged three of them across the street. I told Bobbi I planned to make them into a couch.

The next day I stopped back and told Bobbi I was looking for a part-time laborer job. She said she was looking for a laborer but that it only paid three bucks an hour. I told her I'd take it.

Now I had to convince my boss to let me take time off to try my hand at renovation. I was lucky that Paul valued my work. He agreed, but he limited my part-time leave to six weeks. I was fine with that. I just wanted to get some experience. Three mornings a week I walked across the street to work. It was grunt work but I was on a job site renovating a building from the late 1800s. Every day I was learning.

I spent that first Saturday making my hundred-year-old doors into a couch. I bought a piece of foam on Canal Street and some red corduroy on Orchard Street and some big colorful throw pillows. A week later, I asked Bobbi out. She was one of three women owners, all in their twenties, and this was their first project. Pretty cool, I thought. Things went great on our first few dates; I was in love again and pretty soon we were together all the time. She lived on West 79th. For the time being at least, I was settled in on the upper west side.

Out in Essex County, things were heating up. Phyllis wasn't involved in the district leader campaign except on Election Day when she manned one of the polls. She was in East Orange and she had an organization to build and an urgent issue to win: getting the rent ordinance implemented. She picked up the pace and issued a press release that the East Orange Tenants Association was formed with temporary officers: Jesse Royster, Thomas Bryant, John Atlas, and herself. But Phyllis wanted a *real* organization, so two months later she convened a group of leaders from the buildings she'd been advising. They formed the EOTA Board of Directors, electing Phyllis as its first president. Phyllis put herself in the position she wanted. Now the hard work would begin.

Phyllis became John's protege. She followed his call to organize tenants with a unique and burning passion. It was soon apparent that Phyllis aspired to become an influential grassroots *leader,* not just someone who pitched in behind John. But if she was going to follow John's lead, she expected him to be responsive and accountable to her.

When she called his office on her lunch break, he'd better take her call, or call her back after she was out of school, or at home after her evening tenant meetings. Or on the weekend. Phyllis felt she was being accountable to John and she deserved the same from him. For Phyllis, accountability would always be an essential part of our joint work together.

Ronnie taught Phyllis that a tenants association is not a social service agency; of course, it's a "helpline" that's essential for tenants with landlord problems, but much more importantly it's an organization of its members. So Phyllis insisted that her new board of directors establish a membership policy with annual dues of three dollars for every apartment represented. She pressed tenant leaders to collect money from folks in their buildings and pass it on to her. Sometimes she'd collect cash and checks and issue membership cards on the spot at tenant meetings. She

Part II: The Scene is Set (1970-74)

sent a dollar from each tenant to NJTO and a membership card from the statewide group would arrive in their mail. It was all about building *organization*—grassroots organizations controlled by their members.

Implementation of the East Orange rent ordinance was still in limbo. Phyllis saw this as retrenchment by the mayor and some members of the council, and she felt it as a personal rebuke. She needed to establish her credibility if she was going to keep the tenant momentum going and build a worthwhile organization. Her strategy to motivate the other new tenant leaders after their initial victory was to double down on her public attacks on Mayor Hart.

For three months, Phyllis attacked Mayor Hart in the press for intentionally dragging his feet on establishing a rent leveling board. Hart's political adversaries on the council took advantage and piled on criticism of their own. Mayor Hart, who must have been steaming over the public attacks, confidently assured the press and the council that doing things properly and legally takes a little time. He promised that the law would be implemented soon.

I liked Mayor Hart, what little I knew of him from his public appearances, and I admired him trying to lead his changing city at such a difficult time. He was East Orange's first Black mayor and I'd have been inclined to cut him some slack, but not Phyllis. To her it was a battle. A personal one. Either she was going to win or Hart was. I knew Phyllis needed to prove herself in the public arena, and she wanted EOTA to be the voice of tenants in East Orange. And she was the voice of EOTA.

By May of '73 the Rent Leveling Board held its first meeting with Mildred Barry as its chairperson. Phyllis and EOTA had their first public victory. East Orange tenants were becoming aware of this young and fiery leader and her new organization that represented them. Elected officials and the local press knew her well. In those months, you couldn't pick up the weekly *East Orange RECORD* without reading about Phyllis and EOTA.

Meanwhile, Bill Hart must have felt bruised from the battle. He was usually quite measured in his public responses to her attacks saying things like, "I believe Miss Salowe is new to East Orange and unfamiliar with my long record of helping tenants." But he was unlikely to forget how he was treated by this new firebrand.

When the political battle receded from the headlines that summer, Phyllis sent off a press release to *The East Orange RECORD*. The printed article listed twenty-five buildings that were getting help from EOTA, meaning Phyllis was working personally with them. Looking to pump up the list of addresses, Phyllis included the single family house where three friends lived, with Louis Baron named as the tenant leader. Phyllis probably did give her friends some landlord tenant advice, and I bet she required them all to pay dues.

Legislator Endorsements

That fall, John recruited Phyllis to co-chair an Essex County candidate screening committee. Candidates for State Assembly and Senate who were seeking NJTO's endorsement needed to be vetted. Phyllis agreed but was nervous. Marty Parker from PACT, who was now the president of Orange Tenants Association, was with her when twenty-six-year-old Richard Codey, the candidate for State Assembly, arrived at Phyllis's apartment for his interview. Codey was from a prominent Irish family in Orange who owned the biggest Irish funeral home in Orange. In deeply ethnic Orange there were also two Black-owned funeral homes and two owned by Italians. It mattered that you were buried by your own people.

Codey had the blessing of County Boss Harry Lerner, so he won the Assembly Primary easily. The district was solidly Democratic, so victory in the General was a sure thing, but he still sought the endorsement of NJTO. Codey was what I thought of as a *New Deal Democrat*, a guy who naturally sided with working people and with tenants, but I also think he saw seeking the NJTO endorsement as a gesture of respect, and the establishment of a political relationship, regardless of how new these tenant organizations were. Codey's running mate Eldridge Hawkins, a Black attorney from East Orange, didn't bother and neither did the Republicans.

At the interview, Phyllis's nerves were calmed a bit by the script provided by NJTO, and she and Marty followed it to the letter. What really thrilled Phyllis was delivering the statewide endorsement to Codey and announcing it to the press. This was her first taste of representing the growing statewide tenant group. She might have been nervous, but this bigger political role definitely appealed to her. She'd just gotten started in East Orange, but she already wanted a bigger stage.

I definitely underestimated Phyllis. As her accomplishments mounted, I came to understand her better.

That's Ronnie on the left teaching me a new chord.

CHAPTER 10

This Old House

I was finding my groove. It was fascinating to get to know different cities and the different people who made their lives there. Saving old city neighborhoods was becoming a passion.

Today, rehabbing old city neighborhoods always raises the specter of displacement. When real estate values and rents go up, poor people get pushed out, and there's a culture divide between newcomers and old residents. But back then, big areas in plenty of cities were in freefall. Few people, who could afford the suburbs, wanted to move to the cities, except to places like Greenwich Village. The growing middle class wanted the new pristine life that the suburbs represented. Suburbs were the lure, and what to do about the cities was a hot debate. In city after city, community leaders and elected officials were trying, mostly in vain, to keep the old neighborhoods stable.

I knew Englewood pretty well, and now I got to know every homeowner in this neglected neighborhood. It opened my eyes to the intimate neighborhood and family life of Black families that most White people only knew from a distance, if at all. People were remarkably open to this young, earnest White guy, even if they weren't quite sure what to make of the free federal money and the low interest loans.

The small house in Englewood that I wanted to renovate slipped through my fingers, but the urge to renovate did not go away. Even though I had few actual carpentry skills, I imagined myself one day with a truck full of tools fixing up rundown old houses. I connected with nonprofit groups in Baltimore and with urban renovators working in Philly. And I wanted to be an organizer. I had this dream of communal life and political action, and life as a community organizer. I saw myself as a hammer-swinging, pickup-driving urban renovator.

My life was full again. I was turned on by interesting work and a sense of purpose. And I was in love again. But I was still unsettled. I felt *disconnected*. I loved my neighborhood work in Englewood and my one-night-a-week co-leading teen rap sessions at St. Paul's. But every evening I left that community and crossed the Hudson River to the Upper West Side. My political life and increasingly my social life was now in the Oranges. I was a commuter, a guy without a place that he belonged to. Something needed to change.

I'd made up my mind and was anxious to share my news. I wanted Ronnie to be the first to know. He was working at home that day, and he lived on my route home from Englewood to the Upper West Side. I stopped and picked up a bottle of wine.

His apartment-*slash*-law office was a low-rent garret in the shadow of the George Washington Bridge, on the road down to the edge of the Hudson River. I took the winding stairs to the third floor. The door was ajar, and his long skinny frame was stretched out on the old oriental carpet as he leaned back on some mismatched Goodwill cushions. I smiled as I took in the scene.

The only hints that this was a lawyer's office was an oak roll-top desk and a single file cabinet at the other end of the living room. I wondered how clients reacted seeing the old sofa covered with an Indian print bedspread. Fortunately, he was the most highly regarded tenant lawyer in the state. And luckily, he wasn't totally dependent on legal fees to pay his bills because he accepted a lot of clients who couldn't afford to pay or could pay only a little. His part-time job as City of Orange Treasurer meant a steady paycheck.

He passed me the joint he'd just lit and I managed to casually open the bottle of Almaden red.

I got a couple of glasses from his tiny kitchen, but before I even sat down, I blurted out, "Hey, I'm moving out of the City to the Oranges."

He gave a big smile and threw back his frizzy blond head. "Good to hear. I've been wondering what's holding you back. I know you been itching to make a move, ever since that first PACT meeting. Ya know, you're pretty easy to read, right?"

"I suppose," I said. "So do you know I plan to buy a house—probably in East Orange?"

His eyes tilted skyward as he nodded his head. "Hmmm, I'm not *totally* surprised. I remember you wanted to rescue that house in Englewood, the one scheduled to be demolished. Good for you, man. That's exciting. What kinda house?"

"Maybe one of those beat up Victorians, there's plenty of 'em. I'll get one that needs a *bunch* of work. About the only thing I can afford, really. But I love those old Victorians. There's a ton of 'em slowly rotting away." Taking one last toke, I held the smoke down and added, "I wanna learn renovation skills. And invest in the future of the neighborhood."

"I *love* it," he exclaimed. "But—" then he hesitated, shaking his head. "Don't you worry? That might not be the best place to invest?" He smiled as he added, "You do know? It *is* a *changing* neighborhood."

"Hmmm?" I looked up as if noodling on that thought a bit. "So, my career as a get-rich-quick speculator, house flipper, and block buster is unlikely to take off?"

"That's what I love about you," he said, offering one of his big, gracious smiles. I poured us some more wine. "If I can find a beat-up old house for pretty cheap, it'd be cool to create some affordable group living. Like a *commune*, man. You dig?"

"I do. Sounds beautiful. And I *love* your vision. You got guts. Have you crunched the numbers?"

"Sort of," I said with false confidence. "Of course, it depends on the house. *Obviously*. The size and its condition. With renovation, most of the cost is labor. In my case the only out-of-pocket costs will be for materials, which I'll lay out as I go. I'll be doing *all* the work so I'll draw my pay once I sell it."

"You're amazing. You're so sure it'll work out. Have you got enough for a down payment?"

"I got about twenty-five hundred and another couple thousand for renovation."

He arched his sun-bleached eyebrows and smiled as he scrunched his face. "That *might* do it." I could tell he had doubts about whether I really knew what I was doing when it came to the numbers. But I didn't have time for doubts. It would have to work out.

"I'll do your closing for you," he added. "But you know I don't come cheap." I reached over and clinked my glass to his. "There's a lot of hungry attorneys out there. Maybe I should shop around."

Part II: The Scene is Set (1970-74)

I talked some more about my plans and right out of the blue, he said, "You know, you just might need more cash." I wondered what he was getting at, questioning whether I could manage my dream project. "So, if you're looking for a partner, one who has zero renovation skills, I just might be interested. But I'm not looking to *live in a commune, man.* You dig?"

"I dig. You're a real cool cat. Let's talk." I nodded at Ronnie and smiled. Feeling a deep sense of love and satisfaction, I laid my head back for a few seconds. I couldn't believe that he might do that. Invest in *my fantasy*. We talked some more about my plan to buy a house. Turns out he was dead serious. I knew Ronnie didn't have a lot of savings, but he'd decided. On the spot. If I was going to do this, he'd participate. I was floored. Wow.

So we talked it through. I was floating through the conversation. We'd own the house fifty-fifty. I'd be responsible for basically everything. And once we sold it, we'd share the proceeds based on our hours worked.

"You're amazing," I said as I got up to leave.

His big long arms pulled me into a hug. "I believe in you, brother."

I crossed the massive George Washington bridge. Glistening Manhattan spread out before me, and below the dark slate Hudson River was making its way to the sea and my mind was on fire. *I'll start looking tomorrow. I probably don't have enough savings and I really do need his help. It'll be so much fun together. A friendship like this? Incredible!* A blanket of good fortune had just embraced me.

For a moment, my reverie was broken and I thought about Bobbi. Our relationship was only a few months old. I really hoped she'd move with me. I knew that would be a big ask, that her ties to the Upper West Side were strong.

I had no strong connection to New York; I knew I'd be going. With or without her. This was my chance to be part of a community again. I looked forward to investing in Orange and East Orange and becoming part of the place, not a commuter whose new friends lived there.

My Dream House

I stopped by a realtor's office the next day. My imagination went into overdrive when I read the listing for 31 Chestnut Street, East Orange. Thirteen-rooms, built before houses were electrified, with eight bedrooms, five fireplaces, a wrap-around front porch, two second-floor porches, something called a butler's pantry, and a *solarium* off the dining room. Wow. It was a piece of American history. At $12,500 it was more than affordable. It seemed like a steal. I wanted it.

I drove along the parade of over-sized houses lining Chestnut Street, all built at the end of the nineteenth century. They were all a bit different but all in that catch-all style called Queen Anne Revival. Big porches, fancy trim, big gable dormers, some had turrets, steep roofs. My heart beat faster when I pulled up in front of number 31. I was in love already. I saw a tarnished gem reaching out for me to polish. I was completely blind to how worn out she was, having spent her last dozen years as a rooming house.

In love with this piece of living history and imagining my dreams fulfilled, I ignored that the massive porch was no longer level, burdened by the weight of the second-floor porch above. I focused instead on the tall carved doors with beveled glass that secured the entrance like a pair of palace guards. They led into a protected space where a stately main door gave a peek through its etched glass into the spacious front foyer beyond. I headed back to the realtor and arranged for Ronnie and I to see the house on Saturday.

Flashlights in hand, Ronnie and I stepped into a foyer the size of a living room. It had a fireplace, faced with Victorian-era tile and topped with a carved wooden mantle. Next to it on the right was a stately set of stairs. Decades of young and old hands had worn the top of the carved newel post to a shiny golden finish. To our left, a pair of oak pocket doors opened into a formal parlor with its own fireplace. More pocket doors connected the parlor, the living room and the dining room. Each with its own fireplace.

I could feel the presence of eighty years of occupants, all the way back to when the house was lit with gas lamps. I'd later discover live gas lines in the walls that fueled the now-missing lights. The second and third floors told a more recent story. Screwed into the Victorian door molding on each of the eight bedroom doors was a latch for a padlock. I pictured some older guys living the solitary rooming house life and locking up their few belongings when they went out. Then I imagined the house full again. No padlocks.

As I feasted on the elegant moldings, parquet floors, and stained-glass windows, Ronnie shined his flashlight on the puckered plaster ceilings and the water-stained cracks that mapped the locations of leaking radiators in the rooms above.

I acknowledged that we'd have to do some plaster repair.

"Have you ever done that?" he asked.

"No, but it's not *that* hard," I said. Then I wondered if my complete lack of caution might give him pause. It didn't seem to. Some twenty-five cent washers and a pipe wrench could have eliminated weeks of plaster repair that

I'd face later. That is, once I learned how to mix plaster and, working overhead, how to apply it smoothly with a metal trowel. But that's what I'd signed up for, right? An apprenticeship.

With Ronnie and the realtor waiting near the front door, I wandered again through the first floor, just savoring the craftsmanship—the beveled glass doors, stained glass windows, the ceramic tile, oak flooring, the heavy plaster walls, high ceilings, and the grand staircase. I ran my hands across the elaborate moldings. I admired the quality of the work. All of it was done by carpenters with hand tools. People like my mom's father, Joe Kurz the carpenter.

I loved Papa Joe and loved the thought of taking up his craft. I remembered spending so much time with him when he and Grandma lived across the street. I missed them both and that comfy city block.

As I came back around to the foyer, I was imagining what time-tested observation the chatty realtor might make, so I beat him to it. Looking at him I shook my head.

"They sure don't build 'em like this anymore, do they?"

Ronnie smiled, knowing that it was a tease.

"You got that right," said the salesman. Then he added, "By the way, the house was reroofed just last year. Those new asphalt shingles are guaranteed for twenty-five years."

Without even looking at Ronnie, I told the realtor we'd be preparing an offer. Ronnie asked if the seller would be open to taking back a mortgage. The realtor thought she would. I hadn't thought about how impossible it would be to get a bank loan. But Ronnie had.

I was so appreciative of Ronnie's commitment. My dream was moving ahead. A new chapter was opening. I'd have this big and beautiful old house and become a carpenter like my grandfather. I'd be a rehabber, an old house remodeler. And a community organizer. Things were falling into place.

Phyllis's friends Bernie, Louie, and Larry threw a New Year's eve party at their house on Morton Street in East Orange and invited Ronnie and me. We were each other's date. Ronnie hadn't seen Joanne for at least three months. She decided that she needed to make a sincere six month attempt to make her marriage work. I don't know how he did it. He was way more Zen than me.

We didn't really know this group but we got a nice little ovation when we walked in with our guitars. Phyllis showed up alone. Most of her close women friends were engaged or in serious relationships and a couple of them were already married. Phyllis was tired of being alone and had her eye on somebody she knew was coming to the party. She was looking forward to spending some serious time with Stuie Kaye, an old acquaintance, just back from an Alaska road trip. Stu finally showed up but he had a date. It was a great party, though probably not for Phyllis. Late in the evening, Ronnie and I played and a hootenanny broke out, people sang along. We hooped and hollered at midnight. I made a couple resolutions but one of my wishes was for my best friend to be with Joanne in the new year. Phyllis made only one resolution for 1974.

The resolute stalker got two of her friends to invite Stu over for dinner. Unfortunately, this target of Phyllis's desire had no idea that he was being fixed up and he showed up with a date. Phyllis was foiled again and perturbed being the fifth wheel in this group, merrily having drinks and dinner. That was it. She needed a more direct approach.

The next day, she called Stu and invited him over to her place for dinner. She'd finally got him alone and the dinner went well. The first time Stu spent the night at Phyllis's, he got a picture of the tenant leader's life. All evening long, the *Tenant Hotline* rang constantly. Tenants needing help. That's when she got an answering service. She had a boyfriend now and wouldn't be spending *every* evening on the phone with needy tenants.

• • •

Ronnie and I pooled together a four-thousand-dollar down payment and offered twelve thousand and proposed that the seller, Mrs. Mocille Lassiter, take back a mortgage for the eight thousand balance. She agreed to hold the mortgage but wanted full price. Ronnie asked what we should do.

Afraid of losing my dream house I said, "Let's pay the asking price."

Ronnie figured she would give in if we didn't budge, but I wanted to seal the deal quickly. My dream house was already filling my imagination, so Ronnie agreed. We'd be closing in a month or so. I was out of my mind with excitement. I couldn't wait to be in there as the owner. And start the renovation.

I began talking up the house project with the PACT group. Phyllis said she *might* be interested in moving in and that she wanted to be part of a *communal thing* but was definitely not into shared living.

I was anxious to get a commitment so I made Phyllis a proposal.

"How about a separate apartment? On the third floor there are three bedrooms and a full bath. I'll tear down a couple walls and add a nice kitchen. You'll have one bedroom and a living room open to a kitchen and dining area." I proposed a rent that was less than she was paying on South Munn Avenue, where the landlord was starting to cut back on maintenance.

We had a deal. The militant leader of East Orange's tenants would soon be my renter. On her first date with Stu, she walked him up Chestnut and showed him where she'd be moving to. She was hopeful. She really liked Stu. Meanwhile Ronnie's love saga had taken a delightful turn. Joanne's husband moved out and she and Ronnie could be together. I liked Joanne a lot and was so happy for them.

Soon, my real estate backer and I were heading toward a closing on our big, beautiful monstrosity on Chestnut Street. Ronnie ordered a survey and title search and I checked the Yellow Pages for a termite inspector. I called the first listing: AAA Pest Removal. The title report came back clean and I waited to hear from the termite inspector. I just wanted it to say there's no evidence of termites. This was the perfect house; I couldn't lose it. The seventy-nine-dollar inspection report came back: no evidence of termites. That was the last hurdle. I was on my way.

After the closing, I changed the locks, and that weekend Sam Ferber with his big Chevy Suburban wagon helped me move.

The first-floor kitchen was a disaster area, with one exception: Somehow when we'd first toured the house, I overlooked a vintage six-burner stove. The single stove in an eight-bedroom rooming house was bound to look pretty dingy. This one was disgusting. The name plate said Chambers, a coveted but no longer manufactured brand.

As I scrubbed years of grease, grime, and scorch from the stovetop and the burners, and cleaned the oven and the broiler, I was filled with warm thoughts of my mom, the woman who'd taught me how to clean. I remember watching her scrub roasting pans with a steel wool pot scrubber and Ajax cleanser. So that's how I attacked the Chambers. I thought of her German mother who must have taught her. I was so identified with being Irish that I didn't often think about my German lineage. I valued what those two great homemakers passed down to me. I hoped they'd approve of the job I was doing. I thought they would.

Houses of this pedigree had a "butler's pantry" connecting the kitchen to the dining room. Mine had a sink, a counter, some cabinetry, and open shelves. Maybe it could serve as my kitchen. I ran an extension of the gas line and crammed the Chambers stove into the end of the butler's pantry, then added a fridge. I had a small working kitchen. It was tight, but definitely workable.

I closed off the old kitchen and ripped out the beat-up counters and cabinets. Each layer of vintage linoleum I removed brought images of the cooks and families that made this kitchen hum. The patterns from the forties and then the twenties were distinct. When I got down to the bare subfloor, the kitchen became my workroom, a place to store materials and tools, and the last room to be renovated.

I promised Phyllis I'd get to work on the third floor apartment next. There was a bathroom up there but no kitchen. That would take some serious remodeling. Her lease was expiring so I needed to get cracking. But first I needed to do something about the main bathroom.

The house had one bathroom on the second floor and just a toilet and sink in the basement. In the main bath, the black-and-checked-white floor tile was worn but completely intact. It gave a vintage look to the bath. But the wall tile around the tub/shower was a mess. Tiles were missing and others were beginning to lose their grip to the wall. Water from the shower was hastening that process and some mold was beginning to grow where tiles were missing. I knew repairing those two walls was urgent and would take some serious time. Time I didn't have right then.

I removed the loose tiles, then killed the mold with bleach and bought a nice solid blue shower curtain and a white one that was sort of translucent. I fastened the blue one high on the two damaged walls so that it hung down, just covering the rim of the tub. But the hot and cold handles were now behind the curtain, so I removed the faucet handles, poked two holes in the curtain, and replaced the handles. The new white curtain, I hung from the old shower rod with shiny clips, and it was all perfectly sanitary and usable. That tile work would have to wait for another day. Another year probably. I gave the room a quick coat of white paint and hung a nice big garage sale mirror. A light gray bathroom rug in front of the old free standing sink completed the job. All in one weekend.

With nineteen windows that were eight decades old, the house was drafty. The exterior walls weren't insulated. I knew that come winter, that the boiler'd be pumping steam all day and night to radiators on all three floors; my oil bills would be sky high. Before then I needed to keep out the cold, so I began measuring the windows for triple-track storm and screen units. It would make a big difference.

I needed a truck and one day I spotted a '63 Dodge panel truck for sale. The perfect vehicle for both carpentry and camping trips was mine for eight hundred bucks. It became my *daily driver*. I established contractor accounts at the lumberyard and the paint store and got to work on the third floor. I loved my design for the apartment; I'd raise the ceiling in the kitchen and dining area and open it to the living room. A row of new windows high on the south wall would fill the apartment with light. Exposing the big, red brick chimney would finish off the loft-style look. I began demolishing walls and tearing out the ceiling. The kitchen would be my first real challenge.

Adding a kitchen meant tapping into the hot and cold water lines and to a cast iron drain pipe from the bathroom. *Here's my first test,* I thought. *I'm not calling a plumber.* An old guy in the plumbing section at Epstein's Hardware on Main Street became my guru. He drew me a diagram and coached me on how to tap into the cast iron drain pipe and how to sweat the copper water lines. I couldn't wait to tackle the job, and it took me a couple days but I finally got the kitchen sink hooked up and turned on the hot and cold water. No leaks! But my celebration was cut short. I hadn't really thought about the stove. How would I get a gas line up to the third floor from the basement?

Robert Blumethal, a friend of a friend, was reluctantly working for his dad's plumbing business until he could find something he liked better. I asked Robert how to run the gas line.

"I'll come by on Saturday morning and show you how."

Well, Robert showed up with Larry Looker, a buddy of his. With me as a kind of gopher/laborer, the gas line was up to the third floor by lunch time. When Robert and Larry started loading their truck, I ran out for sub sandwiches and beer. I toasted them as we ate on the big front porch. Of course they wouldn't accept any pay. I loved guys like that. We barely knew each other and they spent a Saturday morning plumbing my house for free.

For the next five years, the old guy in Epstein's plumbing

department guided me as I wrestled with leaking eighty-year-old faucets, an oil fired steam boiler, hissing radiators, and lots more.

Phyllis stopped by most days to check on progress as her apartment took shape. She wanted to participate and contribute some "sweat equity." I knew that Phyllis was a poor candidate for this work, but she was so eager.

Anybody can paint, I thought. *What could go wrong?* I sent her to the paint store and she bought a gallon of bright yellow for her bedroom walls.

When I returned later that day, splashes of yellow were cascading down the side of the house. The source: an open third floor window. Phyllis sheepishly explained that somehow the can of paint tipped over. She'd tried to mop it up with newspaper and threw the newspapers out the window. I rolled my eyes, shook my head, and fired her from the renovation crew.

My vision was emerging. The apartment came out great. The first big renovation challenge was behind me and the house was coming to life. Phyllis loved her custom apartment, and in one weekend we helped her move in from one block down the street.

" . . . there's no way of continuing to engage in direct action and resistance outside of community."
~ Elizabeth McAlister

CHAPTER 11

Community, Nonviolence, Resistance

EOTA kept up the pressure, and during 1974 got a major change to the Rent Leveling Ordinance. The maximum rent increase to a new tenant was reduced to 15% above what the previous tenant paid. This was movement in the right direction, but EOTA leaders were plenty unhappy and prepared to organize for a stronger law. This would be another active year for East Orange tenants.

Meanwhile, life for tenants, especially in the older buildings, was getting tougher as landlords cut back on maintenance and repairs. This slow but steady disinvestment was undermining East Orange. The city was in trouble. Landlords were maximizing their monthly bottom line and no longer treated buildings as long-term investments. The Tenant Hotline was a nonstop stream of desperate tenants who had nowhere else to turn.

Phyllis's lifeline in meeting these challenges was the best pair of advisors anywhere—John and Ronnie. Phyllis was teaching five days a week, so her answering service fielded the constant calls. During lunch, she dominated the lone payphone in the teacher's lounge. With a purse full of quarters, she'd call the answering service, return tenants' calls, and reach out to her advisors. She made call after call while trying not to catch the glaring eyes of other teachers waiting to use the phone.

The Thursday Night Group

The PACT Sunday brunches stopped being a regular thing. Maybe because so much political energy was going into OTA and EOTA, but the social side of PACT didn't let up. I was invited to parties and potluck suppers, and Bobbi and I even went on a couple of camping and canoe trips with my new found group, but I missed the organized political discussions.

Through Mary Tasker, our group caught the attention of Elizabeth McAllister, a prominent radical war resister. Liz asked to meet with us. I didn't know who she was but I knew about her radical Catholic priest husband, Phillip Berrigan. He and his brother Daniel, a Jesuit priest, were famous for their dramatic anti-draft protests. Liz had once been a nun and was now spreading the gospel of community, nonviolence, and resistance. She proposed that if we were interested, she wanted to meet with us weekly. Some of us were still itching for that intense and purposeful political discussion. Liz traveled to New Jersey from Baltimore in the middle of each week and she had Thursday evenings free. The Thursday Night Group was born.

The radical former nun and her husband lived in a Baltimore collective of war resisters, a place they called Jonah House. In May, 1968, Phillip and Daniel Berrigan, and seven other Catholic protesters, made headlines burning the records of the Catonsville, Maryland draft board with homemade napalm. The arrest, trial, and three-year prison sentence of the Catonsville Nine propelled them to national prominence and fueled a Catholic war resistance movement. Nonviolent civil disobedience in opposition to the Vietnam War and the draft grew.

Phil just finished serving his three years in jail when he and Liz made their marriage public. Phil was still a priest. They were both promptly excommunicated.

About seven or eight of us met with Liz that first night. She got right into it, telling us how she and Phil and a group of lay and religious people founded the Baltimore collective that supported the group's anti-war activities. Their work was dedicated to three themes: community, nonviolence, and resistance. Those themes would guide our discussions with Liz.

I was in the thrall of Liz's deep religious courage and her dedication to ending war. We all found her warmth and openness irresistible. Her generous spirit and commitment to a life of active resistance to violence and oppression were a contagious combination. Liz was familiar to me. She had the school-girl looks of the Irish-Catholic girls I'd grown up with. It also wasn't that hard to imagine her in a starched habit with a rosary around her waist. To the Jews, I think nuns were an alien life form. They always referred to her as *Sister Liz*.

Sister Liz drilled down on what it meant to dedicate your life to community, nonviolence, and resistance. Her husband and others had just finished three years in prison and it wasn't their first jail term for war resistance. Liz wanted to know what our group was about. We told her we were dedicated too—to collective action to build a movement of economic justice and we supported each other in that work. We were committed to a cooperative lifestyle and becoming less focused on personal achievement; we believed that "the personal is political," that is, how we conduct our lives and treat others was itself a political act.

Liz asked about our tenant organizing and was curious if tenants' rights was our only public issue. I think she was feeling around for a *moral resistance* issue, that might get us to a deeper level of moral commitment. I don't think she saw our tenants' rights work in the way that she regarded war resistance. It was Joan, I think, who told Liz about PACT's involvement in an Essex County consumer rights project. Liz told us about a group that practiced civil disobedience when they couldn't get chain grocery stores in Baltimore to provide the same quality produce and pricing in the inner city as out in the suburbs. How, when negotiations with the chain broke down they invited the press and threw the rotten produce on the floor of the inner city market and waited for the cops to come and arrest them.

We quickly sensed that when she said "dedicate your life," she meant a different level of commitment than we were prepared for. Liz talked in moral terms about peace and justice. We spoke slightly different languages. For Liz, the work of moral resistance required an inner look at who you are and what your inner commitments are, so she gave us homework: Write about your personal goals and come prepared to publicly discuss them in the group.

Phyllis, Ronnie, and I did our homework and reported back the next week. The copied pages that Phyllis and I passed out were no surprise to anyone. We were both already pretty transparent. We wanted to deepen our commitment to political work that aligned with our deeply held values. Hers stressed more direct action and mine tilted toward building community, but Ronnie went deeper and he clearly laid out what he was struggling with. He wrote that he was challenging his inner drive for status and influence and wanted to be more engaged in *collective* success. He was interested, he wrote, *"in being part of a community."*

We were best friends and I'd never heard him express that deep inner conflict so clearly before. He was incredibly talented and engaging. To Ronnie, status and influence came easily. He moved about with confidence in all kinds of circles, from groups of poor tenants to the politicians who inhabited Orange City Hall. But he was also a very private person. It took some courage to reveal those feelings to the group, but he wanted to make his commitment public. His writing had more clues into his inner life, this time about the *value* of community. He wrote, "I believe it would be easier for me to move in the direction of an integrated lifestyle, devoted to a life of integrity and truth-seeking through a community of people and I want to expend energy in this direction, to explore this. My challenge is to identify those steps that I am willing to take to move in these directions."

That was the key to his decision to help me buy the house. Participating in my venture had been more than the generosity of a best friend; it was him acting on that *commitment* to community. Ronnie didn't have to put his meager savings at risk, but when he was faced with a tangible way to put his words into action, that's what he did. And he seemed to do it with ease.

When Ronnie talked about his commitment to living a life more aligned with his values, I thought about a very visible change he'd already made. He no longer drove that cool Camaro convertible, the car that was an extension of his handsome, tanned persona. He'd traded it in on a beige Datsun compact station wagon. If that look wasn't nerdy enough, he added the rooftop tent option. Ronnie's car choices sent a message about the driver, and the messages could not have been more different.

John didn't respond to Liz's promptings like the rest of

us. He saw the Thursday Night Group as a continuation of the PACT meetings. Rather than explore how he wanted to change, he kept advancing his movement building ideas. John was drafting a political manifesto about linking with other single-issue groups who were also opposed to the growing power of big corporations. His anti-corporate message made sense to me but I didn't quite get how it related to helping tenants deal with their landlords.

While Liz pushed us to connect our discussions of society's inequities to direct action, John was peddling his big vision and it wasn't limited to his familiar call to "unite the poor and middle class around pocketbook issues," or "One foot in the Democratic Party and one foot firmly in grassroots organizing." John was blunt when he stated that organizing tenants was *not* the goal of our group's political work.

Our leader's proclamation stated that our goal was "to build a mass or popular political movement consistent with economic democracy or democratic socialism," and that "people will start demanding a larger share of the economic and political pie." He declared that, "Our common enemy is big business, multinational corporations, and those that directly serve their interests."

I was on board.

In terms of strategy, his encyclical prescribed, "targeting blue-collar, low-income, and minority voters who have suffered most from the policy failures and broken promises," and that "our progressive movement would take on big business that was manipulating our political democracy to benefit those at the top." I was definitely for that.

John's bold proclamation finished with, "Only this movement can solve the basic problems of daily life—the cost of oil, housing, food, and medical care; the quality of our air, water, and consumer goods; and our working conditions, jobs, and pay."

Undeterred, Liz persisted with the direct action discussion and brought up a campaign that addressed the low quality of produce sold in Black neighborhoods, like the Baltimore group had done. There was some interest and I think maybe there was one confrontation at an East Orange market, but that was it. We were too consumed with our tenant work. But Liz didn't give up on us.

The ex-nun and her religious colleagues practiced a type of resistance anchored in bearing moral witness to violence, oppression, and exploitation. They protested with acts of civil disobedience—breaking the law to shine a light on an immoral system, and they were willing to accept the consequences, including jail time. It soon became obvious that we didn't share that level of religious zeal. We wanted to live meaningful lives, lives of purpose, build a movement for change—not bear witness from a jail cell.

We were building a practice of political activism based on local needs and issues. We built a communal social life—parties, camping trips, a jug band, sports teams, and events; and we began to build our own organizations and programs to support our political work that could employ some of us. We admired and loved Liz; she had that deep sense of moral purpose that Dr. King had and she was living out what she felt "religiously" called to do. Some of us found working with her really valuable, but she wasn't gaining converts spending her Thursday evenings with us.

Liz suggested a weekend retreat to bring together her three New Jersey groups. We gathered for a spring weekend in western Jersey, a place called Bushkill Falls. It must have been a summer camp. We stayed in group cabins and had a dining room with a big kitchen. We liked the folks from Passaic County; they were earnestly searching for how to put their values and their politics into action. By comparison, our PACT group had its shit together. We were the only group that showed up with a manifesto and a jug band: two guitars, a banjo, a washtub bass, a washboard, and a bag of kazoos.

Nobody remembers how the folks in Liz's two other groups reacted to John's call to unite the poor and the working class around pocketbook issues and to challenge the rising influence of big business. I suspect most people agreed but just didn't see that it affected what they were doing at the moment. What people did remember was our jug band. We played familiar folk and protest songs. Everybody sang along. The feeling was electric. This group of fellow travelers who'd all just met joined in song around the campfire. It captured the feeling of Liz's message and our shared sense of purpose—*community, nonviolence, and resistance.*

John's manifesto was the first time I got wind of his idea that we should build a coalition with other single-issue groups like labor unions, environmentalists, and women's rights groups. John called them *anti-corporate reform organizations,* or *ACROs.* The acronym never stuck, but coalition was definitely in our future. Still a few years away.

If PACT's chief strategist was disappointed that folks didn't want to adopt his declaration of resistance or even discuss it much, he didn't show it. It was his first attempt at trying out his message on a group beyond just his PACT family. He was just getting warmed up.

I don't recall that the weekend retreat accomplished much. We continued meeting with Liz on Thursday evenings, but she was pregnant and soon stopped coming to New Jersey. She had other concerns too; she was involved in a court case where she'd been illegally wire tapped. Liz didn't say she'd given up on us but I did wonder whether she thought her time with us was well spent. She never asked us about the draft. We all avoided getting sent to Vietnam and none of us were in jail. I wonder what she thought of that.

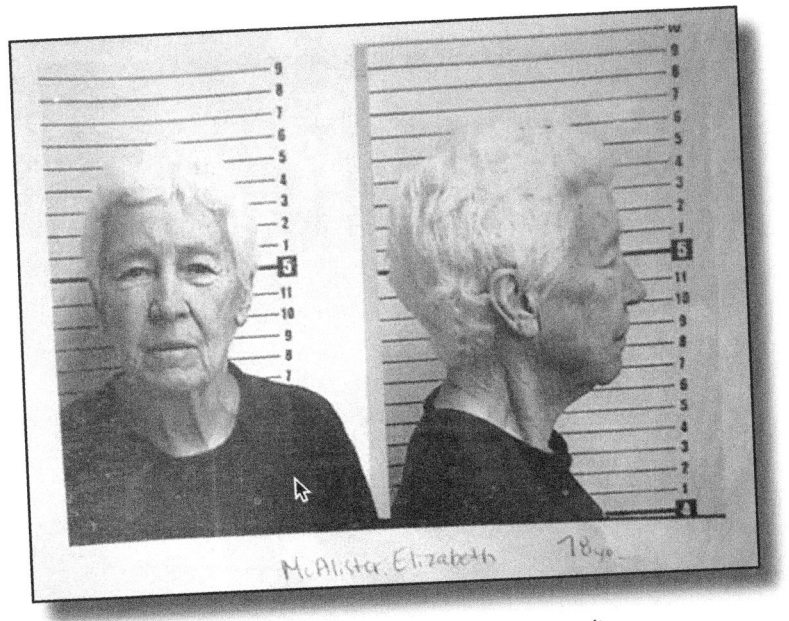

Sister Liz was jailed again for civil disobedience at a nuclear submarine base at age 78.

My daily driver.

Part II: The Scene is Set (1970-74)

CHAPTER 12

Settling In

I was able to lure Bobbi to New Jersey. I wanted her with me and she seemed to like my new community. In my heart I must have known that it was a bad fit for this New York artist who'd grown up on the Upper West Side. She moved in but most of her days were spent in the City. She was still finishing up the second renovation project, another brownstone on the upper west side but she got involved in some other art and political projects too. I was jealous that I might be losing her to New York.

One Sunday we hosted Bobbi's dad, Dr. Helpern, and his lady friend for brunch. Her dad was real nice and seemed to like me but he made me nervous. I suspected he'd have a dim view of his daughter's choice of neighborhood and my rundown house. We cleaned up the house and prepared a brunch spread for the four of us. Dr. Helpern pulled into the driveway and we greeted them on the front porch.

Bobbi said, "Well you found it okay, huh, Dad?"

Doctor Helpern nodded and smiled. "Well, we got a little lost but we just asked directions at a colored fish fry." I looked at Bobbi and she gave me a sheepish grin. The brunch was cordial and pretty brief.

I was settling into my big old house and decided to plant a garden. One morning while the coffee pot rattled, percolating on the Chambers stove, I looked out the dining room window at my dreary backyard. I filled my coffee mug and made my way through the tools and supplies in the gutted-out kitchen and headed down the rickety back stairs. *I'd better fix these soon*, I thought. *Move it up on the list.*

Fully a third of the backyard was patchy gravel, parking for the roomers who until recently inhabited the eight bedrooms. I stopped to survey the solid masonry two-car garage. Shingles on the classic hip roof were pretty new, but those two pairs of heavy wooden doors would need work. The doors were textbook from that period, each with a sturdy outer frame and a cross buck below two rows of four window panes. Heavy hinges and hardware completed the period look. The bottom rails were thoroughly rotted out, but I'd enjoy bringing those hefty doors back to life. It wouldn't be this summer, though. A lot more urgent stuff was on the to-do list. Those shaky back stairs, for one.

The rest of the backyard, scrubby as it was with a mix of grass and weeds, had a private feel, edged with bushes that hadn't seen a clipper in decades. The ubiquitous yellow forsythia, the earliest to flower every spring, were already in bloom. My house backed up to the deep yard of a house just as big on Beech Street, though caddy corner was an aging brick apartment building. Phyllis said the new landlord there was bad news. She'd met with the tenants about their maintenance complaints that were totally ignored.

I stood back, cradled my coffee, and took in the rear facade. To the left was the small porch off the kitchen with its derelict railing and decorative lattice work up top. I shuddered and looked away. It would take some work to rebuild it. Straight ahead a pair of large dining room windows stared back at me. At the far right, slouching and sagging, was a mini greenhouse, a solarium with wood-framed glass walls that looked ready to fall down. Panes were cracked or missing and its short glass-paned roof had begun to separate from the house, letting moisture in.

From the dining room, you entered the solarium through an oak door with a leaded glass window, banked by two oak panels with matching leaded glass. I imagined the small south facing space filled with moist greenery and potted plants. But the floor was badly rotted. My once elegant solarium needed a rebuild, but not this summer. I knew I couldn't save every rotted feature of this carefully built house, but I *was* tempted.

I enjoyed all the details of this house—its crafted details constantly grabbed my attention. The place was a work of art. I couldn't believe it had been so poorly cared for, or that I'd bought it for so little and now owned it—all this carefully made wood work and tile work and carved mantelpieces and parquet flooring, pocket doors, stained glass windows.

That morning I decided to plant a garden. I wanted to stake claim to this place, and a garden might do that. It might connect me deeper to its historic flow. Connect me even to the carpenters who, working only with hand tools, brought this stately house into being and the house next door and the one next to that. Hundreds more in these neighborhoods. I was now caring for, tending, and reviving what they'd created so long ago, back when gas lamps illuminated the newly built rooms and lit the streets at night.

In fact, all of East Orange was once illuminated by gas lamps, and every evening, lamplighters would come and light them. I found this out when I drove onto Woodland Avenue, a spacious street of beautiful well kept homes near the Upsala College campus. A guy from Public Service Electric and Gas was on a ladder fixing one of the gas lamps that lit that street. I stopped and asked him why this seemed to be the only block in the city with gas lamps.

"Well there's Eastwood around the corner; it also has a few. A few years ago with rising crime, the people wanted their streets better lit at night, so we replaced them and installed sodium vapor lamps, the so-called *anti-crime* lights. Listen to this, we sold the gas lamps to a swanky town in Connecticut. Here's the best part of the story though, when all the other streets got those anti-crime lights with the bright yellow glare, well the mayor lived on this street. He wanted"—here the guy added a little french accent—"the *ahm-be-ance of the gas lights.*"

My house faced north, so the rear was full of sun. I itched to start digging that morning, but I had more pressing work to do and planting season was still a few weeks away. I was sure that by late August I'd be eating tomatoes. The image of my grandfather, a carpenter, filled my head. He was a wonderful gardener too. When I was about five he picked a ripe tomato from his garden, took a bite, and handed one to me. I'd never seen anyone bite into a tomato like that, like it was an apple.

He looked down at me and said, "Go ahead." So I took a bite. It was almost sweet. As I wiped some of it from my chin, he said, "All we need is a little salt."

Sitting around the dining room table eating food from a new garden would complete the circle. It was an irresistible *Whole Earth Catalog* fantasy.

I remember it was bright and sunny but still cool in the morning when I started scraping off the layer of grass and weeds before turning over the soil. The dirt was dark and rich, with more than a few worms. Hand digging was painfully slow and I wished for a moment that I'd rented a roto-tiller. I thought instead of the newly arrived immigrants, the ones who'd dug all these basements. Back-breaking work—filling wheelbarrows and running them up onto horse drawn wagons. My garden was only twelve feet by fifteen. It now sounded miniscule.

As I took a drink from the hose, I noticed a dirt-encrusted coin I'd unearthed with my last shovelful. As I rubbed it, the Indian head image emerged. A little water revealed the date: 1908. I knew that was the last year they minted Indian head pennies. I wished I could call Bill Turner, my coin collecting buddy from my youth, but we'd lost touch sometime after college. I put my lucky penny in the pocket of my cut offs and got back to digging. The past was coming half way to meet me. I just had to do a little work. Before I finished, I found another one. 1907.

Marsha Ferber told me what seeds to plant and that I should buy tomato starters, seedlings that were grown in a greenhouse. Henry David Thoreau was on my mind as I planted; I remembered visiting Thoreau's hideaway, Walden Pond near Boston, with Betsy Bauer, who I'd heard joined the Peace Corps in Afghanistan after grad school. I thought fondly of Betsy and smiled remembering when she and I took our thirteen-year-old siblings, her brother and my sister, to a *Monkees* concert at Olympia Stadium in Detroit. *The Monkees* was a mop-headed boy band created by TV producers for what became a popular TV show of the same name. The four actors/musicians recorded a few hit records, all written and produced by a Hollywood songwriting team.

Almost every morning I'd walk the garden, pulling

up a few weeds that seemed to grow faster than even my radishes, the first seedlings to pop through the soil. The summer sun baked the garden each day and I'd water it every evening.

On a camping trip across the Delaware River, I bought a brightly colored hex sign like the ones that adorned the barns of the Pennsylvania Dutch farmers. Hexes were talismans to ward off evil spirits and guarantee a fertile harvest. I mounted it on the front of the garage.

By late August, the zucchinis—that I'd planted too many of and too close together—took over the garden with their long stalks, giant leaves, and their multitudes of green progeny. Meanwhile, the tomatoes, the crop I couldn't wait to eat, were still small and green. There were lots of them, but I wondered if they'd ripen before the first frost.

The garden also produced squash and cucumbers, radishes and lettuce, and while I had plenty of tomatoes, they were still green. Not the darker green they'd been a couple weeks ago but lighter with a slight blush that wanted to turn pink, and then bright red. But the sun was setting earlier. The nights were cooler. I was losing faith that my tomatoes would ripen before the first frost got them.

One day a boy from down the street wandered into the backyard, walking around like a building inspector. Looking down at my plantings he immediately told me I'd planted the squash too close together.

"Do you have a garden, James," I asked.

"No, but my grandma does. She lives with us."

"Are her tomatoes ripe yet?"

"Uh huh, a few are, but she *loves* fried green tomatoes. She's from down South. I love 'em too. She fries them up in a pan and we eat 'em hot. That's what you should do."

He laughed a little, then looked at me accusingly. "You never heard of fried green tomatoes. Did you?"

True, I'd never heard of fried green tomatoes. And James was getting on my nerves.

Summer turned to fall, we ate produce from the garden, and then winter set in.

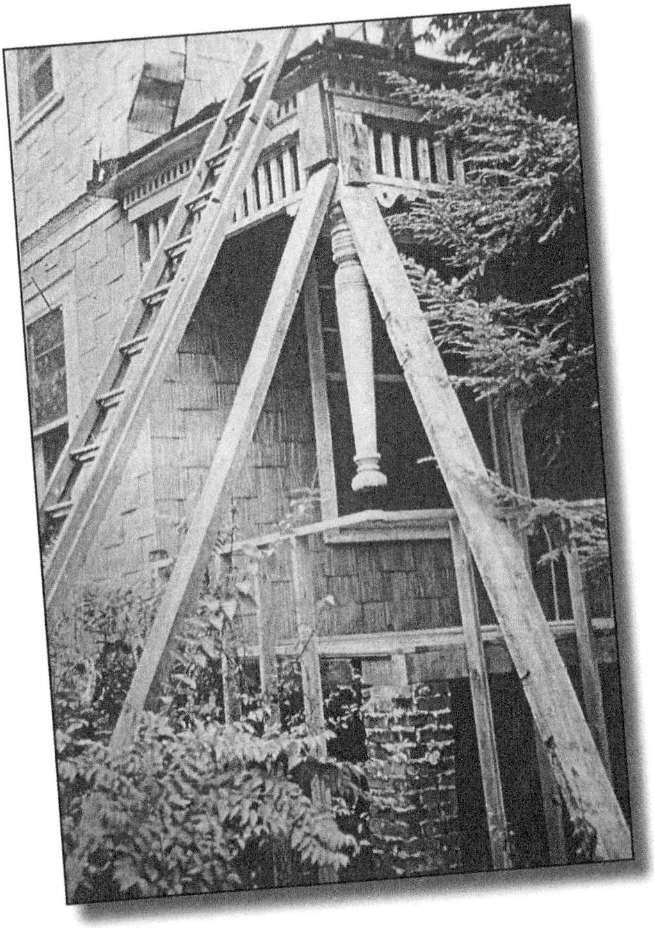

CHAPTER 13

The Battering of East Orange

It was just shy of 7am and the February sun hadn't shown its face yet. Dewey and Magdalene sat with coats on sipping hot coffee in Jackie Cooke's kitchen, her oven pushing out heat through its open door. This was the third day with no heat or hot water. The tenants all looked to Jackie when there was a problem. This time Jackie was stumped. She looked at her two despondent neighbors.

"I called Property Maintenance two days ago and the inspector was here yesterday. Late last night I left a message with the answering service for the Tenants Association hotline. Maybe I'll get a call today."

Jacquelyn Cooke was short and round from a small town in Georgia, with just the slightest touch of a Southern accent, a sweet blend of rural Georgia and something else equally soothing. When she smiled her whole polished, round, ebony face lit up, and she smiled a lot. But when she called EOTA she was damn serious, no sparkle in her dark eyes. There was nothing to smile about—the way their landlord was screwing over the twelve families who paid rent at 66 and 68 Lenox Avenue.

The property was U-shaped with twin three-story buildings attached where the lobby and the stairwells were. The frame and stucco building housed twelve apartments in all. It had never been a fancy place, and by the time Jackie and her neighbors moved in it was well-worn and tired looking. Inside, the tidy apartments weren't large or at all modernized, but when there was heat, they were cozy.

Jackie called the Property Maintenance Department in City Hall regularly. The landlord stopped returning her calls. Last time the heat went off because something was wrong with the boiler. By the time an inspector came a couple of days later, the building was stone cold. No hot water either. The landlord had a story.

"It needs a part that's hard to get. I ordered it right away, what else can I do?" The inspector would threaten but not fine him. Another day or two the heat was back on. Then the front door wouldn't stay locked and it would take a week or more to get that fixed. And on and on.

Then, no heat again. Jackie called City Hall.

"An inspector will be there tomorrow. Will someone be home?"

I lived one block over from Lenox Avenue, mid-block on Chestnut, a quiet street of big homes from the 1890s. We had one apartment house. A quiet one. Mostly older White folks, lots of widows. Chestnut felt like a different neighborhood. On Lenox, one side of the street was all smallish apartment houses. The other side was big old houses like Chestnut. The apartment side backed onto Freeway Drive, at least since 1970 when the east-west interstate was pushed through. Cities are funny that way. Your block can feel like your neighborhood, and a block away? A different neighborhood.

I loved Jackie and greatly admired her. She was so much fun, laughing, telling stories about crazy people from down South, some of them in her own family. She made fun of the city inspectors, teased them about their bad eyesight when she thought they were overlooking code violations. But she was serious and determined. That's what I really admired. Her neighbors all relied on her. They loved Jackie and she'd do anything for a friend or neighbor. But she didn't put up with being played for a fool and taken advantage of. There were lots of shitty landlords in East Orange now. More and more. And there were a bunch of tenants willing to stand up to them. Mostly Black women. Lots of single moms. But there weren't enough like Jackie. Determined, persistent, someone who never gave up. She'd been through a lot with her shitty landlord but things were going downhill. She needed help.

I knew those twelve rent paying tenants would have moved if they could find another place. One they could afford, a place with a decent landlord. Even then they'd need a month and a half security deposit plus the first month's rent, and they knew they couldn't count on getting their security deposits back from the current landlord. None of them had that kind of ready cash sitting around. Besides, they all knew each other and their kids played together. Neighbors who are decent and aren't troublesome? You won't find that everywhere.

That same February morning when Jackie, Magdalene, and Dewey were staying warm by Jackie's oven, Phyllis called the answering service and picked up her Tenants Hotline messages. Before she headed off to teach school, she returned Jackie's message. It sounded urgent.

Jackie told Phyllis that a guy who lived next door checked and they were out of oil. Property Maintenance came to inspect and he wrote a report. Then she called the oil company. The landlord hadn't paid his bills, so they'd canceled his automatic delivery. They were happy to deliver oil. C.O.D. No checks. Phyllis knew what the tenants should do. John schooled her in the basics of New Jersey landlord-tenant law.

Phyllis had to get to school. With her car keys in hand she advised Jackie to pay for the oil, keep the receipt, and deduct it from the rent. Phyllis hurriedly explained that this perfectly legal remedy was called Repair and Deduct. She wished Jackie luck and promised to call her back that evening.

It was just six years earlier that the Repair and Deduct remedy was upheld by the state Supreme Court. When Marie Ireland's landlord refused to fix a toilet that constantly leaked onto her bathroom floor, she had a plumber replace it and sent the receipt to her landlord with the balance of her rent. The landlord moved to evict her and her Camden County Legal Services lawyer took the case all the way up to the Supreme Court. It became a valuable tool for tenants with landlords like Jackie's.

Phyllis advised lots of tenants on how to use Repair and Deduct, how to strictly comply with the law and avoid the risk of eviction for nonpayment. All of Phyllis's organizing work was in response to tenants who weren't getting basic services—heat, hot water—or getting essential repairs made. East Orange was now experiencing what Newark, especially its all-Black Central Ward, had been going through. The slumming of East Orange was once thought of as unthinkable. Now Phyllis and her Hotline were doing double duty.

With no idea how much oil they'd need or for how long, Jackie and a couple of the tenants scraped together some cash. The delivery guy showed them how to fire up the boiler. In the cold basement, their mood brightened as they heard the boiler pump steam to the radiators upstairs.

They hugged and high-fived and one of the women gave the shocked delivery guy a kiss on the cheek. Maybe for the first time, these poor tenants, mostly women, began taking matters into their own hands.

When it came time to pay rent, they deducted for the oil and sent the paid receipt to the landlord. He accepted the partial payments, and thus began their half-assed relationship with their negligent landlord. When something needed repair, Jackie called the landlord. No action. Jackie called Property Maintenance. An inspector came. Notice was sent to the landlord. No action. Maybe a municipal court date was set. Meanwhile, Jackie called a repairman. Jackie and a neighbor or two paid for the repairs and deducted from their rent. I knew what a tiring and time-consuming process this was and that they really had no other options.

Phyllis continued to guide Jackie, promptly returning her calls from the pay phone at school. Together, they were taking the first steps of what would become a years-long struggle to simply hold on to a decent place to live.

But Jackie was getting worn down by the constant hassle with the landlord, the tenants coming to her every week. Repair and Deduct had its limits. It turned Jackie into a part-time property manager and she was burnt out.

Jackie's dilemma was repeated in more and more buildings. More tenant leaders were in Jackie's situation. Code enforcement and the courts, even when they were responsive, had no answer. Finally, Phyllis connected Jackie with one of John's Housing Unit attorneys, Sam Farrington, who agreed to take the tenants' case. Maybe Sam could figure out something.

The Limits of Code Enforcement

EOTA was finding that regulating rents and preventing

rent gouging was a walk in the park compared to trying to guarantee that landlords maintain their buildings. The city was once an upper middle-class mecca so there were lots of large apartments with quality maintenance, and in many buildings there were doormen. In the seventies landlords began splitting the large apartments into two and generally cutting back on routine maintenance. The doormen were long gone.

Some of the new owners were slumlords who milked the old buildings. Collecting rents and making few if any repairs.

Enforcement of Property Maintenance Codes was a game of cat and mouse. The inspector has to verify the complaint, send a Notice of Violation, and reinspect before any action is taken against the landlord. At EOTA we thought most of the inspectors were lazy, on the take, or racist. Enforcement of codes was spotty at best.

EOTA was overwhelmed with tenant complaints. With no control over landlord behavior, our next move was to propose a Landlord Security Deposit—a fund, managed by the city to make emergency repairs when the landlord refused. It was becoming clear that without an alternative to private landlording, poor tenants were stuck with a system that flatly didn't work.

Our group had no experience with rental properties. We knew the law and how to help tenants get what they were entitled to, but we had no real understanding of the details of managing property. I was the lone exception with my four or five rent payers.

With more and more East Orange landlords cutting back on maintenance and some new owners clearly "milking" their buildings, a vicious downward cycle was eating away at the city's stability. In the final stage of "milking," a landlord would stop paying taxes and continue on until the city foreclosed, a process that usually gave the landlord an additional two years to pocket rents with little or no investment in maintenance or repairs. A similar erosion was playing out in East Orange's commercial district.

Saving Main Street

I needed a local place to bank so I headed downtown. Main Street was just a few blocks away on the other side of the freeway. Gibraltar Savings had the modest look of a small town institution, so I went in to open a savings and checking account. I was pretty sure the bank was in the footprint of the Brick Church Urban Renewal Area, but looking up Main Street there was no evidence of that.

I asked the teller what the story was, how long they had before the city moved them out and tore the building down. He smiled and raised his eyebrows.

"You and I don't need to worry about that for quite a while. They did that urban renewal plan about six years ago. Nothing's happened yet. The shop owners talk about it all the time. I've stopped paying attention. We're going to be here. Don't worry."

It had been six years since the Feds awarded almost six million to the East Orange Housing Authority. The plan was to assemble a large site through eminent domain, then demolish the buildings and remake this key portion of Main Street, adjacent to the Brick Church commuter rail station. Brick Church got its name from the imposing red brick Presbyterian church that had anchored the corner of Main and Prospect since the 1800s.

I walked up and down both sides of Main, wondering what the makeover would look like. The area seemed busy enough for a weekday and definitely didn't look "blighted." There were a handful of vacant stores, like a lot of older downtowns that'd been upstaged by suburban malls. I knew that East Orange once bustled with classy brands. Best and Company, an up-market Manhattan based clothier for women and children closed four years earlier. B. Altman, another top Manhattan brand, abandoned Central Avenue back in 1957. My walk was instructive. A sprawling corner department store sported the sign "Muirs," but inside it housed a collection of independent vendors. It was a flea market. Most nearby stores sold lower cost goods, a reflection of East Orange's changing population. The Main Street redevelopment was East Orange's bid to recapture its former glory, reluctant to accept its role as houser of Newark's displaced poor.

Thinking back on what the bank teller told me, I wondered who owned the buildings that housed all these shops and businesses. Maybe the Housing Authority made more progress than it appeared. Maybe they were the landlord, waiting to complete the acquisitions before beginning the demolition. I was curious about the Redevelopment Plan and whether there was a developer already designated. I vowed to look into all that. I was pretty familiar with the workings of urban renewal. I was still employed at the Englewood Redevelopment Agency, now in its fifth year of a successful federally funded Urban Renewal grant.

Kicking It Up a Notch

Meanwhile, Phyllis and EOTA were calling for a referendum to strengthen the rent control ordinance, and launched a petition drive to put a 4% annual increase on the ballot. Bertha Collier from 148 Halsted, who was leading tenants now in their second month of what would be a protracted rent strike, agreed to chair the petition drive, and soon five hundred signatures were delivered to City Hall, calling for limiting the annual increase to 4% and no decontrol upon vacancy.

Phyllis and the Tenant Hotline were swamped, so in February, 1974, we inaugurated monthly workshops at Munn Avenue Presbyterian Church. Frank Hutchins, our comrade from Newark Tenants Organization, was the guest speaker at our opening session. All of us volunteered to staff the workshops. We were mobbed with tenants who needed help. Along with two attorneys from the Housing Unit, we all dispensed legal advice.

We were a growing team. Ronnie was the coach and John was the quarterback. They taught us and led us, always emphasizing *collective action*. Their approach was basic: Teach self-help. There's power in numbers. Promote solidarity. Build strong organizations. Everything we did flowed from those concepts, and that's what we taught at the workshops.

We'd teach people about the law, how to negotiate with their landlord, and how to deal with city inspectors and public officials. The Housing Unit taught people how to represent themselves in court. Our message to tenants was simple: *Collective Action.* One person could maybe get their landlord to make a repair. A group of tenants working together could get everyone's apartments repaired. A citywide group working together could win stronger laws and enforcement of city codes. And a statewide group of tenant associations can change state law and win protections for all tenants.

In Orange I was now the voice of homeowners. My message was that stable tenancy and maintaining apartment buildings was in the interest not only of tenants but all of us homeowners, and we all needed to support the aims of the Orange Tenants Association. In the spring of 1974, the OTA endorsed five candidates for the Orange City Commission: Joel Shain, Tom Kelly, Ben Jones, Frank Panucci, and Melvin Randall. John's press release announcing the endorsement again quoted Pat Morrissy, volunteer accountant for the OTA, who had just bought a home, urging homeowners to vote for the slate because "tenants and homeowners clearly have identical interests because tenants want their taxes kept down because when taxes go up, rents go up" and "we all want safe streets, clean neighborhoods, and responsive elected officials."

PART III

Keep On Keepin' On

1975–76

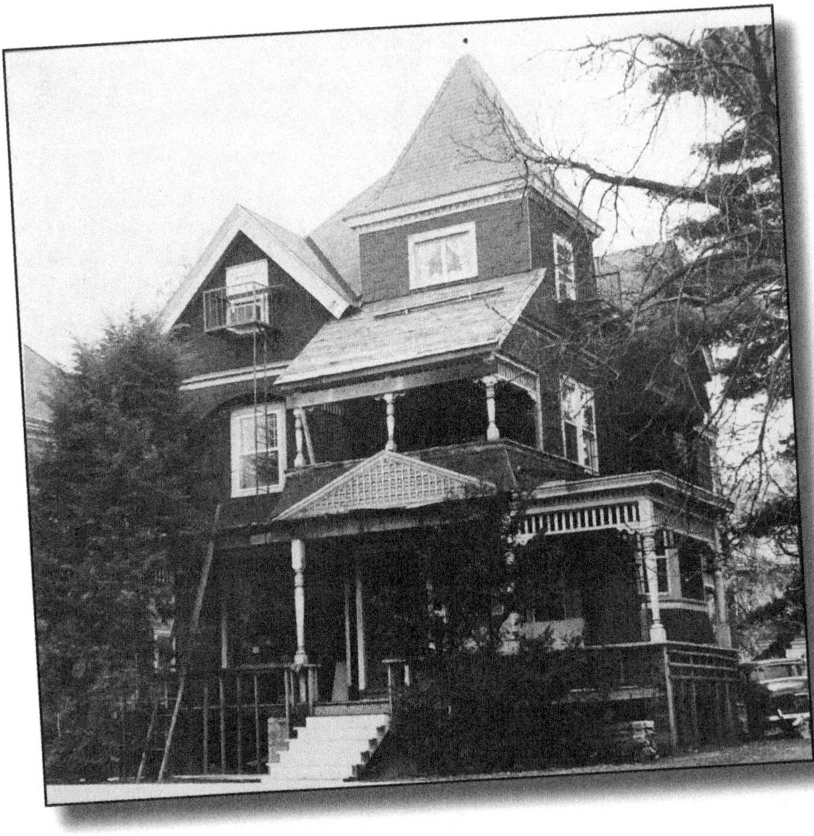

By the mid seventies, activists—young and old, women and Blacks—had achieved so much. They'd brought an end to an unjust war, won important civil rights gains, and changed a lot of consciousness about race and gender and the environment. But the shape of activism was evolving.

The rise of Black consciousness had begun to self-segregate the Civil Rights Movement. The Student Nonviolent Coordinating Committee (SNCC) expelled Whites. The women's movement was by definition all women, but it tended to be mostly educated White women. Environmentalists, who were also mostly White and educated, built organizations focused on pollution and the resulting health hazards. The liberal left was growing but it was being siloed by issue groups. They all shared a belief that their view of a better society was ascendant and within their grasp. Meanwhile, a lot of White working and middle-class people weren't a part of that coalition.

There were two Americas, and trust in government by both sides was at an all time low. According to a 1976 Gallup poll, only 33% of Americans said they trusted the government to do what is right "most of the time."

In city neighborhoods, resident groups were organizing to combat disinvestment. This grassroots upswell sparked the creation of a federal Urban Reinvestment Task Force. By 1976, the Task Force was supporting local organizations called Neighborhood Housing Services in forty-five cities.

Consumer rights crusader Ralph Nader recruited law

students and launched Public Citizen. With careful research, lawsuits, and press exposure, his group fought for auto safety, workplace safety, and more. He exposed the dangers of nuclear power and he publicly and constantly challenged the growth of Big Business.

It was 1954 when the Supreme Court ruled that racial segregation in public schools were separate and unequal, but it wasn't until the seventies that anything was done about it, and the answer was to bus Black children to schools in White neighborhoods and vice versa. White, working-class Americans often saw busing as an incursion, while African American communities viewed it as a necessary step toward equal education. The result was mostly the acceleration of White flight from the cities.

The ideological and cultural split in American society was evident in the Democratic Party, which spawned The New Democratic Coalition, a new faction of middle-class liberals that was fast becoming an influential bloc around civil rights, gender equality, environmentalism, consumer protection, and government reform. A competing vision of the Party was advanced by Michael Harrington, a vision of economic justice, labor rights, and opposition to corporate power. Like the good Socialist that he was, he recognized that you couldn't expand economic justice without the working class.

Federal backtracking on social programs and aid to cities gave way to progressive change at the local level. Lee Webb, a former SDS leader, formed the *Conference on Alternative State and Local Policies* to bring together progressive, mostly young elected officials, spreading the message of how meaningful change could happen locally.

The nation's bicentennial celebrated in the months leading up to July 4, 1976 gave the country a breather in the

Part III: Keep On Keepin' On (1975-76)

wake of the Vietnam War and Watergate. Fashion for men was relaxing as the coat and tie was replaced by leisure suits.

Political change was coming to the Republican Party too. Gerald Ford had only been in office less than two years when he faced a Primary Election challenge from his right by Ronald Reagan, the governor of California. Richard Viguerie, the father of conservative direct mail, propelled Reagan's campaign. Reagan reached out to George Wallace Democrats with a message of grievance and resentment and the slogan *Make America #1 Again*. He won primaries in Texas, North Carolina, and a few other states and almost stole the nomination from Ford.

Meanwhile, Carter avoided a divisive convention floor fight when George Wallace threw his 146 delegates behind his fellow Southern governor. Voters had lost trust in government and wanted an outsider, not an establishment figure like Ford, so that November, they narrowly elected Jimmy Carter.

SHELTERFORCE

APRIL 1975 Vol. 1 No. 1

SHELTERFORCE COLLECTIVE & THE NATIONAL LAWYERS GUILD

Gov't Intervention and the Growth of the Real Estate Industry

profits

HOUSING ACTS
1937   1949   1968   1974

Racism, Planning and "The Tipping Point" ...p. 2

Taking on the FHA ...p. 4

The Housing Act of 1974 A Challenge for Organizers ...p. 6

Book Reviews

Legal Developments

Resource Guides

CHAPTER 14

Connecting Nationally

John Atlas was active in the National Lawyers Guild, the left-wing alternative to the Bar Association. To give an idea of how unlike the Bar Association they were, the radical lawyers held their 1973 national convention at Armadillo National Headquarters in Austin, Texas, a venue normally pulsing with live music and awash in draft beer. John and Ronnie headed to Austin in hopes of getting the Guild to align with the work that they, and now Joan, were doing. They wanted the Guild to recognize and support the lawyers who represented the rights of tenants and the movement for better housing for the poor.

The Guild had a rich history stretching back to the 1930s, when Guild lawyers had helped organize the United Auto Workers and the Congress of Industrial Organizations, and during the McCarthy era, when Guild members represented the Hollywood Ten, the Rosenbergs, and thousands of victims of anti-communist hysteria. In the 1960s, the Guild set up offices in the South and organized thousands of volunteer lawyers and law students to support the civil rights movement long before the federal government or lawyers groups were involved. The organization had been dominated by older radicals, some of them Communists or ex-Communists, but by the seventies, the Guild had become synonymous with the New Left and expanded its membership to include legal workers, jailhouse lawyers, and law students.

John was critical of the Guild because so many of them were dogmatic, ideological, and internationalist. One reason John enjoyed Guild gatherings was his love of political debate and ideological battle with other leftists. His special target were those out-of-touch romantics who were enamored with Third World liberation movements but ignored the struggles of the working poor here at home.

John and Ronnie convinced the Guild to form a housing committee, and after the convention he told Phyllis and me that he wanted to launch a newsletter to reach lawyers, paralegals, and organizers doing tenant work around the country. Our response was basically, "That sounds cool. Good luck."

John said, "No, we should *all* do this. Look, I know it's more work but I think the New York Guild might put up some money. I'm going to ask them for ten thousand dollars."

We liked the sound of that.

A National Publication is Born

Some months later, John approached the Lawyers Guild in New York and he pitched a proposal for a publication to inform housing lawyers, legal workers, and organizers. Never afraid of being too bold, he asked for ten grand in seed money. Apparently there was general agreement about the concept, but, as with everything within the Guild, there was a lengthy debate, probably around editorial content. The committee voted to provide five hundred bucks.

John called a meeting and we met in the dining room at Chestnut Street, which always doubled as our conference room. It was paneled in dark oak with a Victorian fireplace surrounded by a carved mantel in one corner, facing across to the stained glass entry to the solarium. A long, wooden dining table—that I'd made from a discarded base from one table, and a hefty but scratched-up top from another—was in the center. A little sanding and some tung oil gave it the look of a well worn antique. That table hosted a lot of meetings. We gathered around it on mismatched rummage sale chairs as we weighed John's latest *big idea*—launching a national housing publication.

Ronnie and I took a break from some demolition work and I brought out a pitcher of iced tea. Phyllis was the first to arrive.

"So what's this *latest* thing that John wants us all to do?"

Ronnie and I laughed. Phyllis was always skeptical about John's latest proposition but she would always sign on. John and Joan entered together, and John grabbed a couple of folders from his well worn briefcase. Marty arrived, dressed like he was probably teaching a class later that evening. Woody Widrow who lived down the block, was the last to arrive, wisecracking in a voice so loud you suspected he was deaf.

"So I hear John wants to compete with Better Homes and Gardens."

"I could write a home repair column," I added.

Ronnie looked around the room and into the living room beyond. "You should call your column *This Old House*."

John raised his arms palms up and looked at the ceiling in a sigh of exasperation as if to say, "When you guys are done wise cracking . . ." John proceeded to pitch his idea for a newsletter with useful information for tenant lawyers, paralegals, and tenant organizers. Methodical, as always.

"Look, there are other people around the country, fighting like we are for better housing and equal rights for tenants. We have an opportunity with a little seed funding from the Guild to create a publication that can begin to share ideas among that broad community of lawyers, organizers, and tenant groups. No such forum exists. The tenant movement is growing. Everywhere. A vehicle for sharing ideas is essential. This could grow into something big."

The more we talked, the more the idea of a "publication" grew. Marty wanted to analyze big legal decisions like the New Jersey Supreme Court's decision requiring municipalities to allow affordable housing and he wanted to review books on housing policy. Woody had drafted Newark's rent control ordinance and he wanted to be sure we wrote about rent control and that we should always include tenant organizing tips. John and Joan wanted to spread their gospel and influence lawyers to devote more resources to supporting grassroots organizations. Phyllis showed little interest in discussing content but she was supportive. Ronnie was a good writer and agreed to do editing. I saw the publication as a way to bring people together who were toiling on the margins in places like Minneapolis, Cleveland, and Chicago. We could create a sense of belonging, a way to feel a part of something bigger and linked to others like them.

In addition, I thought, as John probably did, that the publication would establish us as leaders in what we hoped would be a growing movement. We were focused on tenants' rights and organizing but I hoped we'd eventually branch out into other housing work, like saving neighborhoods. That turned me on as much as tenant organizing, but I was the only one in the group who was doing community development work. Maybe I'd try to write something for the first issue. By the time the meeting adjourned, we were in agreement. We wrote an initial to-do list and scheduled another meeting in a week. Woody and I agreed to shop around for printers and come back with a proposal. My 1974 pocket calendar shows lots of entries for "newsletter" meetings.

Collective Responsibility

We began meeting every week. There was so much to do. What would be in our first issue? We needed to decide and then generate the content. We didn't know much about design, layout, and the printing process. We needed to gather mailing lists. Someone needed to get a postal permit and figure out how to qualify for nonprofit bulk-rate postage.

We were excited about making contacts around the country. We agreed to share the work pretty much equally. Woody had newspaper experience as editor of the *Hilltop Press*, the college newspaper at SUNY Cortland. John loved to write, Ronnie was a good writer and editor, Marty with his academic bent was interested in deeper analytic pieces, and I was the jack-of-all-trades. I had experience with government housing programs, I was a fair writer, and had a good eye for layout and design. I figured Woody and I could master the mechanics of publishing and getting the thing printed.

Woody brought in Tom Connell, another VISTA at the Newark Tenants Organization. John invited Stan Varon, a tenant lawyer at Legal Services of New Jersey in New Brunswick. Ronnie recruited Kathy Aria from Joel Shain's office. She had some editorial skills. John's wife, Deena, did a bunch of our typing at her job at Rutgers Law School.

Our objective was to connect tenant activists, organizers, and lawyers from everywhere that grassroots activism on tenant and housing issues was happening. Except for John and Ronnie through the Guild, we weren't that well connected to the tenant organizing world. But we soon contacted the Met Council, the New York City tenants organization and the New York State Tenants and Neighborhood Coalition. A New York group that wanted their message in print was Homefront. They were a collection of radical organizers, academics, architects, and planners. That's how I met Tony Schuman, an architect teaching at NJIT in Newark, where he supported housing and community development groups in Newark.

Our goal was not modest. We wanted to help build that movement. The publication would circulate nationally and we declared that we'd be a clearinghouse for the exchange of information about organizing strategies, legislation, and local victories. The publication would inform and help build strong local organizations and connect them to a nationwide movement.

We discussed organizational details, who would do what, how we would operate. Recognizing we were all volunteers and it would be a good while before we could support a staff we easily imagined a committee of equals; we'd share the work and make decisions by consensus. I imagined all of us sharing what we knew and what we were learning, helping each other develop skills, all participating. The idea of calling ourselves a "collective" came easily. It was the opposite of a hierarchy. We were proud of that.

I suggested the name *Shelterforce*. There'd be little doubt about what we believed in. That shelter was a basic human right and we weren't going to achieve it without a political force. It fit our heady vision that this nascent tenant movement would be the vanguard of a powerful movement for housing justice. The group loved the name and we adopted it immediately.

Woody and I rode out to a grubby section of Route 22 to check out Harrop Press, a printer that all the low-budget publications used. Not only were they affordable, but Harrop offered a "union bug," indicating your publication was printed in a union shop. That was important to us. The drab, generic concrete industrial building was a hive of frenetic activity. The cluttered "office" with a few disheveled desks looked in one direction toward the bare lobby with a few cheap formica chairs and a handful of random newsprint publications on a cast-off coffee table. In another direction, the office looked onto the factory floor and its whirling presses. The place was buzzing.

A lady in the office pointed us toward the presses and said we needed to talk to the manager who ran the place. We found him freeing up a jammed press, and we waited next to the pressman who operated it. The manager signaled to start up the press. We stood back and marveled as newsprint began to move between steel plates. In a few seconds, a monster roll of newsprint on one end became folded tabloids spit out at the other end. I wanted to watch the press for another hour and understand all its details. The guy we were waiting to meet with picked one up, quickly examined it, and handed it to Woody. Over the din of the methodic clapping of several whirling presses, he pointed us with his big crescent wrench toward a door near the office that was marked *Layout*. I caught the eye of the pressman and gave him a thumbs up. He nodded.

As we entered the layout room, the no-nonsense manager grumbled as he picked up discarded paper and layout boards and stuffed them into a big trash bin. He cleared off a littered table and directed us to a couple of stools. Then he gave us our first, very brief, lesson in newspaper layout. I was hooked on the whole process—the layout boards and the camera room where each board was filmed and then transferred somehow to a thin aluminum plate, which got attached to the big metal plates of the press that each held four pages. I wanted to know even more about the process, but the guy was only going to spend so much time. Woody asked about the price for a thousand copies of a twelve-page tabloid.

"You might as well order three thousand," he advised us. "It's only thirty percent more. A lot of our cost is in the set up."

"Okay," Woody said. "Give us estimates for both."

We walked out with tabloid samples and twenty-some boards, figuring that we'd screw a few up. I don't recall the price quote but I thought it was remarkably cheap. On the ride back we settled on a folded tabloid so that the cover page was nine by twelve, the shape of a magazine. We'd need a logo, and I figured we should have some cover art if we didn't want it to look boring like the *New York Times* or worse, *The Nation*. I made a mental note to reach out to Joanne Young. Woody and I were now in the publishing business. There was a lot to figure out. The basics of paste-up and layout being just one.

One Saturday morning I went to see Joanne. She was a good friend and a frustrated painter. She spent her days typing away at the Law Commune. I'd never seen her paintings but I'd often see her idly sketching. The unfulfilled artist lived with a group in a big old house facing

Orange Park. She felt stuck in her dead-end secretary job and couldn't support herself as a painter but was dying to join the New York City art scene. Figuring out how to make that move, or more likely getting the courage to take the leap, wouldn't happen for a couple more years. I asked her if she'd consider designing our first cover.

We smoked cigarettes and drank coffee at her well worn kitchen table, and I told her what the *Shelterforce* Collective stood for and explained in too much detail what my centerfold article was about.

She interrupted me, "So, government programs are supposed to help the people but what they do even better is make the landlords and real estate tycoons richer. Is that it?"

"Well, yeah," I said, thinking, *It's a bit more complicated, but for now that's good enough.*

"Okay," she said, "I've got an idea. When do you need it?"

I wondered if Joanne was the type who took deadlines seriously, so a week later I called her.

"It's going great," she said. "Don't worry. I'll have it by Saturday and I think you'll like it."

I was worried. I felt the whole chaotic process of a bunch of amateur volunteers producing a readable, reasonably attractive publication was falling on me.

We arrived early Saturday at the Law Commune. Deena, Joanne, and Ginny Saunders, another Law Commune secretary, typed hand-written articles into three-inch columns on IBM Selectrics while Woody and I cut and pasted the columns onto the boards with rubber cement at the big third-floor kitchen table, trying to leave the proper space for headlines and graphics.

We put down the headlines with Prestype, a dry transfer

method where the letters on a sheet were transferred by rubbing them with a stylus. It was tricky to get the spacing of letters correct and you'd better be sure you don't want to edit the headline later. The paper didn't have a look or a style. Our headlines were a sampling of Prestype fonts.

Joanne was typing away when I asked her about the cover art.

"Don't bother me while I'm doing your typing." Without looking up from her typewriter, she slid me a manila folder. "Now go away and let me type. I don't want to be here til midnight."

I took the folder into a vacant office. Inside was a carefully rendered pen-and-ink drawing. It took a minute for the entire message to register. It was a graph of rising housing industry profits represented by a row of porky, well dressed tycoons whose pockets overflowed with cash as they got bigger over time while people below were being crushed by the fat cats. The title of the graph read: *Govt. Intervention and the Growth of the Real Estate Industry.*

I got goosebumps. It was attractive and packed a rhetorical punch. I loved it. I rushed back to Joanne. She just kept typing. Her lips were closed in a repressed smile.

"Don't bother me. You can buy me dinner tonight."

Hot off the Press

It was April 1975 and Woody was in the passenger seat when I wheeled my old Dodge truck into the lot at Harrop Press. We were picking up bundles of Volume 1, Number 1.

We ripped open a bundle and sat in the front seat thumbing through the twelve pages, admiring our work, mostly hoping not to find too many typos. Woody immediately noticed that part of one headline was missing. Fortunately, it could still be deciphered.

"Shit," I said. "We forgot the union bug. There's no union bug on our first publication!"

The thought that our message to the movement might look like it had been published at a low wage non-union shop nagged us.

But overall Woody and I were pretty happy. In our hearts we knew it looked amateurish, but we'd done it! The first issue was ready to hit the streets. That is, once we labeled each one and dropped them at the Post Office for uncertain delivery as third class bulk mail. Fortunately, none of the content was breaking news. We brought the bundles back to the parlor at 31 Chestnut, where Phyllis helped us stick on labels and sort them by zip code for the cheapest mailing rate.

The National Lawyers Guild nonprofit account got us an even lower rate so the first issue was published by the National Lawyers Guild and the *Shelterforce* Collective.

We soon found out there was a real *movement* out there. Like us in New Jersey, there were tenant organizers and poverty lawyers connected with tenants facing rent increases and maintenance and repair issues who were fighting back. Against the backdrop of protest and organizing, learned from the civil rights and anti-war campaigns, people came together. At another time they might have just complained to each other. Instead they were spurred on to action and we tapped into that.

We filled the quarterly publication with helpful strategies, model laws and ordinances, stories of successful housing struggles, and more. We were becoming a clearinghouse of useful information as well as local news and developments from around the country.

In most big cities there was at least a nascent tenant movement, and we connected with most of them in the early years. The Collective worked out of the front parlor at 31 Chestnut and provided the volunteer labor for everything—writing, editing, typing, layout, and pasting on mailing labels. The house hosted plenty of fundraising parties to cover printing and postage costs.

We began as a quarterly with an annual subscription price of three dollars, but we sent it out free for at least a year to every activist and tenant group whose address we could find.

Our first three quarterly issues were packed with content. Besides resources for tenant organizers, we took on big stories like urban renewal displacement, the sweeping federal Housing and Community Development Act, exclusionary zoning and bank redlining. Marty Bierbaum wrote book reviews. We reported on some high profile landlord tenant battles like the tenants in Federal Housing Administration financed buildings in the Boston area who all banded together to fight excessive rent increases, and a similar fight in Madison, Wisconsin. We reported on a group of squatters in New York City in buildings owned by the Cathedral of Saint John the Divine. Our early news coverage mostly reflected our contacts that were concentrated in New York and Boston.

The collective was committed to equal opportunity. Mary Tasker was still a part-time college student, but she wanted to try her hand at research and writing. Joan Pransky and Lauri Lowell, a Rutgers law student, partnered with her on a comprehensive article in our third issue titled *Battling the Banks*, which covered the fight being waged by community groups against redlining.

The Big Con Game

Marty Bierbaum dropped off a book that he knew would

hold special meaning for me, *Cities Destroyed for Cash*. He left a note that he planned to review it in *Shelterforce*. In this book with the flaming title, the Detroit journalist Brian D. Boyer laid bare the sordid schemes that brought down entire Detroit neighborhoods. The book was a street-level roadmap of the sleazy actors and corrupt transactions that undermined and eventually sank once healthy, working-class neighborhoods.

My blood pressure red lined as I turned the pages of *Cities Destroyed for Cash*. I recognized street after street on Detroit's near east side— Iroquois, East Forest, Ludden, Preston, McClellan, Chene, East Canfield. I knew those blocks. Now I pictured the abandoned houses, burned and vandalized. Houses tight alongside neighbors who were trying desperately to hold onto their humble homes and their once family-friendly neighborhoods. Scubi and I knew kids who lived on those streets from our youth program at Church of the Messiah in '68.

It was a familiar scenario. Whole neighborhoods started their downward slide toward oblivion when banks drew red lines on maps and mortgage money dried up.

In cases that the author documented, the decline picked up speed when well intentioned public policy, easy federal money, bureaucratic apathy, and blatant corruption intersected with private sector greed. It was a horror story repeated in city after city, but Detroit was the poster child, with more federal housing investment and more destruction. Strangely, at the heart of this tragedy was a bold public policy aimed at fighting poverty and giving people a hand up. I believed in the War on Poverty. I had even enlisted. I cringed when I thought about those poor folks just looking to better their lives while the rug was being pulled out from under them. On a good day, the odds were stacked against them. Now the programs meant to help were actually sucking the life out of their neighborhoods.

The main elements of the scandal unfolded like this: The federal government subsidized the interest and guaranteed repayment on loans to low-income homebuyers. FHA appraisers were bribed to approve high appraised values on substandard houses. The developers who bribed the appraisers did shoddy repairs to the old homes and helped gullible homebuyers to qualify for mortgages they couldn't afford to repay. Mortgage brokers placed these shaky mortgages with mortgage companies who didn't really care if the mortgages were repaid because they were fully guaranteed by the federal government. Soon after homebuyers moved in, their houses required expensive repairs, so the homeowners stopped paying their mortgages. Houses were soon abandoned, then vandalized. Whole neighborhoods were ruined.

Detroit was my beloved hometown. I knew the joys of growing up in one of those tight-knit striving middle-class neighborhoods that the Motor City was famous for. I knew that pretty much the same fate awaited the tidy neighborhood of my youth, just a few miles away on the other side of the city.

Boyer's book was a page-turner, like a bad car accident, so horrible you can't look away. Boyer introduced readers to the low-life perpetrators in a drama he called "a deliberate program of urban ruin for profit." The central plot overflowed with a cast of fast-buck artists; property speculators; corrupt FHA appraisers; short-term, high-interest, hard-money street lenders; and run-of-the-mill real estate hustlers. Of course this scheme had no chance of success without a mass of gullible but hopeful and trusting poor families desperate to own a piece of the American

Dream—that is, families who previously had little hope of ever buying a home and had no real choice about neighborhoods.

Boyer, the author, contended that the program was designed by and for private sector lenders. It would be hard to argue against that. Mortgage companies provided the mortgages, with HUD paying 6 of the 7% interest, and the low-income buyers paying just 1%. FHA insured the loans, so if buyers defaulted the lenders were made whole.

I chewed on the bitter taste of federal guarantees to mitigate risk in mortgage-starved neighborhoods red lined by traditional banks. Banks were government chartered. I thought, *Why were they free to stop lending in places where they still accepted people's deposits? Why wasn't the government requiring banks to lend there instead of using taxpayer money to eliminate their risk? The system was rigged.*

As if the bottom line wasn't sweet enough, the mortgage companies tacked on a fee called points at the loan closing. The typical fee on these already federally guaranteed and subsidized loans was equal to 16% of the mortgage amount. Being 100% insured against default, mortgage companies had no incentive to carefully underwrite the buyers. With the points charged at closing, the mortgage company made a higher rate of return the sooner that a buyer defaulted and the FHA paid up. With loans to unqualified buyers, based on overinflated values on homes with major defects; default and foreclosure were inevitable and usually quick.

According to Boyer, Detroit was the most "FHA devastated" city in America. He predicted the Detroit FHA inventory would reach twenty-five thousand houses at the end of the day, and that the cost to the Feds would be between 350 to 500 million. He was careful to point out that all this cash went not to poor people, but to "real estate speculators, con men, criminals, and mortgage companies."

The book confirmed in chapter and verse what I knew instinctively: that the government housing programs unfolding in cities across America, programs that seemed so promising, actually fattened the real estate industry while spending a lot of taxpayer money and delivering little. In this case it wasn't just meager results, but that whole neighborhoods lay in ruins. Like Detroit and so many other cities, East Orange was being battered by the harsh winds of White flight, bank redlining, and the exodus of private sector investment. Fortunately, it had not been the target of the federally subsidized scams that hit Detroit's inner city. If it had, East Orange's battle for survival would've already been lost.

This revolting tale about my hometown was another piece of kindling that fueled the passion I brought to our organizing work and to *Shelterforce,* our national soapbox for housing and urban poverty issues.

But by now I'd lost faith. What sounded promising back then, I now knew were Band-Aids at best, not a serious commitment to equality. It convinced me that so many government agencies were captives of the capitalist system, and *Cities Destroyed for Cash* documented that.

Boyer's Detroit stories about those sleazy predators stoked my anger and it fed my disgust at the government participation. The human misery came through to me as the author recounted how poor homebuyers were hoodwinked, ending up in homes that quickly needed costly repairs they couldn't afford and could no longer stay in. I knew those neighborhoods. They weren't abstract places. From six hundred miles away, I felt I knew those buyers too. Like the Black families I worked with in Englewood and those now in East Orange. Strivers looking to make a better life for their families. Grateful they got this first chance at homeownership.

I also knew first hand the promise of the federal housing programs when overseen by honest people who cared about the noble work they were doing. At Englewood Redevelopment Agency where I worked, the director secured funding for a 100-unit new townhome development from the FHA Section 235 Low-Income Homeownership program, the same program that undermined Detroit's inner city. In Englewood, the program was run by a local agency with committed staff and leadership, and a hundred poor families would get to raise their kids in well built and very affordable homes.

Marty's review was set to appear in the third issue of *Shelterforce* in November 1975. He told the whole pathetic story in depth and added some interesting context, like how the FHA underwrote the suburban migration while at the same time refusing to insure loans in the cities. I couldn't fault anything he wrote, but he brought an academic style and tone that didn't match the blistering critique that peppered Boyer's reporting. His retelling certainly didn't convey any of the outrage that I felt when I read the book.

The story of Cities Destroyed for Cash is a national scandal, I thought. *The people who caused it should go to jail.* That's what I wanted to communicate, so I asked Kat Brennan, an artist friend, to draw a sizzling graphic for the front cover. I knew Kat's blood ran even hotter than mine. She wouldn't hold back. We hung out late one evening with some Kahlua and vodka and over Black Russians I told her the Detroit story.

"Those rotten fuckers," she said, as we started to brainstorm ideas for the cover. "Let's do an old-style political cartoon. We can show Uncle Sam giving out government handouts and a fat cat in a top hat to represent the real estate swindlers. I'll go to the New York Library tomorrow and look up some political cartoons from the 1800s."

She called the next day, excited. She'd found what she needed and was at work on a cover drawing and thought I'd love it. I knew I would. In the finished version, a lanky Uncle Sam stands at a teller's window marked Federal Handouts, depositing stacks of cash while a fat-cat banker with a cane and top hat strolls through a diminutive cityscape with small people underfoot. She was right. I loved it. It balanced Marty's more measured review. I was happy when Marty told Kat he really liked it.

In East Orange we had our share of bad actors, con artists, and sleazy profiteers making money from the city's decline. We had slumlords. We had housing inspectors who looked the other way, and we had judges with a disdain for poor tenants regardless of how bad their living conditions were. Our cast of characters were nearly as deadly as the swindlers who plundered the FHA program. We were determined to beat back the threat. If we didn't, East Orange's fate would be the same as Detroit's and so many other cities. Human misery, neighborhood decline, a city on its knees.

Boyer's disheartening story was motivating to be sure, but there was something else, a haunting feeling that I was loath to recognize. A sense of powerlessness. That regardless of what we did we'd never hold the government and the finance industry accountable. There was a collusion there that was too powerful. Unassailable really.

Some grassroots action gave us hope. A bank protest

Part III: Keep On Keepin' On (1975-76)

movement in Chicago led by Gail Cincotta and National People's Action ignited an anti-red lining movement, and they won a federal law that required banks to lend in areas where they took deposits. We followed her work and reported on it in *Shelterforce*.

Sadly, later we had to report that the persistent efforts by banking industry lobbyists effectively rendered the federal Community Reinvestment Act toothless. It was on the books but it became nothing more than a bureaucratic reporting headache for the banks. It definitely wasn't community *reinvestment*.

It would be a decade before John and Phyllis and I would be part of a campaign in New Jersey to hold banks accountable and make them comply with that same federal law when they wanted to merge across state lines. Getting banks to sign Community Reinvestment Agreements would finally begin to salve that deep ache of powerlessness.

Kat's cover drawing.

That's Woody and Simon on the left. Mary, Michael, and I are on the right. The cat's name was Digger.

CHAPTER 15

The House Fills Up

I got to know Mary Tasker. We were both EOTA volunteers. We originally met at the Liz McAlister weekend retreat. Mary was part of a group in West Milford but she now lived in an apartment nearby with her two young sons, Simon and Michael. They would be a good addition to the house so I went to talk to Mary. She was serious and earnest and such a naturally warm person, and I was charmed by her British accent. She grew up working-class in Sheffield, an industrial city in north central England known for its steel production and famous for its precision cutlery.

When I stopped by Mary's apartment to talk to her about moving in, I gave her the whole picture. Phyllis was moving into the third floor apartment and I'd be looking for a couple more folks to share the first two floors and the house expenses.

Mary's first question was, "What will my rent be?"

I had my mortgage payment and property taxes and I estimated the gas and electric and gave her a number based on four adults plus Phyllis on the third floor.

"But we're three people and we'll need two bedrooms." I knew she was struggling and told her what I'd decided. That we'd all pay the same. A look of disbelief washed over her face. "That means my rent will be half of what I'm paying now. And the boys will have other adults to relate to. They only see their father every other weekend." She hugged me and said yes. On the spot.

The relieved single mom was anxious to talk about life in the house. She made us tea and we started imagining sharing meals and chores, the shopping, and the cooking. Mary had no extended family in the U.S. and said she hoped it would be more like a family. I let her know that's what I hoped for too. We had a deal. I was elated. She was struggling more than I thought and let me in on how precarious her financial situation was. She was getting food stamps and told me she sometimes needed to sell them to raise cash for rent and other necessities. She was cleaning houses a few days a week but she wasn't making much. She'd only been in the U.S. since 1967 and had no family here.

Mary was right. When she and the boys moved in, the house became more than a stopover for young singles. It was more like a family and I loved it. They were the perfect addition.

Simon and Michael were the only White kids in their elementary school and they felt pretty alienated. We all smiled when Simon came home excited one day and reported that an "almost White" kid had joined their class. His name was Keith.

When Mary asked about him some days later, Simon said, "He's a jerk."

Some months later, Mary managed to enroll the boys in the Ironbound Community School, a project of the awesome neighborhood group, Ironbound Community Corporation.

Michael was outgoing and made friends easily, so a few boys on the block started coming by the house. Simon was more reserved. He impressed me with his air of thoughtful seriousness, happy to be alone reading or playing with his baseball card collection. At one point the young Mets fan wanted to be called Dave after his New York Mets idol, Dave Kingman. When he transferred to Ironbound Community School, everyone knew him there as Dave. He'd give me the stink eye if I called him Simon around his friends. Mary recalls that when she got her first job out of high school, as an "office girl," she told everyone her name was Kim. One Christmas at a junk shop I found a wooden box with a snug wooden cover just the right depth for baseball cards and bought it for Simon. Knowing Simon, his cards may still be in that box. I hope so.

I enjoyed the boys and developed a relationship with them. Mary was balancing cleaning houses and college courses, so I offered to take care of the boys every Monday. I'd make them breakfast, drive them to and from school in the Ironbound, and take care of them the rest of the day. I'd make dinner, supervise homework, and then send them off to bed and some nights tell them a story. I retold a few that my dad had told to me and my brother Mike.

After school, we went off exploring all around Newark. Down to Port Newark to watch ships being unloaded by giant cranes. We'd go to the Meadowlands with binoculars looking for exotic birds. We'd visit construction sites or watch buildings being demolished or just play games in the park. All kinds of stuff that young boys (and I) loved to do.

With so many buildings being torn down, I proposed that we start a used brick business. There was a market for clean old bricks, ten cents each. So after school on Mondays we'd pile in my pick-up, search for demolished buildings, and salvage good bricks. The boys loved crawling on the piles of debris, hammers in hand. We could only sell clean bricks, so I taught them how to chip off the mortar. Every Monday we'd add to our stack by the garage. At some point we'd cash in our booty and split up the dough.

Soon after he moved in I met William Wright, a tall lean West Indian electrician with a big family who moved into a big house across the street, a few doors down. His house needed a lot of work. William walked down early one summer evening. I stopped my work and got us a couple of cold ones from the fridge and we began swapping ideas about renovating our houses. Mike made friends with one of his boys, also named William, and young William started coming by the house. Another boy on the block, whose name I've forgotten, started hanging around too.

I'd be there working on the house, rebuilding the porch, and they'd pester me to let them help. So I'd give them scraps of lumber to work with. Then one day when Michael and Simon were there with William and the other kid, I gave in completely and put down my tools.

"Hey, would you guys like to build your own clubhouse in the backyard?"

They all looked at me with the same happy but bewildered expression that said, *What? We can actually DO that?*

I went in the house and grabbed a big sketch pad and some pencils. We set up a piece of plywood across two sawhorses. Our drafting table. We selected a site in the far corner of the backyard away from the house and the driveway and I took them through the design process. I had to dampen expectations a bit like suggesting that a second floor would have to wait until Phase Two. But a ladder to a crow's nest lookout would be a good idea. They liked that.

We dragged out a bunch of salvaged lumber from the garage and I let them measure and saw and nail. After a couple weeks, the four boys had their own clubhouse.

Part III: Keep On Keepin' On (1975-76)

William brought his older brother Glenn to see the club house. The slender teenager introduced himself as Glenny T and told me that he was a do-wop singer and had started his own singing group at East Orange High named *14 Carat Soul*. I was impressed and asked him to sing me something. Without hesitation the teenage crooner slid into a beautiful song right there in the backyard. I followed Glenn's career for a few years, and *14 Carat Soul* enjoyed some brief fame and released a few albums. They even performed on *Saturday Night Live* and toured in Japan.

The one-room clubhouse was finished. The boys hung out there and all climbed up to the crow's nest. One day some other boys, about Simon and Michael's age who lived in the apartment building on Beech Street behind us, began lobbing stones over the fence at the clubhouse. Our boys yelled back but the stones kept coming. That's when Mary stepped in to mediate. She invited the Beech Street boys over the next day. She gathered all the boys together. Mary had a special way of connecting with people and kids were no exception. With a little talking, and by encouraging our boys to give them a tour of the clubhouse and some fresh hot popcorn, she brokered a truce.

Next door was a big rundown house that'd been converted into apartments. Two sisters who lived there, Rhonda and Charlene, came over occasionally. They'd shyly say hi to Mary and she'd ask them about school stuff and what they liked to do. She always made them feel welcome. Simon and Michael were very nice to the girls and made an effort to include them in stuff. Our new neighborhood welcomed us and we felt the same.

Woody lived down the block at 62 Chestnut, a group of six VISTA volunteers shared a house. They all signed on for two years and lived on a meager government stipend, working full time for the Newark Tenants Organization and of course Woody was part of the *Shelterforce* Collective. When Woody's housemates moved on after their two year stints in tenant organizing, he moved in with us. My commune was filling up.

Woody was a good addition, a reliable and flexible housemate who valued an organized home life. Along with Mary and the boys, Woody contributed a real feeling of family. I wasn't always around for dinner but Woody was. We shared food shopping, cooking, and cleaning responsibilities. We ate vegetables from the garden and we swapped recipes, discovering new dishes like basil pesto and noodles with sesame paste. Woody made the best milkshakes with his Hamilton Beach mixer and Fox's U-Bet chocolate syrup. Thanksgiving was a feast. We hosted Fourth of July picnics and Labor Day barbecues. We had a big tree at Christmas and exchanged lots of presents.

Woody and Mary spent a lot of time together but I was on the go a lot or working furiously on the house. Mary suggested that we put aside one weekday morning each week after the kids had been dropped off at school. We'd cook a big breakfast and catch up on each other's lives. It kept us connected.

Renovating the Interior

In the winter months I renovated the interior, which was a little tricky. The house was fully occupied and usually full of activity—big dinners, meetings, parties. Even with thirteen rooms, it was a challenge to take a room out of service to complete its renovation. I completed the entire third floor before Phyllis moved in, but the five bedrooms on the second floor were all occupied. I had to move people around. Woody and Mary had begun sharing a bed some nights so I could move them in together temporarily. The boys bunked in with Mary while I fixed up their room. I renovated my own room without moving out. That was a mess.

Every room needed plaster repair, some floor sanding and varnish, scraping and sanding of baseboards and door and window trim, fresh paint all over. After eighty years, some doors had to be rehung. The hinges were pulling away from the jamb. That was a pain in the ass. Plenty of windows were painted shut and a lot of them had broken sash cords. I learned a lot about one-pipe steam heat. Over the years, condensed steam that had leaked from the radiator vents had rotted the wood floor. This caused the radiators to slant in the wrong direction so the condensed steam wouldn't naturally flow back to the boiler. I'd have to remove the radiator and patch the oak floor. It took me three to four weeks to finish a room.

I averaged about two days a week renovating. When I'd bought the house, my boss in Englewood relied on me a lot and didn't want to lose me, so he let me work part time. I lived off my part-time work and had time for *Shelterforce* and EOTA and I never worked on Sundays.

When John and Deena separated, we got another housemate. John moved into Woody's room and Woody moved in with Mary.

As charming as our house was inside, the outside was dull and downright homely. The exterior was covered in gray wood-grained, asphalt shingles that cast a gloomy shadow over the stately front porch with its charming second floor porch above. Everything about those hideous shingles offended me. They undoubtedly covered over some nice wood clapboard siding. I hated looking at them.

But removing the shingles and scraping and patching

and painting the wood clapboards underneath was just not an option. I hated aluminum siding as much as those shitty looking shingles and I was really bummed when I learned that painting the shingles was not an option either. The shingles were pliable. Fresh paint would dry out and crack.

I gave my old buddy Tom Jackson a call. He'd renovated a few houses and he told me he'd faced the same challenge.

"The answer is stain," he said. "Use Olympia solid body stain. A dark color. And spray it on. It reacts well with the asphalt in the shingles and it won't dry them out."

Sam Ferber, Marsha's husband, was a house painter, so I asked him.

"I haven't heard that," he said. "But I'll ask around." He reported that a couple of painter buddies had used the Olympia solid body stain and said it performed "better than paint on wood." They said the oil-based stain bonds with the asphalt in the shingles and the color is long lasting because unlike paint it never peels. I felt rescued. I loved learning the tricks of the renovation trade.

Sam said, "You'll need about six gallons. When you get the stain, let me know. I'll come by with my sprayer and if you help me move the ladders, we'll have your house painted in a few hours." That was Sam. A lot of people talked a lot about "community." Sam simply offered to help a friend.

The following Saturday morning, Sam's yellow Suburban rolled into the driveway and he unloaded his spray equipment. Like many painters, Sam was a "neat freak." His old truck was spotless. I was surprised when I noticed his jeans were practically new. He wore a blue denim work shirt with hardly a wrinkle and some worn sneakers. I was curious when he took off his shirt, turned it inside out, and buttoned it back up. He winked at me, "A trick my uncle taught me."

Sam mixed several gallons of the deep brown stain into a five gallon bucket. He said separate gallons might be from different batches and slightly different in color. He put one end of his sprayer hose in the big bucket. We set up the ladder and he started spraying. Together we moved the heavy forty-four-foot wooden ladder and he'd scurry up to the peaks of the third floor, leaning out in both directions with his sprayer. The house was transformed in about three hours. Now it was the flaking dull green trim that looked so dull.

There were miles of wood trim that needed to be scraped, then painted with oil based enamel. Two years went by and I was still painting all that trim—a rich mustard yellow that contrasted perfectly with the dark brown siding. A decade after selling the house I drove by and noticed how the painted trim had faded a bit and started to peel again, but the siding kept its rich brown character.

Some months later I got to return Sam's favor. He called and asked for help re-roofing their house. He and I and a couple of friends spent a weekend stripping off the old asphalt shingles and laying down new ones. I'd never done roofing before and fortunately my steep upper roofs had recently been reshingled, but the roof above the second floor porch still had the original slate and that was the roof that was pulling away from the front of the house and badly needed repair. I wasn't looking forward to working that high up on a steep roof.

I liked working with Sam. We spent a weekend building shelves for Marsha's bookstore in Madison. As we measured and cut planks, Sam told me about their vision.

He and Marsha planned to go *back to the land*. Maybe homestead in the hills of West Virginia. His picture of self-reliant rural life made it sound like paradise. Escape the consumer rat race. Grow your own food. Live off the land again. I was impressed at their initiative and I had a feeling it would be a lot more challenging than Sam made it sound. I promised to come down and help them build their house.

Eventually, Stu Kaplowitz, Phyllis's boyfriend, moved in with her and he was a good addition to the house. Stu was an interesting guy with a generous spirit. He worked as an accountant but his real loves—other than Phyllis—were history and music. Maryann Nelson was another good housemate. She was a labor lawyer at the left-wing Newark firm we called the Law Commune. She lived with us a little over a year. She and Mary nurtured house plants and they made the house feel like a botanical garden.

Stu and Phyllis planned to get married in 1975. The wedding in Phyllis's hometown of Bradley Beach was not going to be large, so Mary got the idea that we'd host a big wedding party at the house. She insisted that the house be "spic and span" inside and out. It was the social high point for our big and welcoming house. We organized a huge barbecue and everybody brought their favorite side dishes and desserts. It was a feast that started early and went late with people out back and throughout the house. Our jug band performed on the front porch. Stu and Phyllis loved it.

The Law Commune

Our community included a preponderance of lawyers. I got to know the Law Commune in downtown Newark. It seemed there was an army of young lawyers with left-wing politics coming out of law schools in the late sixties and seventies. That was certainly true at Rutgers in Newark, nicknamed The People's Electric Law School. Smart and idealistic young men and women wanted to put their legal training to work at righting wrongs, defending civil rights, representing unions, defending the poor, and anyone who was being picked on by society.

Two of those Rutgers lawyers were Jeff Fogel and Stu Ball. They formed a left-wing firm in Newark in 1972 with Leonard Weinglass, a well known civil rights attorney.

Lenny and Stu were just back from three years defending the "Chicago 7" political organizers who were charged by the federal government with inciting the massive confrontation at the raucous 1968 Democratic Convention. Straight out of Rutgers Law School, Stu found himself back in his hometown and thrown into the high profile media spectacle known as the Trial of the Chicago 7. Not only was the trial about a huge anti-war protest and a colossal violent overreaction by the police, but it also represented the clash between freedom of speech and law and order. The larger-than-life characters were straight from central casting: diminutive, cantankerous Judge Julius Hoffman was a dictator in the courtroom who ordered Black Panther defendant Bobby Seale bound and gagged and frequently cited the defendants and their attorneys for Contempt of Court. Abbie Hoffman and Jerry Rubin, the leaders of the YIPPIES, mocked the trial with daily theatrics. Defense attorney William Kuntzler was confrontational in defense of his clients. Meanwhile, the rotund Irish, big city Democratic Machine Boss Richard Daley, staunch defender of law and order at all cost, loomed large over the trial.

The politically charged trial captured the country for five months, and five of the defendants were found guilty and sentenced to five years in jail. Two years later the appellate court cited "judicial bias by Judge Hoffman" and overturned the verdicts.

Fogel, Ball, and Weinglass called their new law firm the Any Day Now Collective, but we all knew it as the Law Commune or just 108; the office address was 108 Washington Street. Secretaries answered the phone, "law office." The young firm bought a classic brick townhouse in downtown Newark near the Rutgers campus. Larry Bogdanow, a mind blowing designer, carpenter, and architecture school dropout joined the collective and renovated the building. There were two floors of private offices that had glass openings to the common hallways and brought in light from the big windows in the front and rear of the building. The open-plan third floor was devoted to a large country kitchen with a big table and cozy seating area near the tall front windows. There was a couch or two for sleeping and a bathroom with a shower.

When I arrived on the scene, the firm's stationery read like an establishment firm: *Ball, Hayden, Kiernan and Livingston*. Weinglass had split for the West Coast to teach and Fogel had joined the Rutgers Urban Legal Clinic. The firm operated as a collective with lawyers and secretaries all earning the same.

I first met Ball, Kiernan and Livingston playing basketball at the Rutgers Law School gym. The law school was housed in a downtown office building vacated by an insurance company. The building's aging amenities included a decent size basketball gym with locker rooms and showers. Jeff Fogel worked at the law school's Urban Legal Clinic and managed to book the gym every Thursday evening. When John and I showed up, Ronnie was there along with Kevin Kerrnan. That's when I met Paul

Acinapura, Paul Castellero and a few others. Steve Block and I were the only non-lawyers. The b-ball was a little sloppy. Paul Atch was a great playmaker and a few of us could pass and shoot. Ronnie was the tallest and had sharp elbows, so he was a strong rebounder. Craig was reckless and loved to drive to the basket. We just got out of his way rather than get banged into and he'd often miss the close-in lay up. Stu loved the game. He'd been the team manager at Princeton when Bill Bradley had been the big star there. It was a fun workout and we'd usually end up at McGovern's, the old Irish bar nearby, for beer and burgers. I loved being included in this bunch of smart, political, and fun guys.

Progress on Main Street

Ever since my encounter with the guy at the bank on Main Street, I'd kept an eye out, looking for progress in the Brick Church Urban Renewal area. The only change was the For Rent signs in vacant shop windows. I knew from my work in Englewood that urban renewal work was complicated and lack of visible progress didn't mean there was none, so I looked into the project's history. In 1970, after a couple years of study and preparation, the City Council approved a redevelopment plan calling it, "One of the most important decisions made in the history of East Orange." This big step would buttress East Orange against the winds of disinvestment blowing in from the East. I imagined the city breathing a sigh of relief with this bold stroke, but that had been four long years ago.

Hoping to attract big investors, the council rezoned the low-rise area around the Brick Church train station for twenty- to thirty-story buildings. Council members made big claims about, "One hundred and thirty million dollars in new development that will increase our entire tax base by forty percent."

Those claims were pretty grand but it did seem like city officials had been proactive in the face of suburbanization and demographic change. Because the city had no industry to speak of, just two factories on the Newark border, East Orange's property tax base was particularly vulnerable. Cities that relied solely on their residential tax base were in a deep bind; they either burdened their citizens with high property taxes or they cut municipal services. Those would be bitter pills for a city like East Orange to swallow.

I wondered about the average citizens who'd been there a while and were invested in the place. When might they give up on East Orange? It was a story happening all across the Northeast and Midwest. I thought with sadness of my Detroit home where this was playing out on a much grander scale.

As I looked further into East Orange's very recent history, I found a 1971 front-page story that the Housing Authority had designated a developer to build a large-scale office and commercial development. Structured parking would compete with the suburban shopping malls and corporate parks. Phase one was a thirty-story office building with ground-floor retail and underground parking on Halsted between Main and I-280.

The other four phases were still under wraps, but the announcement was heralded in messianic terms. One councilman announced, "If the city is going to be saved, this project is going to be the thing that does it." That had been three years ago. Construction hadn't begun yet and I thought some more about what the city's mood must be now.

The shopping district's decline wasn't the only fiscal

thorn in East Orange's side. Construction of Interstate 280 had resulted in the loss of thirteen million in tax ratables, and the long delay in opening the highway had left the center of the city in limbo. Daily life around the city still seemed pretty robust, but a sense of uncertainty loomed. The city wondered what its future held and so did I.

Frank Hutchins

Woody Widrow

Betty Hutchinson leads the Judge Albano protest

CHAPTER 16

Showdown in East Orange

Things had moved quickly for me. Life in the house was settling into a cozy routine. Most days I loved renovating the house and only occasionally did I feel like I'd taken on too much.

My part-time work in Englewood paid well and now included special assignments like evaluating proposals submitted for new housing or working alongside the engineering consultants as they prepared plans for street improvements. Stuff I'd never done before. It was all new and fascinating to this young urbanist.

The best assignment was assisting a study team from the Urban Land Institute, who came to Englewood for a week to advise on a development plan for some key areas, including a portion of the downtown. What a twist of fate that one of the visiting experts who I got to rub shoulders with was Edmund Bacon, the Philadelphia city planner who created the Society Hill neighborhood rehabilitation. I prepared all the background materials that they reviewed in advance and got to tag along as they toured the proposed redevelopment areas.

When the Third Ward Councilwoman requested that the Agency make recommendations about a housing rehab program, I was assigned to conduct a Housing Conditions study. I'd never done one before so I hired Bierbaum to assist me and we developed a windshield survey tool to rank all the houses in the neighborhood. We drove every street and from the car we noted exterior conditions and assigned points to each. The councilwoman was impressed with my work and wanted to know more. I told her about a neighborhood rehab effort in southeast Baltimore. She asked me to call them to see if they'd give us a tour. We made the three hour drive early one morning. It was a real eye opener for me to see how this group of residents organized their own "community development corporation." We both loved the idea of a nonprofit organization that acted like a business but was governed by people from the neighborhood. The excited councilwoman wanted to start one in Englewood. All I could think of was East Orange. Southeast Baltimore was different from my new city, but I knew a nonprofit development corporation was one of the things we badly needed.

Every week now seemed full of adventure. Nothing was more exciting than the showdown in East Orange over Rent Control.

Push Comes to Shove

In January of 1975 the City Council approved a revised Rent Control Ordinance replacing a flat 6% annual rent increase instead of the Consumer Price Index calculation and limiting rent increases upon vacancy to 15%. Phyllis told the press, "Tenants can live with six percent." Privately she vowed to win a 4% annual increase and no bonus upon vacancy. She was preparing for a confrontation with the City Council.

After three months of trying privately with members

of the Council and publicly in the press to get another rent control amendment on the agenda, Phyllis decided to pack the City Council chambers with tenants and demand it. She whipped EOTA into action.

Phyllis was the first to speak at the public session that began the Council meeting. She was followed by a bunch of tenants demanding action to revise the Rent Leveling Ordinance. After the public had been heard, Councilman Bill Thomas, who chaired the Housing Committee, was unequivocal: There would be no action on the rent ordinance that evening. Nor would there be any discussion. The Council had other important business, he said, and the rent ordinance was still being discussed in committee. He called upon the Council President to move the agenda and call the first order of business.

Phyllis screamed at Thomas from her seat in the fifth row and other tenants began to do the same. It was a spontaneous confrontation. Whether it was a legitimate misunderstanding by Phyllis or not, she wasn't going home without a fight that evening.

Council President Williams ordered the cops to remove Phyllis, but she was sitting in the middle of a row and the tenants around her weren't going to let the cops get to her. Cops had to carry tenants out of their seats. There was pushing and shoving and yelling. Mary Tasker sat next to Phyllis with Michael in her lap. They carried her out too.

"Let 'em sit in jail for a while. That's what we did in Selma," said Thomas.

Six tenants were carried out and taken to jail. I was standing in the back, reassuring Michael that Mary would be back soon. The tenants all stayed for the remainder of the meeting, and before the meeting was adjourned, all six of the arrested tenants were let go and they walked back

Staking Our Claim

into the Council Meeting, which set off Bill Thomas again. When one of them tried to speak during the Public Session, Thomas wouldn't allow it. Stu Kaplowitz, Phyllis's husband, went to the mic and read her speech.

The meeting was a standoff. The tenants demanded action to lower how much their rents could be increased every year and the Council stood firm. They weren't going to be dictated to by the tenants. But EOTA tenants were more fired up than ever.

It wasn't just East Orange. All across the state, rents were rising faster than family incomes, and tenants were reacting. Some towns enacted rent ordinances and tenants in every town wanted that same protection, but it meant they needed to get organized and engaged in the political arena with their city and town councils. John and Joan and Phyllis were being contacted by new tenant leaders in other Essex municipalities who wanted help from the people who'd won the early battles for rent control. In Essex, it was happening in nearly every city and town. John spent a lot of time advising these new leaders on what it would take—organizing your neighbors, building an organization. One woman who John came in contact with was the emerging leader in Bloomfield, a White working-class town of about fifty thousand that bordered East Orange. Betty Hutchinson was the voice of the tenants in the eight hundred-unit Forest Hills apartment complex. She had organized her neighbors when they were concerned with declining maintenance. She was now fighting to establish a strong rent ordinance in Bloomfield. Betty wasn't a client of Legal Services but she called John a lot. John put her in touch with Phyllis, who helped with her public campaign.

Betty got 180 tenants to turn out to a council meeting fighting for a 5% increase at a time when the CPI was

9.2%. The council approved 6.3% for the coming year. A year later the tenants convinced the council to allow 4.3% when the CPI was 8.6%.

An Essex countywide coalition was in the making and the entire *Shelterforce* Collective was involved. John and Joan and the rest of the Housing Unit were advising leaders in Bloomfield, Irvington, and West Orange. Phyllis was consumed by the EOTA rent fight and I was helping her. Woody worked full-time at Newark Tenants Organization, and NTO was pushing for rent control. John began talking about an Essex County Housing Coalition. He put together a meeting of all the town leaders who all swapped rent control war stories. It was great having them all together. They had such natural camaraderie. Phyllis was elected Chairperson. The coalition didn't have a mission yet, other than mutual support, but that day would come.

Publishing Regularly

With *Shelterforce*, we discovered a whole world out there of local activists. Folks were organizing tenant associations everywhere it seemed, but there was so much more—neighborhood groups, block associations, an anti-redlining movement, groups building and rehabbing homes. Harry Boyte called it a "Backyard Revolution."

Determined to connect with the tenants movement in all corners of the country, we collected mailing lists and mailed *Shelterforce* free to hundreds of organizers, advocates, poverty lawyers, and anti-poverty groups. We aspired to a bi-monthly publishing schedule, but we continued as a quarterly. It was a challenging pace for an all-volunteer organization but one that we mostly kept to. The newspaper was filled with helpful strategies, model laws and ordinances, stories of successful housing struggles, and more. It became a clearinghouse of useful information and best practices as well as news from around the country. The National Lawyers Guild connection fell by the wayside and the Collective solidified. I put a couple of hand-me-down file cabinets and an oak desk in the parlor. *Shelterforce* shared an address and an office with EOTA.

The Collective provided the volunteer labor for everything—writing, editing, typing, layout, and pasting on mailing labels, and the house hosted plenty of fundraising parties to cover printing and postage costs. Our annual subscription price was three dollars, but we were committed to sending it out free for at least a year to every activist and tenant group whose address we could find. Subscription checks soon found their way to the mail slot in the big carved front door at 31 Chestnut. I'd immediately grab the mail looking for subscription checks and I loved reading the letters of support and appreciation for our effort at bringing some coherence to this disconnected, inherently local movement. We all loved hearing from folks like us fighting for affordable, good quality housing in a decent neighborhood and mounting a grassroots movement to get it. It was exhilarating and kept us committed to the task of supporting them.

In the next three issues we ran a three-part series penned by John, Ronnie, and Phyllis entitled *Negotiating Tactics for Tenant Organizations* and we reported on more high profile tenant organizing like the massive Co-op City rent strike in the Bronx. We developed recurring columns that included *Legal Developments*, *Access*, which listed films, books, case studies, and organizing guides. *Keeping the Heat On* featured short news items about tenant groups around the country. Those news pieces reflected our growing reach because they now included Seattle, Dallas, Detroit, Ann Arbor, Topeka, Philadelphia, DC, Hawaii, Cleveland, Columbus, Chicago, Albuquerque, the Twin Cities, Oakland, and Berkeley.

A People's Law School

Locally, we were dreaming up a new undertaking. I don't know whose idea it was but the idea of connecting grassroots tenant leaders to the law school at Rutgers caught hold. We were already teaching people about their legal rights, why not expand that into some classes for adults at the law school in downtown Newark. The idea for a People's Law School was born. Some law students at the Urban Legal Clinic took on the job of writing a legal manual for tenants. They did a magnificent job—forty pages in plain English explaining everything from leases to security deposits to eviction and everything in between that a tenant who's organizing their building needed to know. I asked Kat Brennan if she'd illustrate it, and she created a beautiful cover and half a dozen illustrations inside.

We scheduled a series of evening classes and spread the word. The registration turnout was tremendous. Most of the classes in the series dealt with understanding the law and were taught by Housing Unit lawyers or law students, but I taught a class that we called Facts and Figures, where I explained how landlords made their profit and some basic elements about challenging a landlord's appeal to the rent leveling board for a higher-than-allowed increase. Tenant leaders from all around Essex attended. What a great idea this turned out to be, but we had just stretched ourselves even thinner. We had no ability to say no to a good idea. We needed some help. We needed funding to pay people.

Black-Robed Injustice

The Housing Unit lawyers were doing a great job representing tenant groups and as a result all of us volunteer leaders knew the law. And the laws on the books claimed to guarantee tenants would get what they paid for, a habitable apartment and even poor tenants could get an attorney through Legal Services. The system was far from perfect and those Legal Services attorneys were overworked and underfunded. But there was a bigger problem. Once a tenant got to court they couldn't count on the judge to follow the law.

One Essex County judge had a particular animus for poor tenants and the lawyers who represented them. Judge Nicholas Albano. Tenants represented by John and Joan had suffered under Albano's brand of justice. But one Housing Unit attorney in particular was the target of the biased judge's antipathy, maybe because she was Black or maybe just because she continuously challenged his awful rulings. That was Patricia Thornton. Pat had been thoroughly trained at Rutgers by Annamae Sheppard in the Urban Legal Clinic. John hired Pat immediately upon graduating and she was a great addition to the Housing Unit.

Albano's anti-tenant rulings were well known. Tenant lawyers knew their client's chances were diminished if their case was assigned to Albano. The Assignment Clerk sent all of Pat Thornton's cases to Albano. We needed to do something. We'd fought for laws to protect tenants. We couldn't sit back and allow those laws to be ignored by the courts. Albano had to go.

Unseating a judge would not be easy. They were appointed for seven years and then typically reappointed for life. Albano had been on the bench for four years. A plan was hatched to try and topple our nemesis. We'd need evidence to show his consistent pattern of anti-tenant and anti-tenant attorney behavior and decisions. The main target of Albano's animosity, Pat Thornton, led the effort to gather that evidence. We organized volunteers to sit in Albano's courtroom and take notes.

Once the evidence was compiled our strategy was both legal and extralegal. Pat filed a complaint with the New Jersey Supreme Court Advisory Committee on Judicial Conduct. Her filing charged Albano with judicial misconduct. Meanwhile the rest of us organized a public demonstration outside the Essex County courthouse. We marched with signs calling for the anti-tenant judge's ouster. We were pleased that the protest attracted the press but unaware that a court officer snapped a picture that showed John in attendance. A ruling by the Supreme Court on Albano would take awhile but action by the Essex Judiciary to disbar John came swiftly. Our leader was in trouble.

Amazingly, John took it pretty much in stride even though his livelihood was on the line. He found a noted old left-wing attorney who was glad to represent him. Then Albano tried to keep Pat Thornton from getting admitted to the Bar. John's sharp legal advocate beat back the charges against him and then we heard that the Supreme Court censured Albano. Wow. Two victories! Pat overcame her tormentor and got her license to practice law. But the wretched heartless jurist was still on the bench. Maybe now we could convince Governor Byrne to give him the boot, but Byrne never responded to our pleas. We were stuck with a vengeful judge who now hated us more than ever. Maybe when his seven-year term was up we could convince Byrne not to reappoint him.

Securing Federal Funds

Back when I did research for my first article on the new federal housing law, I realized how the new program could stimulate grassroots organizing. The Housing and Community Development Act devolved spending authority over federal housing funds to local governments in the form of annual block grants. The amount was determined by population and the level of local poverty. Local governments decided how to spend the money within federal guidelines. Funding for public improvements, community development projects, and even subsidies for low-income housing would now be decided at the local level.

We all cheered when "Tricky Dick" Nixon left office in disgrace and his helicopter lifted off from the White House lawn the previous year, and I also knew his main motive with the new housing act was to cut the level of federal support, but local control, a central feature of the new law, created an opportunity for local organizing. In my *Shelterforce* article I had urged local organizers to come up with community plans and pressure elected officials to fund their plans with the federal dollars. Now it was time to practice what I preached—in East Orange.

My first ideas were grand plans. I sketched out a program to take over apartment buildings where slumlords were pocketing the rents, not making repairs and falling delinquent on their property taxes. The idea I spent the most time on was funding for a nonprofit community development corporation. It could rehab and develop housing, like the group I'd visited in Baltimore. I planned to visit Becky Doggett in Newark and see what Tri Cities was doing.

But first things first. EOTA needed funding. The organization had outgrown Phyllis's third floor apartment and

Part III: Keep On Keepin' On (1975-76)

Shelterforce had taken over most of the parlor. EOTA needed money for an office and a mimeograph machine and to pay the answering service. And basics like envelopes and stamps. The new federal law created Community Development Block Grants (CDBG). There was no reason the city couldn't fund EOTA with CDBG dollars. Phyllis could pack the council chambers in support but we needed a proposal, so I got to work. I described the EOTA project in "community development" terms and came up with a program called Tenant Assisted Code Enforcement. I outlined a proposal to Phyllis and then to the board. EOTA would provide advice and assistance to tenants whose buildings were not being maintained to Property Maintenance Code standards. To us it was tenant organizing, but to HUD officials it was a means of enhancing code enforcement.

I picked up an application at City Hall and submitted a funding proposal for twelve thousand dollars. At the federally mandated public hearing, Phyllis and I spoke about the pressing need that the EOTA application would address, and we were followed to the microphone by at least half a dozen tenant leaders. The Council wasn't going to say no to a modest request by organized tenants. Pretty soon we'd have a physical presence, an office downtown where volunteer organizers could meet with tenants. This was a major step, but I was kicking myself. We asked for too little. We should have gotten money for staff. Phyllis and the other volunteers were swamped.

Nonetheless, I was feeling pretty satisfied. I was definitely liking my life in this new place. I had no idea how the rug might be pulled out from under me.

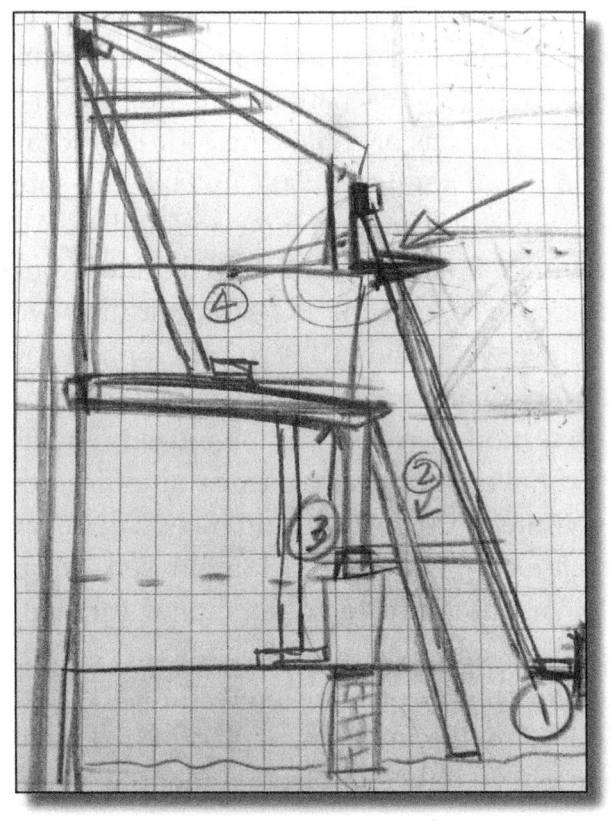

Securing my sagging porch.

CHAPTER 17

I Should've Seen It Coming

Bobbi's second brownstone renovation was nearing completion and would soon be rented up. The Upper West Side market for studio and one-bedroom apartments was booming, and five-story brownstone row houses were being vacated and renovated with two small apartments per floor. Soon she and her partners would have rents coming in from two ten-unit buildings. Occasionally I teased her about being a landlord, which didn't exactly help our relationship.

Now, with the brownstones completed, instead of spending more time in New Jersey, which I had hoped for, she was involved with a group of artists and anarchists in Chelsea and the West Village. I hoped to get her more involved in my community. She made some pen and ink drawings for *Shelterforce* but mostly she got me involved in her New York projects. At one event I was able to play an important role and save the day for Bobbi.

Bobbi was on a committee raising funds for Ramsey Clark, who'd been Lyndon Johnson's attorney general. Clark was an outspoken liberal activist who was now seeking the Democratic nomination for U.S. Senate from New York. The event was a live music fundraiser with Phil

Ochs in a bar near the West Village. Ochs was a big deal in the left-wing folk community. His sharp and biting lyrics were loaded with political meaning. He was also a great guitar player. I idolized Ochs who wrote two of the most famous anti-war anthems—"I Ain't Marching Anymore," a serious declaration that we were done fighting useless wars, and "Draft Dodger Rag," a hilarious spoof on dodging the draft. I thought back on how I stayed out of the jungles of Vietnam.

I Ain't Marching Anymore

It was early in 1971, just half a year before I turned twenty-six, the age cut off for the military draft. My number came up and I refused to go. I had no idea what I'd do if they prosecuted me but for some reason, by that time, the decision came easy. When someone would ask, I'd say, "They can't prosecute us all. There's way too many of us." My brother Mike's experience seemed to confirm that. But every now and then, I felt it hanging over me. It was like the tax returns I neglected to file. Or the career path I didn't have time to devote energy to. I was too caught up in living a life filled with purpose to let all that stuff get in the way.

For a few years, deferments kept all us guys in PACT out of Southeast Asia. Then the lottery made draft dodging a lot tougher. To be fair, we weren't just shirking our duty to serve our country. We were all utterly opposed to the War, morally and politically.

I came late to my anti-war stance. I was a senior at U-D when I attended my first teach-in. I was brought up to support the "battle against godless communism," but when students came to campus from Wayne State University and taught us about American imperialism, my views

Part III: Keep On Keepin' On (1975-76)

started to change. I still hated communism but I supported the right for countries to determine their own destinies.

I still wasn't ready to refuse to go so I got a letter from a shrink and that earned me a six-month delay. I only had to make it to my twenty-sixth birthday. Then in 1970, we learned about the massacre by U.S. soldiers of over four hundred unarmed South Vietnamese men, women, and children at My Lai. That cemented my moral opposition. I filed for Conscientious Objector status. I was morally opposed to the Vietnam War but I'd have fought against Hitler. So I wasn't opposed to *all* wars. Selective Service wasn't letting me off the hook. By January of '71, I'd passed my Pre-Induction physical. An Induction Notice was sure to follow. The clock was winding down; I'd be twenty-six in six months. I was clear in my mind. There was no way I was going into the Army.

My brother Mike was my inspiration. I'd helped him get a letter from a sympathetic shrink. Then at his induction physical, the letter in his file disappeared. In front of the commandant he refused to take that *one step forward*. When the FBI harassed our parents trying to locate him, he showed up at their office in downtown Detroit and read them the riot act for upsetting our mother. He never heard from them again. My younger brother with a chip on his shoulder; he was my hero.

I read an interview with Joan Baez, my favorite folk singer and high-profile war protester, and remembered seeing her at a concert at Kent State University. During her first song, a guy came out from backstage and ordered us all to evacuate the gym. There had been a bomb threat. A couple hundred of us gathered outside waiting for the all clear when Baez came out with a bull horn. She announced they weren't letting us back in for a bit so she serenaded us with a few songs through the bull horn. The protest singer's crystal clear soprano accented with that electric rasp of the bullhorn sliced through the night air and electrified us. We eventually trooped back in and she treated us to more of her luscious singing. Some of us attended her anti-war teach-in after the concert.

In the interview I read, she talked about The Resistance, a group she and her husband David Harris founded. Harris had refused to go and was awaiting trial. He and Joan organized protests and draft board sit-ins and encouraged draft-aged men to refuse conscription. Guys were publicly burning their draft cards. The famous folk singer told the story of a young man who came to her after a concert to give up his draft card. She talked with him about how long he'd been thinking of resisting and suggested that they burn a portion of his card but leave his name and number intact and that he mail it back to the Selective Service.

My scorched draft card and a smoking hot letter were soon on their way to the Selective Service Commission. There's probably a file somewhere with my letter and the remains of my draft card. Like my brother Mike, I was never prosecuted.

All this ran through my mind as I was helping Bobbi set up at the Phil Ochs fundraiser, and I was hoping to get to meet him. As people started to arrive and occupy the tables facing the stage, Bobbi ran over to me in a panic.

"I desperately need your help. Phil Ochs is sitting at the bar. He's drunk and saying that he can't go up on stage. You have to try and talk him off the ledge."

Sure enough, there he was sitting alone at the bar. My hero was drooped over the bar, staring into his glass of whiskey. He didn't look like he was in much shape to go on stage, even if I could persuade him.

Part III: Keep On Keepin' On (1975-76)

"Hey Phil, I'm Pat. My girlfriend, Bobbi, she's responsible for this event and she says you refuse to go up on stage. Is that right?"

He didn't lift his head but turned it toward me, and shifted his eyes up toward mine. "Sorry. I just can't do it anymore. It doesn't make sense any longer. Nothin' I've ever done has ever made any difference." He was pretty smashed.

I took a chance and put my hand on his shoulder, gently guiding him upright. "You're wrong about that, Phil. These people here *love* you. I *love* you. We *love* your songs. We're dying to hear you tonight."

He brightened ever so slightly and looked right at me. "You don't understand," he began and then proceeded without much conviction to rattle off a pre-digested list of evidence to document what a failure he'd become. It was a list he'd memorized, having repeated it in his head so often. It took some more back and forth but I finally felt like he was inching toward agreeing to play. By now, he was sitting up looking right at me as he spoke.

"Hey, what about a cup of coffee before you go up on stage?" I suggested.

"Yeah, that's probably a good idea, huh?" he said with a half smile.

I figured I'd succeeded at my task, but I wondered how capable he was of performing and if he started to fumble on stage whether he might just get up and walk off, or worse, start telling the audience what an imposter he really was.

But that's not what happened. He got up on stage and without hardly looking at the audience, launched right into a song. It all felt weird. I gritted my teeth but when the applause died down, he looked around, flashed a boyish grin, and went right into the next one. His playing and singing of his well worn repertoire wasn't flawless but it was definitely passable, especially for someone that drunk. By the end of the set he was chatting between songs, telling little stories. He played a couple of encores and looked pretty pleased as he acknowledged all the applause and the real love he was being shown.

It was a shock but not a surprise when just a year or so later I read that he had taken his life. It came out later that he suffered from undiagnosed bipolar disorder.

• • •

Bobbi was jazzed about how the event had gone. I wondered if I hadn't unwittingly contributed to her wanting to stay in New York. My Manhattan-loving girlfriend came home one day and announced that the political group she'd latched onto was calling itself Free Space, and they were opening up a coffee house venue where people could be free to discuss and read and hold classes and perform poetry apparently, without being subjected to the dogmatic political orthodoxy of the sectarian left. Free Space sounded way better than the tiresome Maoists and dogmatic Communists with their theories about the preconditions for revolution to happen in this country. But to me, it just sounded like a bunch of people hanging around acting like they're part of the resistance, rather than engaging in the hard work of political organizing. I didn't express my dismissiveness but I suppose it registered. I knew Bobbi's heart was in New York and that she saw New Jersey as too parochial. She didn't want to get stuck in the slow lane, the one we inhabited.

She asked me to help with the renovation of the Free

Space venue, so I brought my tools and went to work erecting partition walls and doing miscellaneous carpentry. A group of us had nailed up sheets of drywall and we were starting to tape and spackle the joints. A guy came up to me and asked if I'd teach him how to spackle the joints and apply the messy joint compound. I looked at his button-down blue oxford shirt, which on his corpulent body didn't look dressy at all and I suggested that he first take off his dress shirt, or at least turn it inside out. He just looked like the type who would make a mess.

He introduced himself. Stanley Aronowitz. I knew the name and was wowed. This organizer-turned-college professor and political author was an important intellectual figure on the Left. He was one of the prime movers of Free Space and was its resident intellectual.

I knew Aronowitz had written about the Spanish Civil War, definitely favoring the anarchists' approach to fighting Franco and the fascists, and he was critical of the dogmatic Spanish Communists. So I proposed a deal.

"I'll show you how to spackle. You'll work beside me and tell me about the anarchists in the Spanish Civil War."

"It's a deal," he said.

I showed him the basics and he began his lecture. It soon became apparent that he had trouble talking without moving his hands, a spackle knife in one and a pan of spackle in the other. And he seemed to need to look at me when he spoke rather than at the wall. I loved listening to him. He was impressive, knowledgeable, clever, and totally engaging. And uniquely unsuited to the work at hand.

Bobbi spent more and more time in the City. Late one evening when she came home, I was at my drafting table in the parlor and she came in all charged up, ready to fill me in on her day.

"We had such a good meeting at Free Space. The new people in the Facilitating Collective are so good."

I put my hand on a few sheets of paper. "Look, I've gotta finish this proposal for Phyllis; can we talk about this in the morning?"

"Yeah, sure," she said, as she turned and went upstairs.

The next morning it came out. She'd met this guy who was part of Free Space, a poet. That really hurt. She apparently needed to tell me about him. A creative type. Dedicated to his poetry. *What bullshit,* I thought. In a couple days she was gone. Not a trace remained of her ever having been there, except a handful of her original drawings that we'd use in *Shelterforce*.

I was rejected. Alone. My *manageable* renovation now felt overwhelming. Suddenly, it was hard to make sense of what I was doing. I didn't have a career path. No real skills. I was following some romantic quest. A quest to nowhere in particular it seemed.

I was usually quick to rebound from tough situations, never willing to let painful emotions sit long enough to understand what I was really feeling and what I wanted next. Never long enough for any learning to happen. I'd always moved on quickly. But this time I was stopped in my tracks.

Something's Rotten

I decided the best way to soothe my hurtin' heart was to put my hands to work. Do something productive and satisfying. So I set to work repairing the front steps. The old and rickety front stairs were beyond weathered and worn. Maybe I'd just need to replace the treads.

The next morning I drank some coffee, grabbed my flashlight, and crawled under the porch to check the supports under the steps. I wasn't surprised. I'd need to rip the whole thing out and build new ones. My flashlight revealed something far worse—something I'd suspected but hadn't wanted to think about. It wasn't just the stairs that needed to be replaced; in the dark and moist underside of my stately porch I found the main beam supporting the porch was marked with the wavy grooves and hollowed out spots of a termite colony. As I crawled around with my flashlight, the picture got bleaker: The cross beams under the entire east end of the porch were riddled with termite damage and would probably need to be replaced. Rotted floor beams meant replacing the porch deck. *Fuck!*

I grabbed another cup of coffee and inspected the entire underside of the porch. The western half had little or no damage, but the weakened beams in the middle had left a sag where the stairs came up. As a result, the second-floor porch was also sagging and its roof had pulled away from the house. I could barely comprehend what this would all mean—the complicated rebuilding, the unknown cost. I'd have to pull half the porch apart, rebuild it all and replace or reconstruct all the decorative wood trim. No wonder my palace was so affordable. It was a money pit. I wondered how to tell Ronnie what we were in for. His confidence in my judgement and abilities would be shaken for sure. How could he not regret his enthusiastic confidence in me. Double fuck.

The wraparound porch with its charming second-floor porch and all that marvelous wood trim, that's what gave this oversized place its charm. I had no one to blame but myself. I should have done a closer inspection. But I knew why I'd been so hasty; I was afraid I wouldn't get my "dream" house. But now, that neglect might mean my downfall. I was screwed.

There was *some* good news. The larger west end of the porch looked solid and termite-free. I made an appointment with Peggy Hayden at the Law Commune. I brought the Termite Inspection Report that I'd gotten before we closed on the house. She took a quick look at the report and the look she gave me didn't hearten me.

"The report is over a year old, and who's to say those termites didn't arrive after they did the inspection?"

"Peggy, any idiot can see this is old termite damage. Termites can't eat half of a huge porch in a year."

She didn't disagree, but she still didn't think we'd get anywhere with my claim. She agreed to write a letter threatening to sue if the company didn't negotiate a settlement. I thanked her and left. I was in trouble.

I took the slow way back to East Orange. I needed to think. As I passed through the once vibrant but now worn commercial strip that Central Avenue had become, I tried to plan my attack on this whole rotting porch mess. But those thoughts mixed with the rotting mess of my life at this point. The porch was just the latest reminder.

I was almost thirty. I had no girlfriend and was pretty convinced that I'd never figure out how to make a relationship work. As a result of my childish optimism, my dream project was about to crush me. When I tried to look on the bright side, I was freaked out that I didn't have a career or even a path to one.

What once seemed like a joyous, fulfilling, organic process of developing into my authentic self now felt like I was just playing at life. None of it added up to anything concrete. I thrived for a while in my new-found identity—the hands-on guy with a truck full of tools, rescuing old houses, who was also an organizer helping poor tenants and doing battle with slumlords. But what about making a *real* living? It wasn't going to be swinging a hammer. I knew that. I had a hard time staying focused on the bottom line so I wasn't much of a businessman. Life as a contractor wasn't it. The life of a professional organizer wasn't it either. The pay sucked, and while I wanted to be a force in my own community, I didn't want to be a teacher of others.

I found myself envying my closest comrades. They managed to follow their hearts and still have a professional identity. John, Joan and Ronnie were lawyers. Phyllis was an inner-city teacher. Marty would certainly end up as a professor. Mary was in college now, getting a degree in Social Work. Woody was plugging away at a Master's Degree in City Planning.

I liked my work with Englewood Redevelopment Agency. Since I got promoted, I only worked on special projects for Paul Yang, the executive director. The new field of Urban Neighborhood Revitalization was taking root. My problem was that I liked *all* that stuff—renovating, organizing, saving neighborhoods. If only it added up to a profession or a job or just a way to make a decent living.

Maybe what I needed was to get a degree, earn some professional credentials. Urban Planning was the only thing that made sense. Things had changed. I wasn't happy here. I must have been deluding myself, thinking that I'd found Nirvana. Maybe I could use a change of scenery.

I went to the library and looked up urban planning programs at University of Oregon and University of Washington and sent off letters to Seattle and Eugene, Oregon, requesting applications to their Master's programs. I was taking charge of my future. Now, what about the fucking porch?

Help Is on the Way

Plenty of contractors were tearing off these old porches and replacing them with a minimal porch and new front stairs. Maybe that's what I'd have to do. But I couldn't face that. It felt like a sacrilege. Without their stately porches, those houses looked naked. My parents and grandparents practically lived on their front porches during the summer. I intended to save mine. If only I knew how. I poured some more coffee and grabbed my clipboard and a pencil and a tape measure.

I walked out to the front sidewalk so I could take in the entire house, all three of its floors and its intersecting roofs. I sipped my coffee and scanned the porch structure. The lower porch sat about four feet up from the ground and spanned the entire width of the house and ten feet beyond toward the driveway. Instead of a railing there was a wall from the ground up to railing height covered with the stained shingles. The kneewall was topped with a wide wooden cap. Roughly in the center of the long porch was a second floor porch off the large front bedroom. That porch had a steep shed roof, and above that rose a kind of tower structure with a steep four-sided peak. The whole complicated structure was elegantly balanced and trimmed with handsome moldings and fretwork. It had been a work of art, and it was so hard to imagine the skill it took to create and erect it back in the 1890s. Now it looked worn and tired. You didn't have to look too hard to see where it was sagging.

Because of the rot beneath the porch deck, the main support beams sagged, which meant that the beams supporting the upper porch sagged too. I could see that the roof of the second floor porch had pulled away from the house. I couldn't get my head around how I'd possibly fix it all.

Part III: Keep On Keepin' On (1975-76)

At a party at Marsha's, I met John O'Hara, the contractor husband of Liz O'Hara, an occasional PACT participant. Blonde and blue eyed, popular Liz was flitting around, engaged in conversation, while husband John was alone picking at some chips and onion dip and looking a little out of place. I introduced myself and told him I heard he owned a construction company. I asked him how business was, that sort of small talk. Then I asked him about my porch. He seemed happy to have someone to talk to, and this subject was in his sweet spot. He listened intently as I explained my structural dilemma.

He nodded at me with a look of certainty. "You need to relieve the weight up above with supports down to the ground. Then you'll be able to rip out the rotted parts below and rebuild from the ground up. That's the basic concept."

I understood the concept, but the how-to was impossible to imagine.

O'Hara grabbed a paper napkin and a felt writer from his pocket and sketched it out. To his mind, each step was elementary.

"Listen," I said, "the second-floor porch roof is twenty-some feet up. How do I construct the supports?"

O'Hara added some bracing details to his sketch and offered to drop off a bunch of old two-by-sixes that I could scab together to make the ground supports.

Wow, what a generous offer. "Thank you," I said, trying hard to visualize pulling off this feat. "But how do I get the ground supports to lift the porch roof? It's fucking heavy."

He smiled at my predicament and sent me off to the kitchen to get us a couple of beers. He clinked his bottle to mine. "Well, first I'd suggest stripping off those old slate shingles. They're just extra weight and they'll need to be replaced anyhow. Then when you get your long supports in place, put a board underneath so they won't sink into the ground. Then drive a heavy wooden stake into the ground to hold the support from slipping backwards." He grabbed the napkin and added these details. "Then with a big pry bar, you inch each support forward a little at a time. First one support, then the other. The porch roof will move. It'll take some muscle, but it'll move. When you get it back to where it used to be, drive a bigger stake behind each support. The whole upper part will stay in place while you rebuild below."

As worried as I was, I had to admit, some *big time* construction work was appealing. I felt my energy flow again. When I got home that night, I redrew John O'Hara's sketch and wrote down his instructions. Monday morning a couple of his guys dropped off the used lumber for the supports. My first task was the most dreaded: Stripping off the old slate shingles. I'd be working on a steep roof twenty-five feet up, and I hated heights.

More help was on the way. Dominic was a building maintenance guy from Orange City Hall and Ronnie gave me his number, saying that he'd offered to help out with the house. I gave Dominic a call and he showed up one Saturday morning with a forty-foot wood extension ladder. After a cup of coffee and a quick overview of the porch project, he helped me set up the heavy ladder and held it steady while I worked above, stripping off slate shingles with a square ended spade. Fortunately, with a long spade I could reach the top row of shingles. I didn't need to actually climb onto the steep roof that was twenty-plus feet off the ground. Reroofing would be a different story. Once we got the roof stripped and we wheelbarrowed all the old slates behind the garage, we made a work plan for the

Part III: Keep On Keepin' On (1975-76)

following Saturday. Dominic nodded as I pointed to my drawing of John O'Hara's plan. He asked some insightful questions and just as quickly answered them. He looked at me, his Italian smile radiating confidence.

"Yeah, we can do this. This week you build the stairs and next Saturday we'll attack the big stuff together."

Great, I thought, *but I need to let him know I can't pay him.*

I got us a couple of cold Reingholds and we sat on the rickety stairs. We talked a little about our boyhoods. I liked Dominic and felt comfortable with him. He grew up in a working-class Italian family. His grandparents, like a lot of Italians who migrated to Orange, came from Alberona, a beautiful hilltop village in Puglia, a region in Italy's southern boot.

It was time to set him straight. "Look Dominic, I can't afford to pay you."

"Oh, I know," he said. "I'm doing this for Ron. I'll be back next Saturday. Look, I had some trouble with a couple of old timers in City Hall. I thought I was gonna lose my job, so I went to Mayor Shain and he asked Ron to look into it. Your buddy took my problem real seriously. He got me moved to a better job. He's a *true* stand up guy. I'd do anything for him."

I'd never built a set of stairs. I'd watched carpenters on our rehabs in Englewood, so I understood the basics, but Dominic insisted I write down the building code requirement.

"The treads need to be at least eleven inches deep. The risers, no more than seven and a half inches. Don't mess that up. I saw a ball-busting inspector make a guy rip out a brand new set of stairs. Any questions?"

I wrote down the code dimensions. Yeah. "What should I build the support things out of?"

267

Dominic chuckled. "You mean the *stringers*? You'll need two-by-twelves."

Two days later, I took the old stairs apart with a crowbar and planned to rebuild my new ones to match. I checked the dimensions of the old stringer and the code must have changed. I'm glad I checked. I set up some saw horses, got my Skilsaw and a square, and started cutting new stringers. I remembered this old Swedish contractor in Englewood who primed the underside of the treads, so that's what I did. By the end of the day, three stringers were nailed in place and the primed treads were drying across the saw horses on the porch.

A week later, Dominic and I muscled the support beams into place, and with a pry bar we inched them forward. Just as John O'Hara predicted, they slowly heaved the roof back up—about a full four inches. *Amazing.*

Dom and I high-fived after we sledged some big stakes into the lawn to secure the base of each support, and then we nailed up some cross bracing.

Dominic helped me scope our next step. The broad lower porch still needed to be supported to take the weight off the porch deck and its rotted beams. We were feeling pretty confident as we nailed up some heavy lumber and repeated our earlier process with the lower porch roof. Two more supports on the second-floor porch would raise the sagging rear end of the roof back to where it was originally. Now that the entire structure was independently supported down to the ground, the rebuilding could begin.

It'd been a long day. We downed a couple of cold Reingholds and admired our handiwork.

Starting to Rebuild

Thankfully, Dominic came back for a few more Saturdays.

Part III: Keep On Keepin' On (1975-76)

In between, I ripped out more rotted lumber and realized I had to replace two crumbling brick piers. I ordered concrete blocks and cement and began my masonry apprenticeship. Then I began to rebuild the entire lower portion of the east side of the porch. It was slow going for this rank amateur. New beams and floor joists, framing the front and side knee walls down to the ground, new decking, cedar shingles. Dominic told me to keep his ladder. He'd let me know if he needed it and that I should call him when I was ready to sand the floors inside. That was his real specialty. I loved this guy.

The front entrance looked more like a construction site than an occupied house, when a city inspector drove by and stopped. He was about to write up his complaint and slap a violation sticker on the front door when my neighbor across the street accosted him.

"How can you even *think* about writing up a violation on this man who's fixing up this abandoned house? Look around East Orange. Do you think this is what should be getting your attention? You should give this man an award!"

The inspector got in his city car and drove away. A Violation Notice arrived in the mail a few days later.

I was pissed and called Ronnie. He joked about it—how "The city was cracking down on us fly-by-night, quick-buck artists who were milking good properties and bringing down property values." He said he'd take care of it. I think he just paid the twenty-five dollar fine. The next time a city car rolled up in front, I'd ripped out most of the porch deck and was laying up two new concrete block piers that would support a big beam, which would in turn support the new deck. I was sure he was going to stop and harangue me about how long this was all taking and how come I didn't have a permit for the work. When I caught his eye, he looked away and hit the gas.

People knew I was renovating my own house, so periodically I'd get a call to do some renovation work. Routine stuff—repair some stairs, build a new set, replace a porch railing, install a window, plaster repair and painting, masonry repair. Lots of small time stuff. I had a truck and tools and liked being a contractor. My consulting work in Englewood wouldn't last forever, so I seldom turned down a request. But I was terrible at estimating the time a job would take. I could price the materials right but I always underestimated the amount of time it would take and most people wanted a firm price. I began just adding 25% to the amount of hours I'd estimate and I'd still end up spending more time than that. I liked the work and it helped pay the bills.

CHAPTER 18

Ain't No Stoppin' Us Now

My Planning School applications arrived from Oregon, Washington, and nearby Rutgers. New Jersey's state university had a good urban planning program and I could attend part time. A few months later, I got acceptance letters from all three. By then I wasn't so ready to leave, so I enrolled in two courses at Rutgers. Maybe I'd become an urban planner.

I'd willed my way through the termite debacle, and though I still had so much to learn, I felt like I was now a legitimate old house renovator. My fears about the termites busting our budget were accurate, but Ronnie took it in stride when we each had to put in another thousand bucks. My thoughts of fleeing to the Pacific Northwest evaporated with each new porch beam and length of porch decking. I enrolled for two daytime courses at Rutgers in the fall.

I can't remember the course titles but the first couple of lectures were torture, so dry and uninteresting. My fellow students were all fresh out of college and seemed like kids. The new campus in Piscataway was sterile and unappealing. There was no ivory tower. I'd left the real world and entered a place where people lay over until they're forced to face their lives. I dropped out after two weeks. I still had no career path but I'd eliminated urban planner from the list. Maybe saving urban neighborhoods would be my thing. It checked a lot of important boxes. I'd somehow figure out how to make ends meet.

I was thankful for my communal family. I still wanted a wife and family but I couldn't shake the feeling that I didn't really know how to make a long-term commitment work. I certainly had a poor track record. I loved kids. I was made to be a parent so I considered adopting and contacted the state child adoption service. I got interviewed at length and a social worker paid a site visit to the house and I got approved. *Maybe this might happen,* I thought. Some months went by and I'd call periodically and be told that I was still on the list, just be patient. I finally got a call and was told they had a child for me. I wasn't prepared for what came next—a thirteen year old boy who'd spent the last few years in different foster homes. I hadn't thought this through. I wasn't ready for an adolescent or teenager who might already have a ton of emotional baggage. I'd have to wait until I figured out the bigger question—how to make a relationship work.

Mary's friend Judy, originally from West Milford, now lived nearby and came by the house a lot with her son, Tim, the same age as Michael. I liked Judy. Like Mary she was struggling as a single mom and was in school getting a degree, but the hardship didn't seem to get her down. She had a sassy attitude and a great sense of humor. I liked her a lot and we began spending a lot of time together.

Judy's son, Tim, was now a regular on my Monday after-school excursions with Michael and Simon. Judy was about to graduate and had her sights set on law school. We made a good pair. She was too busy for a husband and

I was too fearful to take the leap. We enjoyed each other and spent a lot of weekends together. Every summer we'd spend a week or two at a beautiful campground on Cape Cod. We were North Truro regulars for six bucks a night. We'd bike into Provincetown and hang out on the pier, eat clams, and drink beer with the locals and avoid the tourists. I had no idea how long our relationship might go on like that but for the time being, it worked nicely for both of us. Maybe it would last.

The Slippery Slope of Urban Decay

I was making headway on my major porch reconstruction, but I couldn't say the same for Main Street. The commercial district's decline and the pitifully slow progress with the Urban Renewal project was a showcase of East Orange's fall from grace. Each new vacant store was a slap in the face to city officials and a reminder that so far, they were losing the war of attrition. I kept an eye on its progress. It was my measure of whether East Orange's leadership could find a path forward for this challenged city. It was more than the vacant stores. Most of the buildings now looked tattered and forlorn.

The remaining businesses were hurt by the snail's progress of the property acquisition and development. Shop owners battled with an uncertain future as neighboring properties were vacated. Foot traffic was reduced, sales revenues were down. Fed up and furious, the businessmen organized the Brick Church Progressive Business Association to fight for their very survival. Their pain was a reflection of a larger ache felt by the entire city.

The East Orange Housing Authority, with its lack of visible progress, was an easy target. The federal Department of Housing and Urban Development weighed in with a formal letter of criticism stating that, "The Housing Authority has only acquired thirteen properties and relocated forty-five commercial and residential tenants over the past two years at an *administrative* cost of $640,000."

Yikes. Two-thirds of a million dollars! That's a crime, I thought. I pictured a bloated bureaucracy with political appointees gathered around the water cooler while the City went to hell. It was so depressing.

Mayor Hart was sick of being called to task about conditions on Main Street when he had no control over the Urban Renewal project. He repeatedly and publicly called for the Housing Authority to relinquish its authority. The City Council routinely passed resolutions asking the same, and Councilman Steve Thomas called for the creation of a nine-member autonomous authority to be in charge of redevelopment on behalf of the city. Commissioners of the new authority would come from the top offices of large corporations like Public Service Electric and Gas and New Jersey Bell. Some months later, Thomas called for abolishing the Housing Authority. None of this changed anything.

The Housing Authority was still looking for a developer and only found one interested party. Presented with only one option, the City Council agreed to grant a ninety-nine-year lease to a New York City developer. J. Dworman, Inc. was chosen to build Phase One, a fifteen-story building with two stories of retail, five stories of parking, and the remaining floors for offices. The businessmen's group called it "the salvation of East Orange," and they pressured elected officials to approve it, saying, "We're sure none of you want to be the cause of the City of East Orange going down the proverbial drain." Everyone was desperate to see something happen.

Reflections on Our Core Group

My bleak period was over and my move to the Oranges was turning out even better than I'd hoped. The biggest thing for me was that I'd found a group of political folks who I loved. Our cadre worked well together and it was work that really mattered to people's daily lives. It mattered to this place that was suffering because the private sector had lost interest and some were ripping it off. Our tenant movement was growing. The OTA, the EOTA and the *Shelterforce* Collective had all grown and matured in a short time. Tenant leaders throughout Essex joined the Essex Housing Coalition. I reveled in our day to day progress, attracting leaders, empowering them, winning battles and working together collectively. And now we were beginning to connect with organizers across the country. It was exhilarating.

John's Housing Unit was a model of activist lawyering. John had worked his will on the Legal Services director and gotten his wish. Remarkably, he'd been able to finagle a separate location away from the rest of Essex Legal Services, in a suite of offices just a block up Main Street from East Orange City Hall. It was an extraordinary coup. I knew he always feared it could be snatched away when complaints about his radical practice of law reached the director. The Housing Unit would lose its autonomy and he'd be on a short leash. John was aware that he and his attorneys would be taking risks and pissing off some judges and other people of influence. For the time being the Housing Unit was the most valuable resource that the Essex County tenants movement had. I saw it like John did: If lawyers were going to effectively represent the poor then they'd support tenants' ability to organize and fight for good housing. After all, this was a *War* on Poverty we were waging. John was thrilled and energized but he wasn't satisfied. He needed to figure out how the tenant movement could become something bigger and contend for power more broadly.

Phyllis was leading a rapidly growing organization with lots of building leaders. They came out whenever Phyllis called. The EOTA Board of Directors had evolved into an impressive racially mixed group who were feeling the collective power that came from organizing in their buildings and operating in unison as an organization. Their leader was still teaching five days a week in Newark but she was consumed with building the EOTA. The fight to get the mayor and the City Council to put a strong limit on annual rent increases and to force landlords to make repairs and maintain their buildings was a full-time job. Multitasking hadn't come into vogue, but Phyllis was already doing it. The Council had passed another weak rent ordinance that continued to award landlords when an apartment came empty and, across the board, building maintenance was declining.

Phyllis had found her role, but she always felt like she was losing ground despite all her efforts. The passionate tenant leader operated day to day on a gut level. Injustice, uncaring landlords, unsupportive politicians—she took all that as a personal affront and responded quickly and publicly. She trusted her mentors, John and Ronnie, to guide her.

Joan now had a following of tenant leaders who kept her busy day and night. The ardent law school grad had found her ideal job and she was a perfect fit for John's group. She quickly developed her legal skills and believed in the Housing Unit manifesto. She adopted John's view of the role of the poverty lawyer and Sam Farrington's exacting use of the law to represent her clients. She was passionate about representing and empowering them at the same time. Joan found what she was looking for when she joined us. She valued the collective nature of our work. Her sarcastic sense of humor was irresistible. We were lucky to have her.

Ronnie supported all his progeny—me and John, Phyllis and Joan. He was always available and tremendously supportive. Ronnie was the empowerer. His understanding of politics, media and legal justice was so advanced. We all benefited from his support and we were hungry for what he had to offer. It was a perfect match. We'd never have accomplished half as much without him. We valued his friendship as he did ours. A lot of people wanted Ronnie's attention. I think he felt like he could really be himself with us and he valued that above all else.

It was serendipity how our group grew and solidified. Woody Widrow enrolled in the VISTA program right after graduating from SUNY Binghamton and was assigned to the Newark Tenant Organization. It was coincidence that he and five other VISTAs moved into a big house on Chestnut Street. We may not have met him otherwise. His college newspaper background and tenant work made him a perfect fit for the Collective.

Mary Tasker needed a place to land when she left her husband. From the Liz McAlister retreat she knew our group and she brought her two boys to an apartment in East Orange, a block away from our house on Chestnut. When she arrived she immediately volunteered with EOTA.

I was rebuilding that fine old house and learning the renovation trade.

Life at 31 Chestnut was pretty harmonious. In the

winter we'd argue about the heat. Someone, usually Phyllis, would push the thermostat up a notch when I wasn't looking. The boiler in the basement would struggle to deliver steam to its legion of radiators stationed on three floors. Heating oil wasn't cheap so when I walked by the thermostat, I'd lower the temp. Mary was the glue. She and the boys brought warmth and a sense of family to the big house. Renovation was messy but everyone took a little bit of chaos in stride.

I had enough paid work, about two days a week between the Redevelopment Agency and occasional handyman work for someone else. That was enough to cover living expenses. I was banking sweat equity that I'd cash in when we sold the house.

I had time for working with Phyllis and the EOTA, and with *Shelterforce* we had constant deadlines. I was busy evenings and weekends but none of it felt like "work." It all demanded time and attention to detail and it wasn't all fun but I seldom felt burdened by it. I had found my groove. The renovator, the organizer, the neighborhood rehabilitater, the publisher.

Just when I was feeling self satisfied, John was there to remind all of us that we weren't exactly bringing the capitalist state to its knees. I didn't spend a lot of time thinking about replacing runaway capitalism. I was content with building a movement to save urban housing and neighborhoods. Building a better community right here, becoming a clearinghouse for others across the country. That was an all-consuming job. John, in his spare time, was trying to figure out how our tenant work connected to the big struggle. Where lots of everyday people fought to determine their own futures and counter the growing threat of corporate takeover of our democracy.

Part III: Keep On Keepin' On (1975-76)

Your flag decal won't get you into heaven anymore

The U.S. Bicentennial was a constant over-the-top display of flag waving and exuberant patriotism. I wasn't in the mood after all that had happened in the last decade, especially the "love it or leave it" bumper stickers that were still on cars all around. I turned up my radio whenever my favorite folk singer, John Prine sang, *"Your flag decal won't get you, into heaven anymore."*

For some reason, Judy's son, Tim, was excited about the Bicentennial. He knew I wasn't and he loved to razz me whenever we saw a big flag display, "Hey, look, Pat. Bicentennial." Tim made me laugh at myself. I eventually got over my knee jerk reaction to false patriotism and started flying the flag on all the holidays. It was then that I reacted to those bumper stickers with even more passion. *The right wing doesn't own the flag. If anyone does, we do. People who believe in the promise of this nation own it. People who believe in tolerance and free speech and equality.*

I wanted to be like Martin Luther King and Michael Harrington. They were constant critics of what was wrong with America, and they were great patriots. They were my role models.

Lenox Avenue Rent Strike

Jackie Cooke's building was my constant reminder of the importance of our work. The plight of those twelve households was testimony to the inadequacy of the legal system to enforce decent living conditions. By August of 1976, the property file on 66-68 Lenox in the Property Maintenance Department was over an inch thick. Occasionally, the landlord was fined after a court hearing. I doubt he ever bothered to show up. For him, the fines had become just a cost of doing business. Meanwhile, the property taxes hadn't been paid for the last three quarters. The tenants were weary from living without basic repairs, maintenance, and services. They wanted someone to force Mr. Landlord to live up to his end of the bargain. They all paid their rent; he should damn well give them decent living conditions. Jackie called up the Housing Unit. She spoke with Sam Farrington and made an appointment to meet at his office on Main Street.

Jackie thought he could become their secret weapon. Jackie needed a secret weapon. Maybe Sam was it.

Sam Farrington gave Jackie and the other tenants confidence. This man in the wrinkled white shirt and a tie from last century was all business; no chit chat. Sam was smart and he knew the law inside and out. He carefully recorded on his yellow legal pad everything they told him. He asked about dates and other specifics.

Then he told Jackie, "Write this down, Mrs. Cooke. Send the landlord a letter, *Return Receipt Requested*, that way we'll have proof he got the letter. You'll have to go to the Post Office. Enclose a list of all the repairs that are needed, even though you've called him a dozen times. When rent comes due on the first of the month, you'll all deposit your rent in a bank account that Mrs. Cooke will set up. This is what's called a rent strike. By the way, you'll need to get more tenants involved."

They liked the idea. A rent strike. But then Sam added, "You're all going to get Eviction Notices." As the shocked tenants tried to digest that thought, he said, "But that's how it works. When we get to court, we have to tell the judge that you have the rent, that we're holding it until all the repairs are made. That's how you'll get your day in court." The tenants were still thinking about the possibility of eviction while Sam explained that this was all based on a legal concept called the Warranty of Habitability and, "Believe it or not, tenants didn't always have this right. That in exchange for rent you're entitled to a liveable apartment. It's relatively new."

Jackie and the couple of tenants who took off work to meet with Sam walked away a little fearful to be sure, but feeling proud, excited even. They were standing up for themselves and they had their own attorney who would represent them.

One of the women questioned, "He's kind of a cold fish, don't you think?"

Jackie shut her down. "John Atlas says he's the smartest lawyer in the whole of Legal Services. And he's agreed to represent *us*. I like him a lot."

That settled it. They had the smartest lawyer. They were going to get their no-good landlord into court, in front of a judge, and they were going to get justice. They were practically jubilant. This group of neighbors, who had limited housing choices, were thrown together by pure chance, they set out down a road together to pull their families' living conditions together. And Jackie was their leader. They were practically looking forward to their eviction notices.

Jackie had to convince a bunch more tenants to withhold rent and be willing to go to court. That evening she knocked on doors, made phone calls, and invited folks down to her apartment. She didn't get everybody, but Sam had told her she needed to get at least half the building to withhold rent. With all her door knocking, cajoling, arm twisting she convinced exactly half to join in.

Their day in court with Sam Farrington at his lawyerly best proved that the law was indeed on their side. They didn't have to pay rent if they weren't getting services and the judge read the riot act to the landlord. Eviction requests denied.

But now what? Sadly, for the next couple of months, it was more of the same.

In the meantime, Phyllis asked Jackie to join the EOTA Board of Directors, to attend monthly board meetings and help decide policy and strategies. Jackie's experience made her a valuable board member, and she was flattered to be asked. Since I was the one with the accounting degree, Phyllis drafted me as Board Treasurer. I enjoyed the board meetings, mostly strategy sessions about tenant issues coming before the City Council. Phyllis organized the agenda and led the assembled mixture of building association presidents—Marvin Schoenberg, Jackie, Tony Zuzuro, Marilyn Hughes, Lorraine Lavender, and a few other Black women whose names I've now forgotten. Battle plans were made. We needed to pack the City Council chambers. Write a press release. Call certain council members. Lobby them. Follow up with the press. Council meetings were pandemonium, standing-room only.

Phyllis was aware that self management was wearing Jackie down, so she asked me to see if I could help with some repair issues. I visited the building a couple of times. It was full of life, kids playing out front and in back, tenants who all knew each other. There was so much life in this crummy building. I had no idea what advice I'd give this besieged tenant leader. Her apartment was nice and cozy. I supposed the others were too, but the building was falling apart. It needed a ton of work.

One time in her kitchen over coffee, Jackie unloaded her burden. It was becoming too much, way too much. She told me how the boiler broke down regularly, or the oil would run out. Or the roof would leak again and someone's plaster ceiling below would buckle and need patching. She was sick of being treated by some tenants as the only person who could possibly make a phone call and by others as if she was the landlord. She was just plain tired. She'd taken way too much time off of work and she felt unappreciated. She laughed and joked even while she told her tale of woe, but I could see that she was burned out. One thing was clear: Without Jackie, this building would already be vacant and abandoned.

In fact some buildings in East Orange were vacant and abandoned, and plenty more were being held together by the sheer determination of tenant leaders armed with legal advice and sometimes a Legal Services lawyer. This was no recipe for how to maintain a stable community. For the time being all we had was people power, the Housing Unit, and political leadership that desperately wanted to solve the problem but couldn't. I chose to cast off any "worst-case scenario" thoughts about where the city was headed and believed that more people power would be the solution.

There were other buildings with mostly White tenants that were better, but conditions were eroding there too. They tended to be newer buildings in more stable neighborhoods, but services were declining. Tenant associations sprouted in those buildings and they joined EOTA too. Like their Black counterparts they all paid their dues, three dollars a year, to join EOTA. Phyllis would send one dollar to NJTO the statewide organization. We were an interracial movement of the poor and middle class, united at least for now, fighting together for better housing. To me that was thrilling. I chose not to think about the so called market forces that were more powerful than all of us.

Renovation Continues

Over at 31 Chestnut, I was the landlord and all my "tenants" liked me but there were still a lot of repairs to be made. I just kept moving people around as I renovated a room at a time. They joked about being "displaced" but everyone just rolled with it.

When it came time to do something about the eighty year old scuffed, scratched, and stained floors in the living room and dining room, I'd have to move all the furniture and close those rooms off. I wasn't looking forward to the mess and disruption. I'd sanded floors once before and it was a lot harder than it looked. Dominic had said that floor sanding was his speciality so I gave him a call. He told me where to rent a sander and what grit the paper should be and that we'd need an edge sander to get close to the baseboards and into the corners. Early one Saturday morning, we got started in the dining room.

We wore masks because fine sawdust was everywhere. Dominic manned the big belt sander and he taught me how to use the edge sander. It was heavy and required a steady hand. He made fun of me as I either bit into the floor too deep or ran the edger into the toe moldings and beat them up. My beat up floors were white oak and the responded beautifully to Dominic's expert touch. By one o'clock, the floor looked like it had just been laid. It was stunning. I couldn't believe the difference. Just an eighth inch below the surface was virgin oak.

We took a break for lunch and I still had time to give the room a first coat of satin-finish urethane. The dull sheen made the white oak light up.

The next weekend, Dominic was back and we did the living room. The fresh new floors brightened the house. Some used oriental rugs gave it a timeless Victorian feeling.

Part III: Keep On Keepin' On (1975-76)

A carpet store on Broadway in Newark sold the used rugs. Typically, there was a bare spot in one or two places but otherwise the rugs were in decent shape and the colors were still vibrant. I never paid more than forty bucks for a big rug. They warmed up the foyer, the parlor, the living room, and dining room.

Kat Brennan continued to do art work for *Shelterforce* and started hanging out at the house more often. I loved it when she was there and made sure to link my schedule to hers. She'd show up with all her drawing materials in a tote bag and set up at the big drafting table in the parlor. I'd stop what I was doing and we'd kill an hour or so with a fresh pot of coffee at the sun-filled dining room table, mostly just getting to know each other. We'd each get some work done and then break for lunch together and usually a glass or two of wine at the end of the workday before she headed back to New York and her husband Bill.

One day I was painting the living room walls. Kat wandered in to survey the work and said, "You know what you need? Have you ever seen pictures of Victorian homes with a band of stenciled designs just below the ceiling?" I hadn't, but I could kind of picture it. "I'm going to look in some of my design books," she said.

It wasn't long before she showed up with a stencil she had cut and we headed off to the paint store. We spent the rest of the day on two-step ladders, taping and retaping the stencil, carefully brushing the light brown Victorian design up high on the off-white walls. We loved working close like that, making sure the spacing was exact and being careful with our brush work. It managed to take a whole day. The repeating design was stunning. Next to each other on the couch, we laid back, clinked our wine glasses and admired our handiwork. Her design addition heightened the original Victorian feel. It was a brilliant touch that I never would have thought of. I was always drawn to creative and artsy females—Scubi, Claudia, Bobbi, Joanne Young, Mady, who I met in Boulder and taught me to juggle. Kat was a great influence on me. I was in her thrall.

With the decorative stenciling and some built-in shelving next to the fireplace where I put my stereo and albums, the living room looked magnificent, natural cedar backed shelves, refinished oak floors, my couch made of old doors doors from that New York brownstone, a floor lamp with a holophane shade, the oriental rug. It looked like an 1890s re-creation. I was so pleased with the outcome that I hadn't thought about an obvious repercussion.

Ronnie hadn't been by in a couple weeks, so when he did come, I was anxious to show him the finished living room.

"It's magnificent, like a trip back in time," he said. "Like you're planning to live here forever."

Uh oh. I sensed what might be coming next.

He hesitated. "What about our plan to sell the house and recoup our investment?" Ronnie had over four thousand dollars invested in the house. We both did. I didn't have a good answer. I was too preoccupied with restoring the house and creating a home for our group to think about his side of it. He continued, "I may need to get my money out. Joanne and I are looking to buy a house." He was piecing together a living with his private practice and some part-time work. I knew that money was tight.

He made it clear that he wasn't concerned about any profit, not at this point at least. But I couldn't face selling the house. I'd created a secure little world around 31 Chestnut. How could I let that fall apart? But Ronnie was my closest friend, more like family to me than anyone in the world. I couldn't face it if our relationship soured, especially as a result of my taking advantage of his friendship and generosity. I needed a financial solution so I could keep my dream alive and save my relationship with my best friend.

"Look. I understand. Totally. You've been so generous," I said. "And I'll find a way so you can get your money out soon."

I had no fucking idea where I'd get four or five thousand dollars. A second mortgage on the house was the answer but my income was sporadic and mostly off the books. I hadn't filed a tax return in a couple years. I couldn't ask my parents. Even if they had the dough. Fuck! I needed to pay Ronnie and I needed more dough to finish the house. I could feel things unraveling.

I called my brother. I called Terry Carolan. They were as broke as I was. I finally went to Beneficial Finance where I'd borrowed a thousand bucks for my motorcycle a few years earlier. I could get a second mortgage but I'd be paying through the nose and the term was only five years so the monthly payments were really heavy. *Maybe I need to go back to working full time, I thought. Cut back on all my unpaid movement work. Get the house finished working every weekend.* My nicely curated life was pulling apart at the seams.

Without us even talking about it, Ronnie announced one day that he'd arranged a second mortgage with Mountain Ridge State Bank.

"Joel's the attorney for the bank and he's one of the owners. He made it happen." I was dumbstruck. Ronnie smiled broadly. "*You* applied for $7500, enough for me to cash out what I've put in and some more to fund the rest of the renovation. It's all approved. You just need to make an appointment, go in, and sign the loan papers."

I shook my head in disbelief and let out a big smile. "You're absolutely amazing. I'm so relieved. I felt so bad I put you in that position."

Ronnie had bailed me out again. "Don't worry," he said, giving me a big smile. "We're good. We always will be."

• • •

Kat continued to come out from Chelsea in her tan AMC Pacer. It was a truly original car, a compact made by the struggling American Motors Corporation. Its rounded body, wide stance, and expanse of glass that improved driver visibility had a Jetson's look all its own when the other Detroit automakers were mostly producing big gas guzzlers. American cars were changing quickly, with options for smaller, more fuel efficient models, but the Pacer's looks were in a class by itself. Like a vision of a future to come, as if future models might leave the ground, landing on heliports of mile-high buildings. She called it her AMC "Racer."

She'd come for a long day and started pitching in on the renovation. She had a lot of practical skills. With the radio playing we'd patch plaster or paint walls and trim together. We'd stop for lunch out on the porch or on my big couch. We'd talk politics or about her art. Or my dream of building a house in the country. We were getting off on each other. There was a lot left unsaid between us. There was chemistry and some electricity too.

When the workday was over, we'd break out some wine. She'd bring art books from the library and we'd sit on the couch or out on the big front porch. She'd page through

Part III: Keep On Keepin' On (1975-76)

the books filling me with insights like how Art Nouveau decoration was rooted in nature. She'd help cook and stay for dinner and we'd talk through the evening. She introduced me to the aesthetic of the period when the house was built, the Victorian era. She turned me on to Victorian era artists like Aubrey Beardsley.

She'd head back late to Chelsea where she lived with her husband and a couple of friends. Kat worked freelance but not every day, doing advertising layout, a job she was quite good at but that she viewed as drudgery. The money wasn't bad, as I remember.

Kat yearned to be a political artist. She admired the WPA artists of the Depression and learned silk screening. By the time I met her, she'd done only a couple of posters, the best one being a profile portrait of the shrewd leader of the Oglala Sioux tribe, Chief American Horse. It was a photo silkscreen created from a photograph and rendered in three rich colors on poster paper the color of soft barley. She'd created a print run of two hundred and it adorned the walls of many of our friends. She brought me one, rolled in a fat cardboard tube, along with pieces to a bright orange metal section frame.

"You need to buy some glass and I'll put together the frame for you."

It looms above me as I write this.

Kat told me she was part of a women's art collective in New York, and one day she said, "What do you think about a silk screened poster to raise some money for *Shelterforce*? I've been thinking about a design."

I loved the idea. She hadn't yet finalized the imagery but we agreed that it needed to support the slogan, *Housing for People Not for Profit*.

Organizers Came to See Us

Shelterforce struck a chord with folks all around the country. People were organizing in urban areas everywhere. One of our first contacts in California was Mike Rawson, who was a tenant organizer with the Santa Barbara Tenants Union. The whole state of California was the latest hot bed of tenant organizing. People wrote to us and sent along local news clippings, copies of their newsletters. Messages with, "Keep up the good work! Enclosed is my check for a subscription." Occasionally, a letter recounted a personal tale of woe and would always end with asking where they could find an apartment they could afford. Others wanted to know what our secret was and ask how they could get rent control in their city or town. The Collective shared the responsibility of writing back, asking people to keep in touch, and often requesting them to send more info so we could report on their work in an upcoming issue. We were slowly building a national network.

Occasionally, some folks came to visit. They'd stay over, sleep in the living room or the parlor. One group from near Boston stayed a couple days. Eric Sherzer brought two of his close comrades from the working-class city of Brockton, just twenty miles south of Boston. During the day they'd go around and meet with tenant leaders, tenant lawyers, get to know our community, and in the evenings we'd stay up late talking shop—tenant organizing, politics, and the ins and outs of building a grassroots movement. The Brockton folks were heavily involved in tenant organizing and were on the verge of bringing together tenants in three thousand apartments in greater Boston owned by a landlord who developed the housing with government subsidy but was not maintaining the apartments well. The group was called the Tenants First

Coalition. It was a heady experience to have these people travel to meet with us.

The three intrepid organizers told us about The Brockton Project. They published a community newspaper and ran a food co-op, a daycare center, and a nonprofit community development corporation. They organized around environmental issues. Some in the core group ran for office. In study groups, the small band of committed socialists read and discussed political theory and studied liberation movements. They called this calculated and intentional campaign, The Brockton Project. Except for the sheer breadth of initiatives it was like our group that morphed from PACT into the Thursday Night Group and now the *Shelterforce* Collective.

Eric from Brockton ended up in New Jersey and got a job in a chemical plant and became active with the union. When we reconnected with him five years later, he was an official with the Oil, Chemical and Atomic Workers Union. When I saw him recently, he looked back on his time in Brockton and laughed when he said, "We were determined to create socialism in one town in two years."

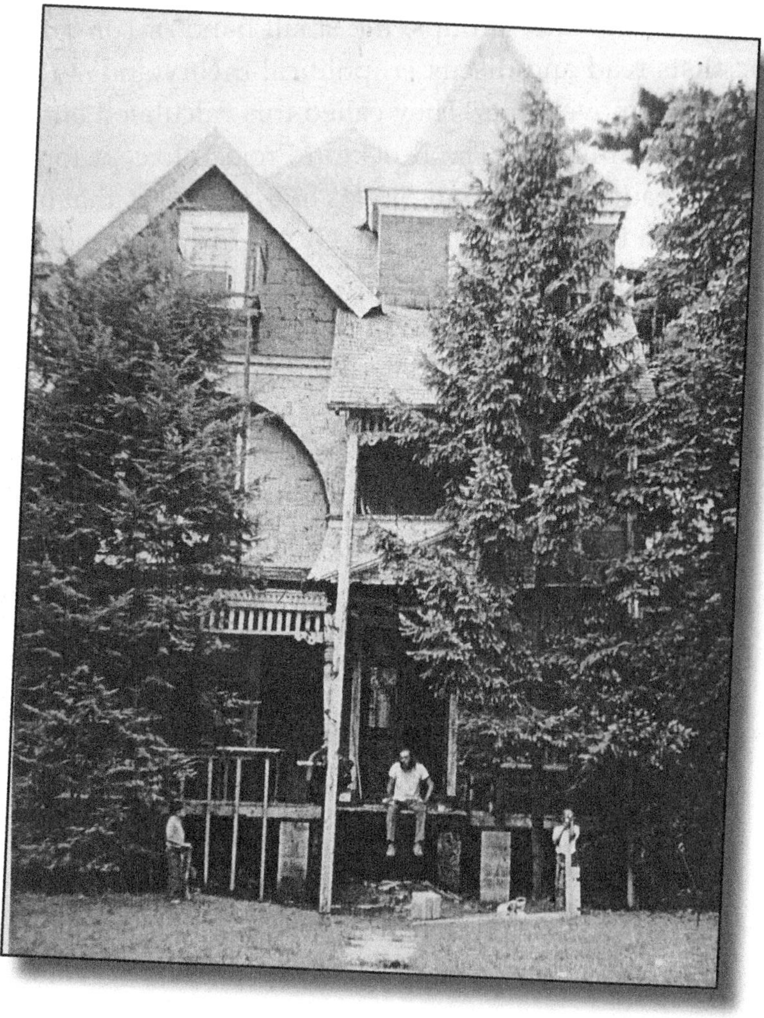

PART IV

Stayin' Alive, Stayin' Alive

1977

Spacey Richard's art on my panel truck.

I was rooting for Carter when he was sworn in but he faced a stubborn economy with unemployment at 7%. Inflation had budged, but it still hung there at 6.5%. Meanwhile, rising competition from Europe and Japan made economic expansion tougher. Poverty increased and consumer prices rose. The only good news was for homeowners, who saw their home values increase.

Americans were weary from the gritty realism of the Vietnam War, all the social commentary following Watergate, and the economic recession. Then *Star Wars* broke onto movie screens, with interstellar adventure and groundbreaking special effects and an optimistic vision of the future. A weary public enjoyed the respite.

Then came Disco, a dance and music culture that had its origins in Black and Latino clubs and in the gay culture. The craze suddenly captured a remarkably diverse audience, and, most surprisingly, among White working-class kids. Disco really went mainstream with the hit movie *Saturday Night Fever*, starring John Travolta with music by the Bee Gees. What was surprising to me was that Travolta's character, Tony, a working-class Italian kid, achieved upward mobility through an art form that originated in marginalized communities.

I kind of liked President Carter but he was a bit of an enigma. He'd campaigned as a moderate on civil rights but in office he supported affirmative action and he posthumously awarded Martin Luther King the Medal of Freedom. The Southern governor and peanut farmer wore his Baptist religion on his sleeve, and when he was running for president he enjoyed the support of religious fundamentalists. But once in office he ordered the IRS to revoke the tax-exempt status of religious schools that racially discriminated. This pissed off those same people and fed into the growth of the Religious Right.

At that same time, Big Business took the gloves off and flexed its political muscle. The Business Roundtable fought an AFL-CIO Bill that would make it easier for workers to form unions. Then the business lobby killed off a Consumer Protection Agency, an idea championed by Ralph Nader. But nothing highlights the ideological struggle of that time between government intervention and free-market principles like the *Humphrey-Hawkins Full Employment Act*. The far-reaching bill would mobilize the power of the federal government to beat back unemployment and inflation. Because the Act set precise percentages for government action on unemployment and would create public jobs; it went to the heart of the *free market vs. government* debate. In the end the bill was significantly weakened. Specific targets for unemployment and a public jobs program were eliminated.

The disruption of oil flow from the Middle East prompted President Carter to create the Department of Energy to move the country toward energy independence and to promote renewable sources of energy and energy conservation. The president hosted E. F. Schumacher, the author of *Small Is Beautiful*, at the White House.

As the decade's weak economy wore on, cities of the Northeast and Midwest continued their downward slide. Good manufacturing jobs were departing for the non-union South. Suburban malls proliferated and downtown retailers were lured to the suburbs. Meanwhile, the federal government was steadily reducing its commitment to cities. Elected officials and civic leaders fought to hold on to their cities, but they had few tools to combat the economic shrinkage.

CHAPTER 19

No Easy Answers

Shelterforce's following was growing. Early on we connected with tenant organizers and advocates in New York and Boston, and then Philly and DC. But now we were in regular touch with groups in the Midwest, Southwest, and California. Groups sent us letters, news clippings, newsletters, and typed articles they hoped we would print. We loved filling our pages with their local victories and sharing the learning.

Woody decided to hit the road, see America, and visit the tenant groups we were writing about. He contacted folks in thirteen cities and arranged meetings and tours and free lodging. He caught a ride to Chicago and then traveled by train to a dozen more cities—Milwaukee, Madison, Minneapolis, St. Paul, Cleveland, Columbus, Cincinnati, Louisville, Indianapolis, Topeka, Dallas, and Fort Worth.

Everywhere, tenant organizing was tough work. Just like us in EOTA or Newark Tenants Organization, where Woody had worked, they were all overwhelmed with individual tenant complaints but determined to devote their precious time to organizing and building strong organizations. They all collected dues and believed in members supporting their organizations and making the decisions, but there was never enough dues revenue to support paid staff. None of them had the protections in state law that we had in New Jersey or that New York tenants had. Those battles were ahead of them and none of them had rent control. We'd been blessed with a liberal Supreme Court that upheld our first municipal rent ordinance.

Woody was playing a bigger role on the editorial side of the newspaper and his trip enhanced that. His personal contact with groups of organizers broadened our role as the national clearinghouse for tenant organizers and housing advocates.

Whitey's Call to Action

I hadn't heard anything about Whitey Goodfriend for at least a year, and then he called John with a big plan. The once formidable labor leader and political organizer was something of a local legend among the folks in PACT. He'd been a fearsome labor organizer in his day, but events had passed Whitey by. The Communist Party of which he'd been a member was now known for the atrocities of Stalin rather than the powerful role they played in strengthening the union movement and supporting civil rights. People in PACT still admired him but he'd become bossy, judgmental, and dogmatic.

John called me, told me about his call from Whitey, and he wanted me to come to a meeting. John switched to a convincing imitation of Whitey's gravely staccato voice.

"John, I want you to organize a meeting. Invitation only. I'm going to lay out a plan for how we can shape the direction of the Democratic Presidential Primary. Invite only your most dedicated organizers, no more than twelve of 'em. Let me know when you got it organized."

Part IV: *Stayin' Alive, Stayin' Alive (1977)*

I laughed at John's Whitey impression. *How could I pass up a meeting like this?*

The meeting was in Phyllis's third-floor apartment. Whitey began by telling us that our group of twelve could move the national debate to the left and dramatically influence the direction of the Democratic Presidential Primary. He made it clear that this meeting was for us to hear his plan and sign on if we wanted, but that "no questions would be allowed," only suggestions about how to move the strategy ahead. No one visibly rolled their eyes but we all exchanged knowing glances. *That's Whitey, alright.*

Whitey laid out in short order a scenario with little detail. A small group, no bigger than the twelve of us, would elevate an agenda of yet-to-be-decided progressive issues, and these policy positions would be so widely popular that any candidates seeking the Democratic nomination would sign on and adopt the policies as their own platform. Those policies would then naturally form the Democratic Platform adopted at the August nominating convention.

When Whitey finished his brief description of a bare-bones strategy, someone asked what we'd all been wondering, "What makes you think that just the twelve of us could pull this off?"

Whitey began to explain that all successful political movements were launched by groups even smaller than this, and then he caught himself and stopped mid-sentence. Red-faced and angry he stared at the questioner. "I said no questions! This is what's wrong with people like you. You want to discuss things to death. I don't know why I'm wasting my time here."

The meeting descended into complaints like, "You can't expect us to sign on to a major project but not be allowed to ask any questions," and accusations from Whitey that we were "all talk and no action." The reality was that all of us were invited because we were organizing people and building grassroots organizations. We were fighting for and winning real change in peoples' lives. Just the types of things that Whitey cared about. But that night Whitey saw us as "arm chair revolutionaries."

We never heard another word about the presidential primary strategy. Whitey moved in with a girlfriend in New York. I seldom saw him after the Big Meeting. He'd given up recruiting people who couldn't resist asking questions. For John and people who had been mentored by Whitey, it was painful to watch his decline. He had become a relic of the Old Left, but his ideas about coalition-building and pragmatic radicalism remained relevant.

Speaking of asking questions, we didn't discuss really big questions that the armchair revolutionaries debated all the time. That is, "What will replace this form of capitalism that we have now?" We made fun of the doctrinaire Leftists who split hairs over whether a version of Maoism or Trotskyism would awaken the proletariat to cast off their chains of capitalist oppression. We rolled our eyes when friends who belonged to the CPUSA hawked *The Daily Worker*, the Communist Party newspaper, door to door in blue collar apartment complexes.

We seldom talked about what kind of *-ism* we adhered to. We definitely weren't Communists and we certainly weren't Capitalists. So we must be Socialists. That's how I saw it. If someone had asked and they probably did, I'd say, "The group of us? We're all Socialists."

A funny recollection comes to mind. I was sitting back in the dentist chair, my mouth, wide open. Fred Jaker, our beloved local Commie dentist, had just stuffed cotton

Part IV: *Stayin' Alive, Stayin' Alive* (1977)

alongside my gums when he stood back and looked at me with his most serious dentist demeanor.

"You and John Atlas, you know, you're just Social Democrats. You know that, right? You guys aren't trying to overthrow the capitalist system. You believe it can be reformed so that it's fair and equal to everyone." He finished his tirade and leaned back as if waiting for my response. I was ready to have the discussion but with all that cotton, I couldn't get any words out. Fred smiled and grabbed his drill and went to work in my mouth.

John did think about all these things. His appetite for political analysis was insatiable. The serious debates on the Left drew him in. He was as passionate about figuring out the political path to a just society as I was about renovating old houses. On political thought, John was my mentor.

John's passion was to find a way that organizing like ours could connect to a broader more powerful movement for change. John said, "We're not just looking to be a successful consumer movement, making sure that people get value for the rent they pay. We're building something bigger, a broad based movement that can challenge the prerogatives of capitalism. We're challenging the whole system of housing for profit. It's important that we keep that in our sights." But that was a tall order. I couldn't imagine how tenants who were getting screwed by their landlord might come to think of themselves as part of something that was challenging the power of capitalism. How would ordinary folks become *politicized*?

John was a follower of Michael Harrington, a democratic socialist. In 1973, Harrington founded DSOC (*dee-sock*), the Democratic Socialists Organizing Committee. John introduced me to Harrington's political writings. I had devoured Harrington's seminal work, *The Other America*, in grad school. It provided me with a class-inflected way of understanding this country in the late-sixties. The book was credited for putting the idea for the War on Poverty in President Kennedy's head.

Harrington was a practical Socialist who now proclaimed his politics as "the left wing of the possible." He knew that if Socialists were going to be relevant to the bread and butter concerns of ordinary working people, they had to work with people who shared those goals. For Harrington, that meant building strong coalitions with the labor movement, the civil rights movement, church groups, campus groups, and the liberal wing of the Democratic Party.

But Harrington was ready to criticize Democrats, as he did when Carter's administration drifted rightward. This might have been what convinced John that we devote an issue of *Shelterforce* to critiquing Carter's urban policy. I was so happy to see Carter defeat Ford that I kind of missed the point that Carter was such a moderate. John called Carter a conservative. Carter was the first president who governed as a "neoliberal."

Harrington understood that neoliberalism was a retrenchment from the decades-long New Deal consensus respected by labor, business, and government, and which built the world's largest middle class. Big Business was now influencing politicians and demanding a bigger share of the economic pie.

John was adopting Harrington's political analysis and practice and I was adopting John's, however slowly. That was the course of my political development, secondhand from John mixed with my day-to-day work in East Orange. Unlike John, I was deeply distrustful of politicians of all stripes. I hated Republicans and didn't care for corrupt big-city Democrats. I had a special distrust of liberals, but that was softening because so many of them were ardent Peaceniks. But for the most part, liberals wouldn't support rent control because it didn't affect them. They were all homeowners. I thought they had too little empathy for the poor or the working class.

John tried out his latest Harrington stance on me. "We should have one foot inside the Democratic Party and our other foot planted firmly in grassroots organizations. That's where we need to be."

I pushed back. The reality was that we had few relationships with Democratic officials. I was hard-pressed to think of more than a few. Elected officials like Byron Baer were the scarce exception.

But John pressed on. "During elections, people are focused on candidates, on issues. We're already endorsing pro-tenant candidates, publishing our endorsements, helping them get elected. We have a rightful place in the Party, but just one foot in."

I didn't outright disagree, but I thought it was a stretch to talk about our rightful place in the Democratic Party. I said I thought we were like labor unions. An organized constituency that the Democratic Party needs to recognize.

John latched onto that statement. "Walter Reuther (the president of the United Auto Workers union), he's a Democrat. He doesn't stand outside the Party looking in. He's very much a part of the Party machinery. You're from Detroit. You must know about Reuther."

Of course I knew about Walter Reuther. In our family he was a hero. My dad told me all about the Reuther brothers who lived not far from us on Detroit's northwest side. When I was about seven, my dad drove me down to see the Ford Rouge Plant, the world's largest auto assembly plant, where Dad had started on the assembly line at age twenty. He stopped along Miller Road and pointed to the pedestrian bridge crossing from the vast parking lot to the plant gate and told me the story of the Battle of the Miller Road Overpass. Striking workers were met by Pinkertons hired by Henry Ford.

"A lot of union men got their heads busted by Ford's goons that day," he told me.

John was testing out a concept, thinking out loud.

A concept without a reality, I thought. So I pushed back. "So what do we do? Go to meetings of the Democratic Party? Listen to Boss Lerner tell us how it's gonna be?"

He laughed. "Sure, what's wrong with that?" His humor always disarmed me. He continued, "I see the problems with what I'm saying but I just think that needs to be a goal for us—one foot in. We don't give up anything by doing that."

I wasn't so sure about that last point.

It would be another couple years before an unusual set of conditions presented a real opportunity to claim our seat at the Democrat's table, and John would push Phyllis and me to do it. And it would pay off in spades.

CHAPTER 20

Blow Up Your TV

Another group of people our age had a completely different response to the dominant culture they'd come to despise. Drop out. Don't participate in the competitive consumerist rat race. Move to the country. Live simply and in harmony with the land. Share, barter, cooperate. Love your neighbor. The aim of the movement was to find ways to live simply but well, outside the economic institutions that dominate the U.S. and its consumerist culture. People talked about being self-sustaining from the land they worked—feeding themselves, selling at farmers markets, and bartering with other farmers. Plenty of them were creating intentional communities, with utopian visions organized around cooperative or socialist ideals, with gender equality. Some were collectivist models that challenged the idea of the nuclear family. They all farmed organically, respecting the long-term life of the soil to regenerate and enhance its inherent fertility mostly by returning to some traditional pre-corporate, pre-fertilizer farming methods.

Going back to the land wasn't for me. I thought it was kind of a cop out. People should stay and fight, not drop out. But I understood the appeal.

Sam and Earth Mother Marsha had been talking for more

than a year about jumping off of the consumerist treadmill and establishing a farming commune. The would-be farmers from West Orange heard that in rural West Virginia outside of small towns, there was a lot of cheap land. Land was cheap because the underground rights to natural gas had been sold off, leaving little demand for the land itself. They went down and looked around. People told them, "Land is cheap up in them *hollers.*" On their second or third exploratory trip they purchased nearly thirty acres, up a hollow in Calhoun County, isolated a few miles away from a little town. The hilly, rocky place was not known for its farming. It was coal and gas country.

It always seemed like a far-fetched dream, but it wasn't long before Sam and Marsha sold their house and they set off with their young boys, David and Michael, to make their stand. Marsha had boundless energy for building a community of willing disciples. Back to the Land types often had little farming or carpentry experience, but Sam had a ton of skills needed for building and I figured he'd get the hang of farming. Our intrepid friends from West Orange shared this ardent belief that life in Middle America was corrupt and hollow and they wanted to get off the consumer treadmill. They had a utopian dream and they planned to live it. They called their homestead *The Mudd Farm.*

I'd miss Sam and Marsha. Their idea sounded borderline impossible and a bit naive, but I admired their guts.

Sam came back up to the Oranges periodically to earn some money painting houses, and he kept trying to lure me down, to stay for awhile, pitch in and help establish the place. I was sure he could use a pair of capable hands and I promised I would, but the demands of fixing up Chestnut Street, keeping our organizing going, publishing

Shelterforce, and juggling my consulting and outside renovation work to pay the bills always came first. Though occasionally, I took off to meet up with my college buddy Terry Carolan.

Terry was unique among my old college friends. Most of us grew up in cities, but Terry spent his youth in Decorah, a small northern Iowa town near the Mississippi River. Terry was as big as a bear and sometimes called himself a bohunk, which I always assumed meant like, big farm boy. This bohunk was a gentle, kind, and thoughtful bear.

Terry was a year or two behind me at U-D and we knew each other from the Saint Francis Club. We hung out a lot one summer when he came east and lived in Greenwich Village. Then Scubi and I caught up with him a year later in San Francisco on our coast-to-coast adventure. In San Francisco, Terry met artsy Ann Kotcher, also from U-D. They were an adventurous pair and bought a beat-up old house in the Bernal Heights neighborhood and started renovating. Mid-renovation, they set off on a cross-country trip and showed up at my apartment on West 89th in their 1946 GMC "wagon." It was a unique vehicle—long with running boards that swept from the front fenders to the rear. It looked like a World War II general's command car with five gallon tanks stashed in the front fenders. Perfect fit for Terry and Ann.

Terry's mom got cancer and they moved to Decorah to care for her. Terry's designer and builder's mind was bursting with ideas, so he bought a vacant lot near his family home and began building a house that, in the ice cold winters of northern Iowa, would rely solely on the sun for its heat and hot water. I was blown away. This was long before solar was considered practical.

Their time in Iowa got extended, and then Terry's mom

passed away. When a four-story brick factory in downtown Decorah came up for sale, my friend, the innovative builder, couldn't resist buying it with a vision to renovate it into an artist's workspaces. It was a big project, but the local bank knew Terry and his family. A big loan was easy to come by. My friend and role model was breaking new ground—building with solar and renovating, making affordable space for local artisans. I was impressed. My thirteen-room house renovation seemed miniscule. Well, soon high inflation was wreaking economic havoc even in Decorah, and the friendly small town bank began jacking up the interest. When he couldn't keep up the payments on his adjustable construction loans, they stopped the flow of funds. He and Ann were living in Terry's family home, but it had been mortgaged as collateral for the new projects. That's when the stressed out innovator found an ancient hospital building in Highlandville, a blip on the map fifteen miles from Decorah, available for five thousand dollars. With the bohunk's real estate portfolio overextended, they put the new acquisition in Ann's name, and it's good that they did. It wasn't long before deeds to his two uncompleted projects and his family's house were no longer in his name. I was sick when I heard the news.

It was a stressful time but Terry's spirit was indomitable. He managed to always look forward and joked about having earned his PhD in real estate development in Decorah. Their second daughter Mary Beth was a few months old when he proposed a mini college reunion in Highlandville. Lois LaFond and I met up there, and among other things we participated in the first firing of the ceramic kiln that Terry and Ann built. Then we all traveled back to Leamington, Canada, on Lake Erie in their vintage one-ton cargo truck.

Part IV: *Stayin' Alive, Stayin' Alive* (1977)

One time when I called Terry, he asked me if I wanted to ride shotgun from Iowa on a West Coast adventure. We drove an old beer truck full of Iowa "antiques" he'd bought up at farm sales, and he planned to peddle them at flea markets. I was plenty busy, but any adventure with Terry was irresistible.

Soon enough Terry had another renovation project in San Francisco and I went out to help him. This one was a small gem, one of few that survived the 1906 earthquake. Terry added a big addition to the back with a rear wall of oversized windows that he salvaged when a downtown hotel was being renovated. The centerpiece of the addition was a family-sized hot tub, the first I'd ever seen.

I did eventually get down to the Mudd Farm. Marsha and one of the young guys who'd joined the Mudd family were in town, and they stayed with me. I laughed when he introduced himself as Mark Mudd. Everyone who joined the family assumed the family surname. Marsha Ferber was now Marsha Mudd. Mark and his brother David were from New Jersey, and at ages sixteen and eighteen were on their way to California in their '49 Dodge pickup when they connected with the Mudds in Calhoun County. They saw no reason to search for Nirvana on the West Coast when Sam and Marsha's utopia was recruiting family members. Marsha convinced me to drive down with them. I could catch a ride with someone coming back the following week. Off I went in Mark's '49 Dodge pickup to the Mudd Farm.

At the farm, a main house and an A-frame cabin were already occupied. A spacious outhouse with gas heat was operational. I knew that Sam was pretty ingenious, but what he'd accomplished with this group of hippies was just short of remarkable. The natural gas, which also heated the house and powered the restaurant-size stove and the king-size hot water heater, was free. Sam had tapped into the piping that came up out of the ground and passed across their property. Sam and Marsha owned the land, but investors owned the natural gas rights. Marsha and Sam reasoned that since the gas came from their land and was being extracted and sold by capitalists, there was nothing wrong with imposing a slight "tax" on that production. They were not the only folks in the county who were heating and cooking with free gas.

I stashed my backpack and my sleeping bag in the dormitory, a single room that spread across the entire second floor. A dozen of us, maybe more, slept there. The outhouse was a hike from the second floor dormitory, so there was a three-gallon jar to piss in. The piss jar was emptied every morning. The sounds of sex, mostly hushed, drifted and hung there in the open dormitory, but by midnight the only sounds were snoring, an occasional fart, and the crickets outside. Or the tinkle of someone using the piss jar.

It was late spring and the family was expanding their garden, doubling its size. After communal breakfast, I joined the work crew. Mid-morning I came in looking for a cup of coffee, and Marsha showed me the big pot of tea steeping on the stove.

"It's peyote tea, not very strong but it's just the right thing to mellow your gardening experience. So help yourself. We leave it simmering all day."

I ladled out a cupful and stopped back a few more times during the day. Marsha was right. Just the thing to enhance a day in the garden, a soothing mind-expanding dose that didn't get in the way of getting things done.

The Mudd Farm accepted anyone who came along and

was willing to work and share. They attracted a varied group of vagabonds, utopians, and young people looking to find themselves. Free love was definitely part of the ethos and Marsha was its greatest advocate and practitioner.

After a week I caught a ride back to New Jersey. The other passenger sprawled in the back was a hippie artist who Mary remembers as Spacey Richard. We arrived at Chestnut Street and I was grabbing my bags and thanking our driver, when Richard came alive.

"Hey, Pat, I don't have anywhere to stay; can I crash with you guys for just a couple days? Your place is enormous. I can just crash in a corner, out of the way somewhere. You won't even know I'm there."

I wanted to think of some reason we couldn't accommodate him for a few days, but I thought of Marsha and her earth mother spirit. How could I tell her, "Richard asked to stay a couple nights and I turned him away." So I said, "Sure, Richard, but just a couple days. Grab your stuff, come on in."

Spacey Richard

None of us can remember exactly how long Richard was with us but it wasn't a couple of days. His art appears in two issues of *Shelterforce*, which came out three months apart. Richard had no money but helped out around the house with cleaning and cooking, always washing dishes. He was good enough company at our big dinner table. Michael and Simon got a kick out of him and the off-the-wall things he said. We became fond of him, like a cherished weird uncle.

Richard wanted to pay his way and he was an amazing artist, so artwork for *Shelterforce* made sense. Woody would sit with Richard and explain what the articles were about and Richard would create the accompanying artwork, beautifully executed but always with a rather obtuse connection to the content. One cover for the newspaper, in the spirit of nineteenth-century political cartoons, was an elaborate tableau with characters from Alice in Wonderland. The issue was about the complexity of federal housing subsidies. We wondered if it might brand us as less than serious, but the artwork was first rate, and cover art is hard to come by, so we went with it.

Richard was grateful that I'd given him a place to stay and he told me often. Then one day he asked if he could paint a scene, kind of a *logo* he said, on the side of my panel truck. I took the opportunity to tell him it was time to start looking seriously for another place.

He agreed and said, "I've been thinking about this beautiful truck of yours and I've got a dynamite idea." But when I asked him to explain it, I got weary trying to understand what he meant. We walked out and looked at the truck.

I loved my '63 Dodge D-100 panel truck. I bought it for eight hundred dollars off a Puerto Rican guy who'd added some salvaged white aluminum side windows, and inside was a nice faux leather front seat from a high end sedan. The back was one big open space with a blue shag carpet and strung with little blue bangles around the inside. Not quite my look, but I admired his artistry. I eventually replaced the windows with a couple of black slider windows, but I immediately replaced the blue shag with a piece of old oriental carpet. I was tempted to keep the bangles. I added a radio/tape deck and some decent speakers. It was my daily driver and the perfect truck for renovation work. A year later, I bought a 1950 Dodge pickup from an Iowa farmer on another visit to Terry Carolan.

Part IV: *Stayin' Alive, Stayin' Alive* (1977)

I showed Richard the space on the side of the truck behind the side window where his "logo" could go but explained that I used my truck a lot, so he'd have to work around my schedule. I realized that Richard had just extended his stay with us until the art project was done, so I told him again that he needed to start looking. But I knew that one day I'd have to basically evict him.

That weekend the side of my truck had an image of an open mouth with rounded red lips, no teeth. I scratched my head and laughed at myself for granting Spacey Richard this commission. Over the next couple weeks, the *logo* started to take shape. Sparkling white teeth were added behind the luscious lips. The paint work was beautiful. It was becoming impossible to imagine painting over it. Richard acknowledged that he was having kind of a creative block, having trouble with the concept of the open mouth and what it was *saying*. He was clearly considering the idea that a lot of people were opening their mouths and what they were saying was, what? Not worth listening to? Deliberately misleading? Vacuous? He didn't know how to articulate the concept brewing inside. I told Richard that I loved the quality of the brushwork and looked forward to how it would evolve. I smiled as I walked into the house. My truck was being adorned by a guy who was operating on another plane. I enjoyed this artistic process and anxiously awaited his next step.

But the next step, a week or so later, still left the mouth just a gaping opening. Richard had added alternating rays of yellow and reddish orange emanating outward from the lips to a squared off border, the limits I'd described to him. The *concept* remained elusive. I drove around with a painting of a wide open empty mouth on a background of bright rays. It was the seventies, and there were a lot of vans with strange stuff painted on them—surfing scenes, peace love flower power, the great outdoors, Black Power images, even factory-produced vans with abstract designs. Mine wasn't that unusual.

Soon, the mouth was completed. Through the frame of the red lips and the white teeth, the open sky was visible. White clouds against a blue background. What it *meant*, I had no idea but I loved it. A strange bit of hippie art that seemed to say something, but what it was saying, no one knows. A piece of abstraction that the viewer can attach their own meaning to. A perfect Spacey Richard production.

Another artist approached me about a project. Freda Jaffe was a talented photographer who I think taught at Independence High, and she wondered if I had room in my big house for a darkroom. The basement was the only possibility, so Freda and I took a look. Her photographer's eyes lit up when she saw the small room with no windows in the corner of the basement. Its rows of wooden shelves I imagined had at one time held jars of canned peaches or tomatoes every winter.

I told Freda she could outfit it for her darkroom. Near that corner of the basement were the laundry tubs and a bathroom so she'd have everything she needed. The basement had a separate entrance and I gave her a key. Unlike Spacey Richard, Freda came and went, sometimes late at night, and we weren't even aware she was down there in her basement darkroom.

CHAPTER 21

A New Role and Big Dreams

It was late August, and a small fan barely cooled my sweaty body. Over the sound of my transistor radio, I thought I heard the phone ring, so I hustled down off the step ladder, ran my dusty hands on my jeans, and picked up the receiver. I was happy for a break from pulling down a sagging portion of ceiling and breathing in all that plaster dust. It was Gretchen MacBryde, a woman I didn't know all that well, but this was a fortuitous call.

Gretchen and her boyfriend Steve Krinsky had migrated up from Austin, Texas, and now they both worked at an alternative high school called Independence High in Newark. Steve taught history and Gretchen was head of the Arts Department. She got right to the point.

"I know this is incredibly short notice but Stash, our carpentry teacher, had a family emergency and went back home to Milwaukee. He should be back next semester. Is there any chance you'd consider coming to work for us, part-time, starting right after Labor Day? It's half a day, two days a week. You'll have complete freedom to teach whatever kind of carpentry you want. You're the only person we could think of to call. Sara said she thought you might say yes. Please say yes."

I told Gretchen to take a deep breath and that the idea did sound interesting. I had plenty of experience working with teens, and Independence had a cool reputation—progressive, *experimental*, I guess. I'd be working in Gretchen's four-person department. My good friend Sara Mastellone, who'd recommended me, was a mainstay on the small faculty. I thought it best to tell Gretchen that I wasn't exactly a skilled woodworker. What I didn't tell her was that I was only midway through my own on-the-job training, but it was clear that whatever skills I had would be just fine. I said I was definitely interested but needed a day to figure out if I could make it work with my cluttered schedule.

The chance to work with teens again thrilled me. I got back to my ceiling repair, my head brimming with thoughts of what my curriculum would be. I'd keep it simple. Simply getting students involved in making things would be my goal. In the end, they'd have used tools and made something. They'd have confidence going forward that they could do it again. Then I thought, *Why not have them each design their own project? Let every student make something different.* Suddenly I was fired up.

My work schedule was definitely cluttered but pretty fluid. Consulting work at the Redevelopment Agency had slowed to about a dozen hours a week so I was also taking on small renovation jobs to make ends meet. I didn't have anything bigger than handyman-type stuff in my pipeline. Keeping the books and financial reporting for EOTA was flexible. I could do that in the evenings. My house renovation hours were completely flexible, though I needed to keep up a steady pace. I had my *Shelterforce* commitment and helping Phyllis with EOTA organizing tasks. I called Gretchen back that evening and told her I was in. We planned to meet at the school the next day.

That night I worried that I'd acted too impulsively. My schedule was already too full for me to lock down two half days every week. I obviously couldn't call Gretchen and tell her I'd changed my mind. I'd just have to figure it out. I really was excited about trying my hand at teaching. I convinced myself it would be fun. And, anyhow, it was probably only one semester.

I liked Gretchen immediately. She was open and engaging, with the scattered enthusiasm typical of artists. She showed me the shop. It was adequate, not that well equipped, but spacious enough and most importantly, it had a table saw. I imagined a drafting table where I'd teach students to design and draw up their projects. I asked Gretchen if there was money in the budget for a used draftsman's table.

"We'll find some," she said.

She left me alone in the humble shop, in reality just a corner of this turn-of-the-century factory. I wandered the empty school and the reality of what these intrepid educators were up against began to sink in. It didn't feel like any school I'd known, but its makeshift charm is what captured me. All the mismatched second hand chairs, tables, desks. The way the place was laid out and all the posters, artwork, and signs on the walls communicated both the gritty hand-to-mouth financial existence they faced, but also there was an irresistible energy of discovery and optimism. I was glad I'd be a part of it.

A day or two later, I went to Atlas Used Furniture on McCarter highway, and they had a few old oak drafting tables. They were things of beauty. I picked out one with a sixty-inch top, the one with the least marred drafting surface, and bought it for seventy-five bucks. While I was at it, I bought a seventy-two-inch one for myself. After I dropped off the drafting table at the school, I started having doubts.

My woodworking skills are really minimal, and what if I end up with a tough group of kids in my class? How'm I gonna handle that? I've never done this before.

In my enthusiasm, I'd lost sight of the practical challenges that high school teachers face, especially working with kids who hadn't succeeded before. I was now somewhat dreading my first day of teaching. I'd been too impulsive. A familiar habit. *Too late now*, I said to myself. *You'll manage.*

Independence High was housed in a converted venetian blind factory deep in the Ironbound across from Independence Park, and it got its start in 1970. It was a pleasant surprise when I learned that this humble alternative to the public schools that had failed a lot of kids, was the work of former members of SDS, *Students for a Democratic Society*, the radical left-wing student movement that began in the early sixties. The school founders were Steve Block and Carol Glassman, political radicals who began as inner city organizers, and Norm Fruchter, a filmmaker.

The radicals-turned-educators had come to Newark with SDS founder, Tom Hayden, to organize in Newark's all-Black Central Ward. They were all alumni of the SDS revolutionary student movement who tried their hands at changing the real world by building a bottom-up movement to abolish poverty and extend democratic participation. The dedicated radicals had been part of NCUP, the Newark Community Union Project that organized mostly around poor housing conditions. They organized folks against greedy, uncaring landlords and lax code enforcement by City Hall.

That inner city work and the simple beauty of this

alternative high school in a working-class, White neighborhood clashed with my view of SDS. I'd seen news photos of privileged Ivy League students occupying the university president's office, feet up on his desk, smoking his cigars. I viewed them the same way my parents did. Spoiled kids vandalizing their privileged university while their parents picked up the tab for tuition.

But when I read the 1962 SDS founding manifesto, *The Port Huron Statement*, drafted by Hayden when I was still a clueless high school junior, I was pleasantly surprised. The radical manifesto wasn't the hyperactive screed against capitalism that I expected. It didn't mince words about the growth of corporate influence and power but, surprisingly, the radical proclamation read a lot like our PACT bagel brunch discussions. The document centered on two essential themes: participatory democracy and living authentically. It discussed personal freedom, social responsibility, and meaningful participation in a democratic community. Reading it, I wished I'd been there at the birth of this generation of activism.

By 1967, with the rebellion and police riot in Newark's Black ghetto, and the rise of Black nationalism and Black self-determination, Hayden's group of young, White organizers wasn't that welcome in the Black ghetto. That's when the Independence High School founders decamped to the Ironbound, a lower middle-class, White neighborhood south of Newark's downtown. Ironbound is a teeming peninsula of dense rowhouses, small businesses, and industry surrounded by railroad tracks. Ironbound was its proper name, but most locals would say they lived *down neck*.

Meanwhile, most of SDS focused almost exclusively on ending the war in Vietnam. Hayden left Newark to join

The Mobe, the National Mobilization Committee to End the War in Vietnam, and later played a major role in the protests outside the 1968 Democratic National Convention in Chicago.

Block and Glassman and a couple of other SDS-ers created the Ironbound Youth Project, a storefront youth center. Then they launched the Ironbound Day Care Center and Early Childhood Program. The youth center attracted a bunch of teens who'd dropped out of high school. The dropouts wanted an alternative to the local high school that hadn't worked for them, or frankly didn't want them.

Steve Block found a building and recruited Norm to work with him and Glassman. Norm's research found that the regulatory requirements for running a high school were surprisingly minimal.

The three organizers-turned-faculty/administrators imagined a school that was democratic and student-centered. They had pretty clear ideas about how to make high school relevant and appealing to working-class teens who'd been alienated by the regular school curriculum and environment. Soon, they had about eighty students enrolled.

I was more than a little anxious on my first day. I gathered a T-square, some rulers, a big pad of newsprint, a roll of masking tape, and a handful of pencils and left the house early. I grabbed a coffee and a glazed donut at Leo's Dinette in Harrison before crossing the Jackson Street bridge over the Passaic River into Ironbound. I arrived plenty early, so I nervously ran a broom around the shop, waiting for my students. Four boys and a girl appeared. I still remember three of them well. Maria was Puerto Rican. Derrick was Black and always had a joke. Danny was White with medium-length long hair and wore a flat Irish

Part IV: *Stayin' Alive, Stayin' Alive* (1977)

cap like mine. I welcomed them, showed them the shop, then we gathered around the drafting table.

I explained slowly, looking at each of them, "This semester you're going to design and build a project out of wood. A project of your own choosing." I let that sink in.

"*Anything* we want?" asked Maria.

I nodded. "The only limitation is that all five projects have to fit in the shop, with room for the six of us to work."

They looked at each other and back at me.

"But first," I said, "let's take a walk. I want to introduce you to the lumber yard. It'll help you imagine your project."

The lumberyard was only three blocks away. IHS had a house account and I'd been in earlier, the previous week. We walked in and I introduced them and told the the guy at the counter they were students from the high school a couple blocks away. I told him that they were going to be designing and building their own woodworking projects and that they were here to take a look at materials.

Looking at them, he clapped his hands together. "You came to the right place. Feel free to look around at all the different types of wood we have. Let me know if you need any help."

We wandered around the stacks of wood, and I pulled boards of different sizes from the stacks, explaining the difference between pine and hardwoods. I pulled a sheet of plywood partway out and invited them to rub their hands over the tight, grained surface. "This is plain plywood but with a thin coating of birch called a veneer. If you give this a light sanding and then some varnish, this makes beautiful furniture." I didn't stop rubbing so neither did they. I could see that they'd entered another universe. I'd captured their interest in the first hour. We didn't stay long. I just wanted to open their minds before they started their design process.

Back in the shop, we sat around and brainstormed ideas—a bookshelf for the living room, a dog house, a jewelry box for Mom. Maria wanted to build a desk for herself. When I explained that it was a big project for one semester, she wouldn't be deterred. It didn't have to be real big, she said, but at home she wanted her own desk.

On the drafting table was my big sketch pad, a T-square, triangles, pencils, and erasers. Soon, the walls held project sketches, a student name in the lower right corner of each. At the beginning of the second week we were back at the lumberyard selecting our wood.

The table saw was my one worry. I had one in my garage and used it a lot. I knew how dangerous that saw could be. I told the kids a story from my teenage summer when Bill Turner and I worked in a makeshift factory with migrant workers. We came in one morning and there was blood on the table saw that we all rotated on and off of. A Mexican on the night shift had lost a finger. I remembered that morning. Vividly. We were sixteen. When Bill wheeled his '49 Olds into the parking lot, the Mexicans were all huddled around, everyone speaking at once. Our high school Spanish couldn't pick up what was fueling their edgy mood. They were looking or nodding toward the old onion barn that was our "factory." Bill and I walked in. Yellow tape cordoned off the area around the saw. There it was. Blood on the blade and on the cutting table. My four-hour shifts on that saw were never the same. I could picture the blood. I now had righteous fear of that speeding blade.

The students cringed at my gruesome example of what could happen if they were careless or inattentive. I made it clear: They were *never* allowed to use it without my direct supervision. Stash, the regular carpentry teacher, had rigged a short two-headed connector plug that was needed to power the saw. I kept it in the locked tool cabinet.

Early on, Steve Krinsky, a social studies teacher, stopped in the shop and introduced himself. When Steve joined the faculty, two years earlier he lived off of a VISTA stipend for the first year. Steve was a political activist with a passion for communications, film, and music. He'd left Austin, a counter-culture oasis in Texas full of weirdos and a legendary music scene, and abandoned his graduate studies just short of writing his dissertation to follow Gretchen north to New Jersey. IHS fit him well. His blue collar roots in Revere, Massachusetts, where his father had been a textile cutter and active with the garment workers union gave him a connection to the students who were mostly from working-class families. He was a dedicated teacher and the students loved him, with his Boston accent and his Red Sox cap over his thick, long hair. He taught a brand of American history that told America's story from the bottom up, focusing on the lives and the plight of the hard-working people who built this country.

One afternoon, I attended an all-school assembly and was shocked to see that on policy matters, everyone had a vote, faculty and students. At that meeting, the first issue brought up was that a teacher's purse was missing from her classroom. The adult leaders of the meeting said they wouldn't conduct anymore business or adjourn the meeting until the guilty party came forward. This was a group of young and pretty inexperienced educators. I was really curious to see how this would be resolved *democratically*.

Everyone—adults and teens, engaged in the discussion. Questions flew from every corner. What classroom was it?

When? After what class? What was in the purse? Did anyone look in the waste baskets or the dumpster outside? Students implored whoever did it to fess up. Finally after more than an hour, a couple of students proposed that if the teachers would leave it up to the students and adjourn the meeting, they would find out who did it or at least get the purse back. All that discussion hadn't gotten them any closer, so all agreed to adjourn.

My students told me the following week that the crime had been solved; the purse got returned and though the perpetrator's name was not revealed, the administrator was told that the thief had been dealt with.

What an interesting way to run a school, I thought.

I loved my two mornings in the shop each week. I arrived early with my coffee and I'd eyeball their projects, thinking about how I'd guide them through the next steps. They'd greet me and immediately go to their works-in-progress, always ready to work. I'd jump from student to student, sometimes bringing them together to brainstorm an issue on someone's project. Seeing their own designs materialize was the magic that fired them up. I loved these five students. Our shop period was extra long but it always flew by. Occasionally, they'd ask me to stay through lunch so they could keep working. I couldn't say no to that. And didn't want to.

For two days a week I was part of a grand experiment. Dedicated educators creating a place for young people left behind by the system. And those left-behind students were learning, thriving even. They were graduating. I adored IHS for that and I loved being a small part of such a thoughtful community that was bucking the system and succeeding.

With the Christmas break and end of the semester

approaching, I reminded my would-be furniture makers they needed to leave time for sanding and a couple coats of varnish or paint. I offered one optional Saturday in the shop and had nearly full attendance. In the end, they all finished in time for Christmas.

Maria told me she had no way to get her desk home, so we loaded it into my truck. Her older brother was clearly knocked out by his sister's beautiful work. Maria looked at me shaking her head, and then back at the brother.

"I told you how nice it was. Didn't I? You didn't believe me."

I wished them a Merry Christmas and headed home across the Jackson Street bridge to East Orange, thinking how grateful I was for Gretchen's call. She got me back into working with teens again. Sadly, Stash was due back right after the holiday break.

Community Organizations

Meanwhile, our work in East Orange and Orange was heating up with more complaints about shitty landlords. More buildings were in a downward spiral and more tenants were suffering—no heat, no hot water, plumbing leaks and sagging plaster ceilings, broken door locks, roaches, and rats. It was mostly the smaller buildings with twelve to sixteen units. There were so many of them and they were particularly vulnerable. Buildings like Jackie Cooke's that were bought by inexperienced, undercapitalized landlords and quick buck artists.

I wished we had an organization like the group I'd visited in Baltimore. But it was hard to imagine a nonprofit with the capital and the expertise to step in and take over all these beat up, mid-sized apartment buildings. In cities everywhere, citizens were taking matters of neighborhood decline into their own hands by creating neighborhood-based nonprofits, but the odds against having a real impact in the face of disinvestment was a long shot, and there was no such organization in Orange or East Orange. The lone exception was the Fourth Ward Urban Renewal group that had built Kuzuri Kijiji, and they weren't poised to go beyond that one large housing development.

In Newark, there were a handful of noble efforts aimed at stabilizing neighborhoods, and it's worth noting that there was little or no funding and support from government or philanthropy during the late sixties and the seventies. In Newark's Central Ward, a Catholic priest, Father William Linder, founded the New Community Corporation to provide affordable housing, childcare, and later job skills training. Father Linder was the most successful of the Newark groups. Early on he tapped into federal subsidies and built hundreds of subsidized apartments.

In Newark's Italian section, Steve Adubato's North Ward Educational and Cultural Center was a study in combining social services with bare knuckle electoral politics. Adubato amassed local political support to build a program of job training, child care, senior citizen housing, and recreation programs.

Nearby in the Puerto Rican section of the North Ward, a capable organizer, Ramon Rivera, gathered together a group of families in 1972 and founded La Casa de Don Pedro. Rivera was a leader of the Young Lords, a militant Puerto Rican organization modeled after the Black Panthers. The program he created to serve the Spanish-speaking community included the same range of social services as Adubato's Center. Both these organizations were a bulwark in the face of suburban exodus and urban decline.

Ironbound Community Corporation (ICC), was

Part IV: *Stayin' Alive, Stayin' Alive* (1977)

founded in 1969. Their first program, the Ironbound Children's Center, served a handful of children and families, but in 1973 the *Ironbound Community School* opened. ICC's mission was to engage and empower individuals, families, and groups in realizing their aspirations and, together, working to create a just, vibrant, and sustainable community.

On the other side of town where the West and Central Wards meet, Becky Doggett and Ed Andrade launched Tri-Cities Citizens Union for Progress. In addition to a People's Center, they began acquiring and rehabbing three family homes into a limited equity cooperative.

These groups all had a couple things in common. They were meeting essential needs of neighborhood residents and they created a sense of community and cohesion in places that were in various stages of change. The other thing they had in common was that there was so little philanthropic and government support for their efforts. It would be another decade before community development corporations would be fully recognized as an alternative to the private sector for housing and economic development, and meager funding would become available.

Meanwhile, the need was great for some alternative to the private sector. For the most part, housing in the U.S. was all in the hands of the private sector, unlike in Europe where social housing was a substantial sector, especially under Social Democrats.

An education effort closely tied to all this urban neighborhood work was the innovative urban studies Public Policy Program at St. Peter's College in Jersey City. The program was unique because it aimed at preparing adult neighborhood leaders who didn't have a college education and getting them qualified for the new jobs opening up in urban housing, social services, and education.

The creators were an impressive and dedicated group that included Norm Fruchter, who I knew from Independence High; Michelle Cahill, a young instructor in Urban Studies who grew up in Jersey City; Jeff Arimstead, formally trained in urban planning and economics with a background in housing organizing; Wilbur Haddock, a long-time statewide labor activist and community leader from Newark; and Elayne Archer, who taught writing skills in an integrated way with the urban studies curriculum. Norm and Michele first created a Certificate in Community Organizing program that quickly grew into an Associate's Degree in Public Policy. They were now on the verge of becoming a full fledged Bachelor's degree program in Public Policy.

I was never involved with the program, but I admired the creators' passion for urban education and their inventive approaches. Classes met for full days on Saturdays, and in three-week-long intensive, retreat-like experiences. Student assignments included readings, films, and writing. These were adult students with work experience and roles in their community. The average student age was thirty-six. After completing the program, graduates took on leadership roles in city government, housing, community development, education, and some ran for elected office. I saw the program as an essential building block for taking control of declining cities with residents in power instead of outside experts.

Build a Statewide Coalition

Our tenant-organizing work was an important part of the bigger fight for economic and social justice and building a society that worked for everyone. But uniting our

Part IV: *Stayin' Alive, Stayin' Alive* (1977)

work with organizations with other issues and constituencies and bringing together a coalition that could win legislation on a broad range of pocketbook concerns, that flatly eluded us. There were plenty of concept papers in the left-wing press about how that could and should happen. Bringing it to life, that was John's current dream. Occasionally, we'd get called to a meeting by someone with a strategy to bust out of our isolation and build a winning coalition of the liberal left. We were all ears.

It was mid-November 1977 when John invited me to a lunch meeting deep in Ironbound at Tony DaCaneca's—a favorite, out-of-the-way Portuguese restaurant that Ironbound natives say is the best food and one of the most affordable of Ironbound's massive offering of Spanish and Portuguese food. The fact that it's so difficult to find separates the tourists from the insiders. Norm Fruchter, who I knew from Independence High, was the one who called the meeting. The former SDS radical-turned-education-reformer was a massively talented and creative guy. When John and I managed to find our way to the restaurant, Norm and Steve Block and Jeff Armistead were already there. I was thrilled to be among this accomplished group of teachers, school administrators, and urban education advocates.

Norm didn't waste time and dove into one of John's favorite topics, a strategy to launch a statewide left-liberal progressive coalition that could contend for power within the Democratic Party and drive debate and policies to the left. Like us, these guys were looking for a way to unite the various constituencies that would support a program and a set of policies that could be implemented and move politics in a more progressive direction.

Norm laid out the process. Recruit a broad range of

organizations, organizations that want to move the political process—from labor unions, senior citizen organizations, community, and neighborhood groups, ecology and environmental groups—the whole gamut. Create a research center to help develop and refine pragmatic but progressive policies. Recruit and help elect candidates.

The coalition would be launched behind the candidacy of a unifying left-liberal candidate in the 1981 New Jersey gubernatorial Democratic Primary. We'd make it clear that this candidate and the organization would only run as a Democrat not as a third party alternative in November. Admittedly, there was little chance of winning the first time out. The plan was that the organization would outlive that particular election and continue to build its base around a progressive platform and more candidates.

Somebody said we should recruit Becky Doggett, that a Black woman candidate with Becky's organizing and political background would be perfect. To me the idea of using a gubernatorial campaign with a candidate like Becky was brilliant. It seemed well thought out, realistic, and doable. It spoke to my aversion to involvement in the Democratic Party because we'd be involved on our own terms. The three politicos talked of building an organization rooted in the grassroots and membership-based constituencies who felt unrepresented in politics. I could imagine being a part of this inside/outside relationship to traditional party politics.

We agreed to meet again. Norm said he'd write up and circulate the discussion from this one. I loved meeting with these smart and serious guys who thought so practically about political power. This was another world to me: Meeting at a legendary eatery tucked away in a deep corner of an ethnic neighborhood. Mapping out big plans to live our political dreams and contend for power on a bigger stage. It was heady stuff. I wanted more of it. And the food was delicious.

Nothing came of that first lunch meeting that so captivated me. Norm dutifully sent us all a carefully worded strategy document, but I doubt that anyone talked to Becky. We never had a second meeting. I was captivated by the grand plan. It needed to happen, but I'd leave that to John.

A Citizen Labor Movement Is Born

Norm wasn't the only person pursuing this idea. John knew about other states that were forming multi-issue coalitions. I was of two minds; I was drawn by the thought of a broader political organization that could really contend for power, especially now when all the progressive efforts seemed so small and local. On the other hand, Orange and East Orange needed a powerful citizens organization if these two great communities hoped to resist the economic forces that threatened their stability. John didn't share my passion for that work, building locally. He recognized it as important, essential even, but he was focused on the big picture. He made the point that the chances of building a strong resistant community without the backing of a political coalition was a long shot without the political muscle to fight politically for resources.

The few progressive coalitions being founded in other states all differed slightly, but the basic coalescing around a common agenda was the same. Connecticut Citizen Action Group was a statewide consumer interest group, founded in 1971 by Ralph Nader, the anti-corporate consumer crusader and Toby Moffett, who would later become a congressman. In 1975, a group of labor unions, senior citizen, church, and community organizations, led by former SDS-er Ira Arlook, formed the Ohio Public Interest Campaign. The Citizens Action Coalition of Indiana was founded a year before that and made its name by challenging utility company rates. That same year, Robert Creamer, who had worked with Saul Alinsky, the legendary community organizer, founded the Illinois Public Action Council, a statewide coalition of progressive organizations that included unions, farm groups, senior citizen organizations, community groups, consumer advocates, environmental, and peace organizations. In 1976, Tom Hayden formed the statewide Campaign for Economic Democracy immediately following his second place finish in the California Democratic Primary for U.S. Senate. Another essential piece of this movement was the creation of the Midwest Academy training school for organizers, formed in Chicago in 1973 by Heather Booth and others.

It was clear that if we hoped to make any real change in New Jersey, we had to unite with other issue organizations, especially labor unions. It would be another four years before John got me involved in helping to initiate that coalition. In the meantime there was plenty to do in the Oranges.

Main Street East Orange was suffering and the redevelopment around the Brick Church train station seemed completely stalled. The area was now in a state of mid-abandonment. The city owned at least half the vacant retail buildings. The once-bustling shopping area looked more and more distressed. Newspaper reports ping ponged from depressing to hopeful and then back again. The latest item reported that the ink was barely dry on a ninety-nine-year lease with a developer, when negotiations broke down over sharing the costs of the parking deck. For the

Part IV: *Stayin' Alive, Stayin' Alive* (1977)

public, the emotional roller coaster continued and public concern turned to dread. And then when optimism was fueled by some new announcement, hopes were dashed and cynicism grew. I could feel it. East Orange was hungry for change but folks were quickly losing faith in what their public officials were telling them.

Soon the public was assured that the conflict over parking was almost resolved and then construction could begin. But the next bit of news was that Dworman, the developer, was having financial difficulties. The financially shaky developer chosen by the City was also involved in litigation on a previous project. That was not a good sign.

It seemed like Dworman was history and the city would be back searching for a developer, but suddenly he and the Housing Authority announced that, "Construction will commence on the Phase One building with one floor of retail and ten floors of office space by June 1977." The pie-in-the-sky project with the bankrupt developer had morphed again. A skeptical public just rolled their eyes. Me too.

Meanwhile, the same Main Street on the Orange side of the border was intact with not a single vacant storefront. I surmised that the difference between the two downtowns was that Orange was never upscale, just lots of stores with goods that average people needed. But things in Orange were changing too. Eventually, the 1200-seat Empire movie theater shut down, and there was a hair salon in what used to be its lobby and one of the two bowling alleys in town had closed. Retailers came and went up and down Main Street, but the shopping district stayed lively.

HOUSING FOR PEOPLE
NOT FOR PROFIT

CHAPTER 22

Two Steps Forward

Phyllis and the EOTA leadership kicked off 1977 by publishing a list of demands and placing them before the City Council and the mayor. The laundry list included both some urgent issues and others much less essential:

1. Rent to be lowered if services decline.
2. An Emergency Repair Law backed up by a Landlord Security Deposit.
3. No increase in rent for a year if the landlord fails to comply with the rent registration law.
4. Reduce the allowed annual rent increase from 6% to 4%.
5. Limit parking fees and garage rentals the same as rents.
6. Eliminate the Tax Surcharge, the automatic pass-along to tenants of any increase in the landlord's property taxes.

The Council promptly responded. They intended to introduce the tax surcharge amendment but were completely silent on the other demands, especially anything addressing declining maintenance and provision of essential services. The vast majority of complaints heard by EOTA counselors and the Housing Unit attorneys were related to quality of life. Apparently, there would be no action by the Council on the Emergency Repair Law or the Landlord Security Deposit or anything to do with maintaining services in apartment buildings. That was depressing.

City Council members continued to hear complaints from tenants in their Ward, and plenty of tenants were coming to council meetings. One small advance was that Councilwoman Bernice Davis joined with EOTA to demand an investigation of the Property Maintenance Department. I doubted that anything would come of it.

And at the end of January, the city held a public hearing on its proposed federal Community Development Block Grant funds. Funds to support EOTA's tenant services were a miniscule amount of the total funds to be received, but a majority of the fifty-two residents who went up to the microphone spoke in favor of funding EOTA. The Council approved the EOTA funding, but when the mayor signed the resolution, he zeroed out the EOTA funds. He was sending a message to Phyllis, but she flew into action and the Council voted to override his veto, so Hart reversed his stand. Phyllis had won another round.

While we battled in Orange and East Orange, NJTO kept winning important rights for tenants in Trenton, the state capitol. Landlords couldn't evict tenants in retaliation for complaining to public officials or organizing a tenants group, but landlords could still refuse to renew a lease or evict a family when they gave birth to a child. Ronnie and NJTO wanted to push for a comprehensive state law that would protect tenants from arbitrary evictions.

Byron Baer, the young Assemblyman who represented the Bergen County District where NJTO got its start, worked with Ronnie and NJTO leadership to craft a far reaching law that limited landlords' ability to evict tenants. The Just Cause Eviction Act prescribed the limits on specifically which grounds that a landlord could evict. It was a major step for tenants. The far reaching law was introduced by Assemblyman Baer and enacted in 1974. Often, tenants didn't know their rights, so NJTO pressed for a Truth In Renting law that required landlords to give tenants a copy of all their rights under state law. It was passed in 1976. New Jersey was becoming the leader in protecting tenants. In most states, they were still powerless.

We Need a Poster

Kat brought by a photo she'd found during one of her searches at the New York Public Library. It was a modest, old, vacant house in Oregon that had been foreclosed during the Depression. She proposed it as the central image for a poster to raise funds for *Shelterforce*. The old house was a strong image but we were organizing tenants. I wasn't sure what Kat had in mind, but I certainly wasn't going to discourage her.

A week later she was back. We stood at the drafting table and she unrolled a mock-up. The foreclosed and abandoned-looking house sat in the foreground against a forest green background with a dense and prosperous-looking high rise cityscape in the near distance. The message *Housing for People Not for Profit* sat prominently below. I was amazed at how she brought together images and created a powerful but pleasing visual impression. She explained that *we* would be using three colors—the forest green, a medium sky blue, and a deep brown.

I planned to help with the printing and she said that we'd be working at the Women's Interart Center on the west side. As far as she knew, it was okay for a man to be working there.

"Anyway," she said, "we'll be there at night. It's the only way to get enough uninterrupted time in the print shop. Nobody will even know you're there."

We'd be hand-printing a run of a hundred, so I gave her money from the *Shelterforce* till for paper and inks. I marked my calendar for my overnight in New York with Kat, silk screening a hundred posters. I couldn't wait.

The Women's Interart Center was a special place with a rich political history, started by a collective that was an outgrowth of Women Artists in Revolution. WAR broke off from the male-dominated Art Workers Coalition in protest over the Whitney Museum's 1969 Annual that only included eight women of the 143 artists shown. The collective wanted a place where women artists could get away from the male dominance of the art scene. The female artists secured some state arts funding and a lease on two floors of a city-owned abandoned building on the far west side of Manhattan.

I picked up Kat, we loaded supplies into the back of my truck and headed up to West 52nd Street. It was already dark and there was plenty of overnight parking in this scrappy old industrial area adjacent to Hell's Kitchen. Kat piled the three screens on top of the 120 sheets of thick poster stock already in my outstretched arms. Her tote bags were full. Jars of poster ink, rags, turpentine and a thermos of coffee. We headed into the empty building and onto the freight elevator to the 9th floor. I was in love with the whole scene. The hundred year old loft building was worn and grubby but even when vacant it pulsed with creativity. Paint and ink spotted the work tables. There were drying racks, trash bins, artwork everywhere. Posters, drawings, paintings. Old school lockers with padlocks for supplies. We had this creative space to ourselves.

Hand screening the posters was a two person operation. Kat and I worked shoulder to shoulder as I placed each sheet underneath the screen and Kat pulled ink across the screen with a squeegee. Then I stacked each freshly inked print on the drying rack and we'd repeat the process. The whole process took most of the night. I was thrilled by the sight of 120 freshly printed posters drying on the metal racks, waiting for their next color. It took a while to clean the screen with turpentine and put everything away. Sometime around six we headed down Eleventh Avenue to a diner.

The poster was a sensation. We quickly sold all 100 signed and numbered hand-screened posters for $10 each, a bargain even back then. A year later we had 150 printed commercially and sold those for 5 bucks.

Sometime later, Kat revised the image and the lettering and we went back into the studio and screened a hundred or so *Housing for People Not for Profit* tee shirts for a National Lawyers Guild conference on housing held in New Brunswick, NJ. We could have sold a hundred more.

Lenox Ave. Next Step: Receivership

Conditions at the Lenox Avenue building continued to decline. One morning Sam Farrington, the tenants' Housing Unit attorney, huddled with Jackie and Dewey and Magdalene in his office. "There are no good choices here," he said. "If you don't take charge of your own building, nothing will get done. I checked at City Hall. Your landlord's almost two years behind in his taxes. He's walked away and he's not coming back. He still owns the building so you should keep leaving him messages and keep all

Staking Our Claim

your receipts, just in case. But I sincerely doubt you'll ever see him again." The tenants wondered if that was the good news or the bad news. But Sam had a plan.

Sam suggested they petition the Court to appoint a Receiver, a professional who would collect rents and manage the building and be answerable to the Court. So in November, 1976 they were back in court, this time in front of Judge John Dios who was new to the Superior Court bench and New Jersey's first Hispanic judge. Sam was pleased. Dios was born in Cuba and came to the states when he was seven. The judge grew up in Newark and was no stranger to hardship.

Sam as always was well prepared and he'd rehearsed Jackie's testimony. Mary sat with the other tenants through Jackie's testimony. The case was pretty straight forward and Sam played it that way, presenting the evidence in his dry, matter of fact way with everything documented—Property Maintenance Department reports, oil bills and repair receipts. Nothing much was in dispute, really. But Judge Dios was somewhat incredulous that things had gotten this bad at the building. He suddenly announced, "I want to see for myself. Let's go look at this building." The Judge and his court clerk traveled together to East Orange and when he arrived, Jackie and Mary and some of the other tenants had convened out in front of 66-68 Lenox Avenue.

When the judge got out of his car a boyfriend of one of the tenants charged at him, cursing him up and down. Jackie rushed over. Dios quickly realized the guy thought he was the landlord and he calmly turned to Jackie, "Let's go inside, Mrs. Cooke."

Jackie conducted the tour while Sam stayed close to the judge and his clerk. Mary and the other tenants trailed behind. After his big show, the irate boyfriend disappeared and pretty quickly Judge Dios had seen enough. He asked Sam to meet them back in his courtroom. He was prepared to rule on granting the appointment of a Receiver.

The tenants were relieved, especially Jackie. The weight of all that responsibility—corralling tenants to pay rent, missing work to oversee repairmen, dealing with paying bills—was off her shoulders. She gathered with Magdalene and Dewey back in her kitchen and they knocked back drinks talking about their cool new friend and ally Judge Dios, their shitty landlord and their whip smart attorney, Sam Farrington. Finally things had turned a corner.

Soon Jackie was working for EOTA, teaching tenants how to navigate the system when their landlord wouldn't do the right thing. She helped them to organize a group of tenants in their buildings and dispensed legal advice. Together Phyllis and I had secured nearly $60,000 in federal grant funds from the City and County. With the economy reeling from stagflation the feds funded a Comprehensive Employment Assistance Act known on the street as CETA. EOTA now had four part-time organizers including Woody and Jackie.

Jackie walked to work at the EOTA office on Main Street just across the interstate. She didn't have a car, and never learned to drive. She loved her job, always working extra hours helping tenants.

Back on Lenox Avenue, things were a little better. But all the deferred maintenance required a lot more attention than the Receiver was prepared to put in, for the monthly fee the Court allowed. Jackie needed someone who took this assignment more seriously, someone she could work with. She called Sam to ask if he could ask Judge Dios to appoint someone else.

I was beyond surprised when I heard that the *Shelterforce* Collective's scholar-in-residence was now the court-appointed Receiver for Jackie's building. Marty Bierbaum had just earned his law degree; he'd passed the Bar exam and was working toward a PhD in Urban Planning. Marty was our writer, book reviewer, urban theorist, and historian. He was still teaching part-time at Rutgers. I thought he was an unlikely choice to manage Jackie's aging, neglected, apartment building. That was no small commitment. I was impressed and soon realized that his wife, Joan, was part of the management team. When Judge Dios agreed to appoint him, Marty and Joan stepped onto a slippery slope, the beginning of their two-decade roller coaster ride with Jackie, Dewey, Magdalene, and the tenants of 66-68 Lenox Avenue.

I hadn't seen as much of Marty and Joan since they moved to Free Acres, the progressive community in suburban Union County, and their daughter Lauren had been born. Free Acres was a special place. It was founded in 1910 with eighty-five households on seventy-five wooded acres, built as a social experiment, modeled on Henry George's economic theory of a single land value tax. It was a beautiful place to live, full of eclectic houses carved into the woods with a community pool. The place was loaded with old Lefties and now young progressives like Marty and Joan were starting families there. Part of me felt like they'd abandoned us and fled for the burbs, but I also envied their idyllic life in Free Acres, free of the chaos that was East Orange.

Eventually, the City of East Orange foreclosed on Jackie's tax delinquent building and it became just another "abandoned building" lost in the city's inventory. Except this one was fully occupied with mothers raising their kids and Marty as its manager. It was a strange amalgam. The Receiver had been appointed when there was a negligent owner. Now the city was the owner, effectively nullifying the Receivership Order. Marty simply stayed on. Now *he* got to be treated by a few of the tenants as the landlord.

Marty and Jackie made a great team. We were all in awe of the determination that Jackie and the tenants showed and the Bierbaums' commitment. It was thrilling to think that there'd be a happy ending to this dismal slumlord story. But in reality, this could only go on for so long. The roof got patched and repatched. It needed to be replaced. With no ability to borrow money, capital improvements were off the table. Repairs of all kinds became more frequent and even though the building had no mortgage to pay and they didn't pay property taxes, the modest rents barely covered the utilities and rising repair bills.

The building had been milked dry and was on its last leg. If this building with a solid structure was going to stay intact, a long-term solution was needed—an extensive renovation inside and out. But that was costly, probably twenty thousand per apartment. A quarter million dollars. It would take a miracle to pull that off.

• • •

The limits of our housing work was becoming apparent, to me at least. The private sector had waning interest in places like East Orange. The economic model for so many buildings was now, "Maximize profits for as long as possible even if it means depleting the asset." Lots of landlords no longer invested for the long term. They didn't upgrade mechanical systems. They kept patching roofs rather than invest in a new roof that would last twenty-five or thirty years. Without alternatives to private sector investment, the housing stock was withering. Abandonment was prevalent in the worst neighborhoods, but deterioration was everywhere.

City Council members fought with the mayor to step up code enforcement. We fought like hell to enact provisions that tied rent increases to Property Maintenance Code compliance. EOTA pressed for an Emergency Repair Ordinance where the city would step in to make emergency repairs and put a lien on the building. That was Joan Pransky's passion, and she proposed a Landlord Security Fund, similar to a tenant security deposit. Those tools were important in the event of real emergencies, but in reality, the city government was ill-equipped to manage things like contracting for emergency repairs in apartment buildings. They had enough trouble just picking up the garbage and sweeping the streets. The mayor was noncommittal, and while some City Council members told us they supported an Emergency Repair Ordinance, we knew it would be a fight.

East Orange tenants were between a rock and a hard place. Our group had no experience owning or managing rental properties. I had four or five communal rent payers. Marty's receivership was our first real foray into the broader field of community development. We knew the law and how to help tenants organize and get what they paid for. I was hard-pressed to figure out how our side was going to win this war. We needed the private sector, but they saw East Orange only as a short-term investment.

In other cities, committed folks like us were starting up nonprofit community development corporations (CDCs) to own and operate low-cost housing. We wrote about them in the pages of *Shelterforce*, and I'd visited one of the best groups in Baltimore. Next door in Newark there was New Community Corporation and Tri Cities Community Union, but there was nothing in Orange or East Orange. CDCs were an important part of the answer to better housing in urban areas, but an army of CDCs couldn't backfill the yawning hole left by withdrawal of the private sector.

Marty schooled us about social housing in European countries with Social Democratic traditions. In the U.S., the meager nod to government low-cost housing was the federal Public Housing program. It was rapidly becoming "housing of last resort," only chosen by the most desperate families. There were a few equally meager government programs that subsidized the private sector to provide low-cost housing. The U.S. government's pathetic contribution to social housing was dwarfed by the massive homeowner tax deduction that benefited the middle class and was particularly generous to the wealthy. The bigger and more expensive your house or houses, the more the tax break was worth. In *Shelterforce* we dubbed it "The Mansion Subsidy." Under Nixon and even under Carter, the federal government was backsliding from its earlier commitment to backstop urban disinvestment.

We were propelled forward by our own sense of urgency and our small victories with the City Councils and in the courts and the streets. But in reality, the war was being lost. Little by little, year by year. We just weren't powerful enough. And there were no resources.

Mayor Joel Shain when Rheingold Brewery proclaimed that Orange was their hometown.

CHAPTER 23

Beware the Wrecking Ball

Economic challenges in Orange and East Orange weren't limited to the housing and retail sectors. Businesses and manufacturing played an important part in the economic health of a city. They provided jobs. Commercial tax ratables paid property taxes but required little in municipal services and didn't add kids to the school system. East Orange didn't have any industry to speak of except in one small area on the Newark border. Orange had a long industrial history. In its heyday from the mid-1800s until about 1920, the Valley neighborhood was known as the "hat making capital of the world." Hat-making was long gone, but the old hat factories still housed a variety of industrial and manufacturing uses. Orange's biggest employer was right in the center of town, the Rheingold Brewery.

I drank Rheingold beer and still remember the jingle on my truck radio.

My beer is Rheingold, the dry beer. Think of Rheingold whenever you buy beer. It's not bitter, not sweet; it's the dry flavored treat. Won't you try extra dry Rheingold beer?

It was May of 1977 when I drank my last sip of Rheingold beer. I was grabbing a coffee to-go downstairs from the EOTA office. Two regulars sitting at the counter told me the story. Just that morning, the brewers, mechanics, and truck drivers arrived at the Rheingold brewery in Orange. A sign on the padlocked gates read: THE BREWERY IS CLOSED. INQUIRE AT YOUR UNION OFFICE.

Seven hundred good paying jobs. Gone. Overnight. This same scene, in multiple industries, was playing out across the Northeast. I was told that Rheingold had squeezed the City of Orange for a million dollars in property tax relief, promising not to leave. Suddenly, when the tax breaks dried up, so did the jobs. The loss of the tax revenue and all those jobs was a crushing blow to the small city so recently assaulted by construction of the interstate right through its middle and the slow draining of its middle class by suburbanization and White flight.

It was corporate greed, pure and simple and it made my blood boil. This company cared so little about the struggling city that had been its home for so long and it had even less loyalty to all those workers. I told everyone who'd listen, "Stop drinking Rheingold. The bastards who own the company just raped the city and fucked over all the employees."

The clean taste of Rheingold was what made me a loyal consumer, and it was brewed just a few blocks away. Its dry crispness reminded me of Stroh's, my "fire brewed" Detroit beer that sadly was unavailable east of Ohio. I was beerless. Ballantine, Pabst, and Budweiser were brewed in Newark, but they were poor substitutes, though Rolling Rock from Latrobe, PA wasn't bad.

More Main Street Woes

Meanwhile, the Brick Church Urban Renewal saga played on. Hounded by angry taxpayers, a frustrated City

Part IV: *Stayin' Alive, Stayin' Alive (1977)*

Council called for the Housing Authority to terminate its relationship with Dworman, the financially shaky developer. The writing on the wall seemed clear. The June groundbreaking date came and went and in September the Housing Authority finally announced it was canceling Dworman's contract, citing his "failure to provide necessary information and failure to show up at scheduled meetings." It sounded to me like Dworman had just disappeared. Everyone seemed to be asking, *Why can't something be done? Why is this so difficult?* Even the mayor and the City Council felt powerless.

Local businessmen were particularly incensed, and the owner of the popular and swanky Suburban Cocktail Lounge sued the Housing Authority for "deliberately destroying the area without rebuilding it." The owner claimed his business had been irreparably hurt by the delays, the uncertainty, and the vacant buildings that were now his neighbors.

The vacant buildings on the Phase One site continued to rot in place. A fire burned a row of stores at Brick Church Plaza and Main. The Fire Department announced it was the result of an "incendiary device." The area looked more forlorn than ever.

I pulled up in front of the vacant church on South Harrison. The front doors were open. The massive empty church was stunning and scheduled to be demolished any day. I thought about the cities that were repurposing old churches for theater groups, arts and craft bazaars, offices for nonprofits. It made me crazy that the city was ravaging its own downtown while spending good money to tear down this 1800s gem. The city officials had no vision. Dazzled by the dream of a suburban mall, they were blind to the treasures right in front of them. It was disgusting.

I grabbed some tools from my truck and joined a group of tradesmen who were removing solid oak doors, decorative trim, brass hardware, windows, and other fixtures from the magnificent structure. I filled my truck and dropped my load off at home and came back to load up again. Minutes later, the East Orange cops arrived and rounded us all up. They told us what we already knew, that the city owned the building and that we were trespassing. They stopped short of saying that we were stealing. They knew it was all headed to a landfill. They said we could keep whatever was already in our trucks but if we came back we'd be arrested. A few of the guys argued that all this beautiful wood work would soon be destroyed so why not let us take it and reuse it. The cops said it wasn't their call. Insurance problems and all that. We cleared out.

For the next month, the mixed Byzantine and Gothic gem sat quietly, with big boards crudely spiked to its ornate doors. I drove by often, and I could picture all that carved woodwork inside. All that richly carved detail would rot in a landfill. The thought made me nauseous.

Then one day driving up Main Street, I spotted a big crane by the church. As I drove closer, a thousand-pound wrecking ball was bringing down the upper stone work and knocking it inward through the roof to the stone floor below. I shivered each time the big iron ball smacked against the cut stone walls high above. The crane would stop as a excavator gobbled the big pieces of masonry and spit them into waiting dump trucks. I could only watch for a few minutes and drove off shaking my head. East Orange was *fucked*.

The city was lost in an identity crisis. It still thought it was a suburb. Its schizophrenic civic leaders had one

Part IV: *Stayin' Alive, Stayin' Alive* (1977)

foot anchored in the genteel past. Even if they hadn't lived in the city back then, it was a hard vision to give up. So appealing, so liveable. A great place to raise a family. The people who created and populated that earlier place had walked out and didn't look back, but the new leadership couldn't accept that East Orange was a city now. And that it had been dealt such a lousy hand.

The tenants on Lenox Avenue weren't a part of this *top-down* urban renewal, they were charting a unique *grassroots-up* approach. Marty Bierbaum, the Lenox Avenue property manager and overly smart lawyer, was researching his PhD dissertation topic on the revitalization of Hoboken, a gritty riverfront city on the Hudson River facing Manhattan. That's where he met Sal Santinello, Hoboken's Director of Housing. Marty shared his East Orange dilemma with Sal. The old building on Lenox Avenue needed a full-on renovation, but the rents needed to stay affordable and would only support a modest mortgage. And, just to complicate things further, the City of East Orange now owned the building.

Sal loved knotty housing problems. Admittedly, this one was a stretch, but Sal had some immediate suggestions for at least two pieces of the puzzle. "First, get the City to deed the property to a corporation set up by the tenants. The corporation will be a *limited equity housing co-op*. By limiting the equity of the tenant owners, the units will remain affordable to future purchasers." Sal and Marty agreed that this part should be easy. The city didn't want to own and manage yet another apartment building.

The second piece, raising low-cost capital, was daunting but Sal had some ideas. "There's a low-income housing grant program that just got announced at DCA, the state Department of Community Affairs. If we can put together the other sources, the DCA grant will cover at least a quarter of our renovation costs."

Sal continued to noodle as Marty took notes. "Federal tax law is complicated, but there's a way to raise investment capital by selling off the accelerated depreciation deduction that rental real estate enjoys. Sell the *depreciation tax shelter* to high-tax bracket investors while still keeping ownership of the building. It's called *equity syndication*. We'll have to spend some dough on a tax attorney but it's done all the time. If we can raise some additional grant funding and secure a small mortgage, we could do this."

Sal was excited. He was the president of the Ethical Culture Society, a liberal group that met on Sunday mornings. They were sort of a secular church for agnostics and atheists. He thought the Society would be willing to act as the nonprofit sponsor for the project. Another piece of the puzzle.

Maybe the tenants on Lenox had a chance after all. Maybe their success would be a model that could be built on. While Marty and Sal and Jackie continued down that road, a surprising opportunity was about to present itself to us.

PART V

Taking Our Shot

1978

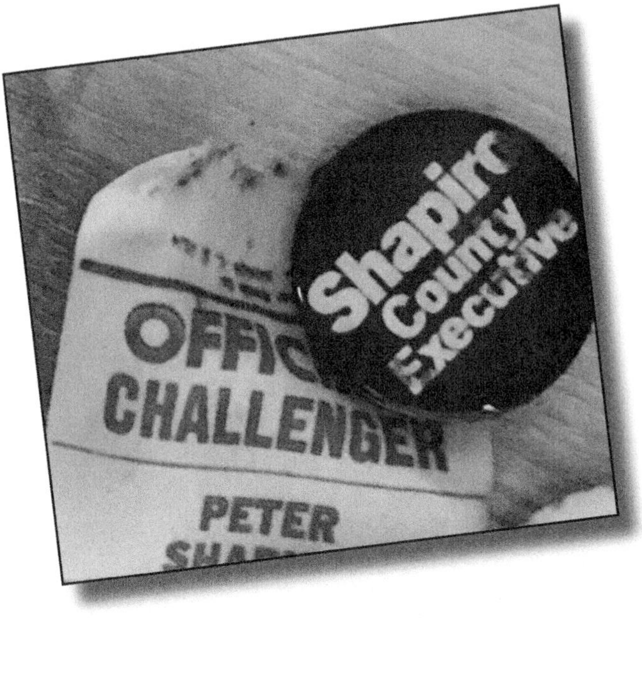
County
Executive
CHALLENGER
PETER

The seventies wore on and Carter's approval rating slid. A majority of Americans believed that inflation was the nation's most important problem, but they were divided on whether the solution was government intervention or market-based solutions. Locally, a California tax revolt overwhelmingly approved Proposition 13, which cut property taxes and limited future increases.

Across the country, business interests continued their efforts to chip away at the power of unions with so-called Right To Work laws. These laws made payment of union dues in a unionized workplace optional. A federal Civil Service Act in 1978 gave federal employees the right to opt out of their union and greatly limited their bargaining rights. Meanwhile, in Ohio, a Right To Work ballot initiative with strong business backing was defeated by the voters.

If the business lobby was bruised by the Ohio ballot defeat, Carter soothed the pain when he signed the Revenue Act of 1978 that reduced the top tax rate from 48% to 46% and lowered the capital gains tax from 39% to 28%.

On the global scene, Middle East peace inched one step forward when Carter brought together Menachem Begin of Israel and Anwar Sadat of Egypt. They signed the Camp David Accords that outlined a framework for peace between Egypt and Israel and laid the groundwork for broader peace in the Middle East, including resolution of the Palestinian issue. In China, Deng Xiaoping assumed the position of Vice Premier and initiated market-oriented economic reforms. In Iran, there were widespread protests against the U.S.-supported Shah.

In the name of energy independence, Carter initiated deregulation of natural gas, a move that would surely drive up prices. In response, leaders from the New Left brought together more than seventy citizen and community groups, labor unions, senior citizen groups, and farm organizations to fight back. They formed the Citizen Labor Energy Coalition.

Cities especially in the Northeast and Midwest continued to struggle fiscally, and even under a Democratic president, they got little help. Neighborhood groups fighting back against disinvestment saw a tiny glimmer of hope when Congress chartered the Neighborhood Reinvestment Corporation. Within two years, Neighborhood Housing Services organizations in 126 cities received annual funding and technical assistance.

In 1978, Newt Gingrich and Dick Cheney were first elected to Congress.

Peter Shapiro

CHAPTER 24

The Dems Come Calling

As John was fond of saying, "We need to have one foot in the Democratic Party and the other firmly planted in our grassroots organizing." As good as that sounded when Michael Harrington said it, we never had more than a toe in the Democratic Party. That was about to change.

Once Essex had turned majority Democrat, the Democratic Party Chairman Harry Lerner consolidated power; he could designate who would run for office on the Regular Democratic Organization ballot line. Chosen candidates were bracketed on the Chairman's ballot line as a slate. Once that line had won the Primary, the November general election result was a foregone conclusion. County employees and their families were expected to donate money and get out the vote for "The Line." Lerner's finely tuned machine maintained a balance of power that put him in control of every bit of county government, every dollar spent, every person hired, every appointment made, and with control over the Democratic organization, all the state legislators from Essex answered to him as well.

Lerner's ballot line, the Regular Democrats, always occupied the top and most visible spot on the ballot—Line A. Ballot position was allegedly chosen at random by the

County Clerk, and yet in the Primary Election, the Regular organization always drew Line A, and in the General Election the Democrats always got Line A. County Clerk Nicholas Caputo's perfect record in "randomly" choosing the top spot for the chairman's line earned him the nickname, "The Man with the Golden Hand."

So reliable was Caputo that it was rumored that The Machine had a warehouse full of election posters—for the June primaries and the November general elections. The blue posters' simple message urged voters to vote the entire slate: "VOTE LINE A ALL THE WAY."

Since county office holders were elected countywide, Republicans who had majorities in a few suburban towns had no chance of sharing power at the county level.

Lerner's job was to keep enough local political bosses happy and loyal to the Regular Democratic Organization. Those bosses were the heart of Essex Democratic politics. Some were local mayors or the leader of an ethnic clan that had its origins in the immigrant strongholds of Newark's old neighborhoods. The County Democratic Chairman needed the allegiance of enough of them to form a winning slate in a given election. He held together a sometimes fragile, often fluid coalition by distributing patronage—contracts, jobs, and perks—accessed by individuals through their boss's relationship with the chairman.

Backroom, patronage-driven government had plenty of detractors, especially among disenfranchised minority groups and a growing *good government* movement anchored in the suburbs. But Lerner seemed unimpeachable.

The County Chairman was selected by a vote of the County Committee, people elected from the six hundred or so voting districts (precincts) and known as District Leaders, whose allegiance was usually to their municipal

Democratic Chair. The County Committee, District Leader system was, on the one hand, a model of grassroots party democracy, and yet in Essex in the 1970s, it was the backbone of machine domination of the levers of government power. Democratic Party power was rooted in some strong ethnic power bases.

The Irish

The roots of Irish political power were back in the *old neighborhood,* the Vailsburg section of Newark. Generations of sons and daughters of Erin had now moved west and dominated politics in South Orange, Orange, West Orange, and Maplewood. The Newark Saint Patrick's Day parade originated on Sanford Avenue in Vailsburg near the original Cryan's tavern and ended in downtown South Orange near a newer Cryan's watering hole. Ireland-born John Cryan was the County Sheriff and the West Ward Democratic Boss. A solid base of Irish loyalists were the fraternal organizations like the Ancient Order of Hibernians, The Friendly Sons of St. Patrick, and the Emerald Society, the group of police and firefighters. Prominent Irish families all had civic associations that were social, political, and charitable—The Giblin Association, The Cryan Association, and The Dillon Association. Governor Brendan Byrne from West Orange was a product of this political Irish stew.

The Italians

The seat of Italian political power was the North Ward of Newark and extended to neighboring Belleville, Nutley, and then west along Bloomfield Avenue through Bloomfield, Montclair, and Verona, where most of the mayors and council members were Italian. Robert Curvin, an early civil rights leader, wrote that North Ward boss, Steve Adubato, "built his power on three things: a network of highly successful social programs, a disciplined cadre of election workers who are superbly trained and expert at getting their constituents registered and getting out to vote on Election Day, and a network of loyal politicians and carefully placed government workers, including the key staff at the Essex County Election Commission, who owe their paychecks to Adubato." In an interview once, Adubato answered a question about his leadership style as Machiavelli might, "I'd rather be feared than loved." Adubato never held office but from his base in the North Ward, he became one of the state's most powerful political bosses.

The Blacks

Black political power in the fifties and sixties emanated from the segregated Central Ward of Newark, and later after the Jews departed, from the South Ward and then it followed Black migration from Newark along Central Avenue into East Orange and Orange and along Springfield Avenue into Irvington. For years, Eulis "Honey" Ward was the Black Central Ward Democratic Chairman and the Payne brothers, Donald and Bill, led the South Ward. Kenneth Gibson was elected Newark's first Black mayor in 1970, a year after William S. Hart was elected East Orange's first Black mayor. That same year, Black political representation in Orange grew with CRG, the Citizens for Representative Government.

The Hispanics

Puerto Ricans who lived in a tight portion of the North Ward and the Portuguese who took root in the Ironbound were just beginning to have political influence.

Leaders of ethnic factions and small-time political machines shared one relationship in common. They were either in with the County Democratic Chairman or they were on the outs. Without the Chairman's largesse to pass around—jobs, contracts, appointments, political favors—it was hard to keep followers happy.

Our First Insiders Meeting

It was early in 1978 when Phyllis and I reported our big news to John. He was hot to know how our first meeting with the reform Democrats went. I leaned forward, excited to report that we'd been cheek to jowl with Essex County's politically powerful.

"There were a few heavyweights. It wasn't just the ECDC crowd. We met in Tom Cooke's conference room on the second floor of East Orange City Hall. Besides Mayor Cooke, Ken Gibson was there. Phil Freedman, Governor Byrne's law partner. Shuchter was there and some of the suburban liberals. Joyce Goldman, Jackie Yustein, a couple more." I knew it was significant that the county's two most powerful Black politicians were in the room—Cooke and Gibson.

John nodded. "Nice." Anxious to know more, he leaned in. "So how did it go? What was decided?"

We briefed John on the plan taking shape. It was a strategy to make sure that the Essex County Democratic Boss Harry Lerner and his political machine didn't capture control of the new form of government—the one the reformers had worked so hard to create.

This would be a knock down, drag out battle for control of Essex, the state's most populous county. For the first time, a County Executive would be elected along with a group of county legislators, four at-large and one each from five geographic districts.

It was 1978 and political reform was in the air across the nation. Liberal Republican John Lindsay had been Mayor of New York for a few years now. The McGovern Commission had rewritten Democratic Party rules that opened the party process to women and minorities and weakened the control that party power brokers had over the nominating process. Jimmy Carter had become the 1976 presidential nominee through a system of wide open primaries with little influence from traditional party bosses.

But "Boss" Lerner and his machine hadn't kept their grip on the reins of power by losing elections to a bunch of Black political leaders and suburban liberals. The anti-machine forces knew if they were not united around one candidate, Lerner and his machine would simply take control of the new form of government and nothing would have changed.

At that meeting in Tom Cooke's conference room, I tried to make sense of this alleged "anti-machine" coalition. We knew Mayor Cooke well and certainly never thought of him as a reformer. We had won and strengthened rent control in East Orange over his strong opposition. This would be the first time we were aligned with him—on anything.

As each of the participants arrived I continued to wonder, *Will this coalition hold together? What if Lerner tries to buy them off? Are we naive to believe that some of these people who are presently on the outs with Lerner wouldn't join him under the right terms? What if a Black candidate emerges for County Executive, will that split the coalition?* I was excited to be at the meetings and getting my political education, but I also wondered what role we'd play. How we'd justify sitting at this table.

This was a coalition of strange bedfellows. I admired Gibson, Newark's first Black mayor, and was happy I got to sit next to him at the meeting. In 1970, he ran an anti-corruption campaign to beat the incumbent Hugh Addonizio, who later that same year was convicted on charges of extortion and conspiracy. But after a brief honeymoon, Black nationalists who had helped elect Gibson now branded him a "neo-colonialist." Politics was a tough game in Newark.

The suburban liberals, called "goo-goos" by some because of their passion for "good government," made for an odd pairing as well. I'm sure they hadn't imagined themselves aligned with Tom Cooke, maybe with Gibson. And even though we knew some of them from the Peace Movement and other liberal causes, most of them opposed rent control, our Holy Grail.

Folks filtered in and took seats. Tom Cooke came out from his office and sat at the head of the table. He surveyed the assembled group, gave a tight smile and a knowing nod when he noticed Phyllis and I, and called the meeting to order.

"Let's go around the table. Introduce yourselves. I'm Tom Cooke, Mayor of East Orange." Cooke looked to his left. "Ken?"

Mayor Gibson's head was down, reviewing the stack of three-by-five cards that he always kept in his shirt pocket. I watched him making notes, erasing items. He barely looked up. "Ken Gibson, Mayor of Newark."

Physically, Cooke and Gibson were an odd pair. Cooke was handsome, tall and slim and an impeccable dresser, while short and stocky Gibson looked every bit the nerdy engineer that he was trained to be.

I was next. I couldn't help feeling that we'd crashed the party and everyone around the table knew it. My mind went to that meeting with Pete Shuchter two weeks earlier when it was decided that Phyllis and I should show up and just assume we were part of this group.

Another Plan Hatched in a Diner

The meeting with Shuchter, the behind-the-scenes operative of the political left in Essex County, would be pivotal to our county-wide influence as tenant leaders. Shuchter's passion was anchored in the peace movement with New Jersey SANE, though currently he was the legislative aide to Peter Shapiro, the twenty-five-year-old Kennedyesque State Assemblyman who represented Irvington, South Orange, and parts of Vailsburg. We knew Shuchter's mom, Lillian Maurice, a dogmatic Old Left tenant leader in Irvington. Like plenty of old Commies, Lil was brittle and judgmental. But her son was the opposite—open, warm, patient with folks. He had a delightful, somewhat sardonic, sense of humor.

With his customary and irresistible sly grin, Shuchter welcomed us to his booth in the East Orange Diner. "Step into my office. Welcome to the coup that will topple the evil empire that controls *your* county government." As we slid into the booth, he leaned in, looking each of us in the eyes. "I need to swear you to absolute secrecy," and then with a mock whisper, "not a word of this can get out."

We all chuckled and were anxious to hear the inside dope of the brewing battle between the reformers and the old Machine boss. We hadn't been involved in Charter Change, the movement to modernize county government that promised to break the hold of the Democratic Chairman. In fact, we were pretty unaware of county government. There was a large two-year college, an important institution. A few large and beautiful county parks. Administration of the courts and the welfare system were all housed in the antiquated Hall of Records on Market Street in Newark, the county seat. I'm sure there was more to it than that but I was skeptical.

I asked Shuchter, "Why is county government so important?"

"Yeah you wouldn't necessarily think that it is, right?" said Shuchter. "But the annual budget is a hundred and eighty-eight million dollars. The County Executive of Essex will be the second most powerful elected official in New Jersey."

Everyone called him Shuchter, not Peter or Pete, just Shuchter. He always looked the same, dressed in a coat and tie but somehow he never managed to look dressed up. He had two tweed sportcoats, one for summer and one for the rest of the year. He was overweight and rumpled, always wore a tie and the same pair of scuffed up but comfortable shoes. The political operative had the familiar look of an old time news reporter, one who pounded a city beat and then raced back to file his story before deadline.

Shuchter took a swig of Diet Coke, his constant caffeine source. "So, there's this group taking shape, organized by suburban liberals, who were part of Charter Change. Do you know the Essex County Democratic Coalition, ECDC?"

We nodded.

He continued, "They're openly at war with Lerner. They're now talking with some *not so liberal* pols who are on the outs with Lerner, who for one reason or another want retribution for Lerner having cut them out of sharing in the patronage pie that is *your* Essex County government." After ordering another Diet Coke, he went on, "They're having their first meeting on Thursday in East Orange City Hall. Tom Cooke's a part of this." He smiled and took in Phyllis's skeptical expression. "Look, this is strange stuff. Get used to it. Welcome to coalition politics. But you guys should be at those meetings."

I was incredulous. *We don't belong there. What would our role be? And we wouldn't be welcome*, I thought. I looked at Phyllis, who obviously had doubts too, though neither of us spoke up right away.

John jumped in, "Shuchter's right. We need to be in those discussions."

John probably knew that Shuchter's young boss Peter Shapiro had his eye on running for County Executive as the reform candidate, and John thought that we should use this opportunity to establish our relationship with Shapiro who was an obvious *up and comer*, and a progressive too.

Shuchter wanted us there. He knew we'd help his boss get elected and he believed in what we were doing—grassroots organizing. He probably knew that some folks wouldn't necessarily welcome us.

John saw that Phyllis and I were skeptical. "Look, we have as much right to be there as anyone else, maybe more so. We represent a constituency that depends on good government. And we represent a lot of votes. Nobody's going to waste energy objecting to us participating." That's what I loved about John. Where I recognized the unwritten boundaries and thought we needed to be invited, John was an insurgent. He broke down barriers. He went on, "Phyllis, you need to be there. Say that you represent the Essex County Housing Coalition, all the tenant associations in Essex."

Back in Tom Cooke's Conference Room

That was two weeks ago and now here I was. I remembered Shuchter's words, "Get used to it. Welcome to

Part V: Taking Our Shot (1978)

coalition politics." I was next to introduce myself. I looked up and down Tom Cooke's long conference table. Then I straightened my back.

"I'm Pat Morrissy with the Essex County Housing Coalition. I'll let Phyllis tell you about our group for those of you who may not know us."

Phyllis was determined to carry out the responsibilities that John had laid on her. She looked down at her notes.

"I'm Phyllis Salowe-Kaye. I'm the President of the East Orange Tenants Association." She smiled and looked to her right. "Hello, Mayor Cooke. And I'm here to represent the Essex County Housing Coalition, a group of city- and town-wide tenant associations throughout Essex."

She looked like she was about to say more when Mayor Cooke interrupted, "Welcome Mrs. Salowe-Kaye."

And the introductions continued. Apparently we were now part of the group, confident that even if we didn't get notified of the next meeting that Shuchter would let us know.

Essex is the state's most populous county. It turned solidly Democrat in the late sixties. Its over nine hundred thousand residents were governed by an archaic form of government overseen by a nine-member body with an equally archaic name, the Board of Chosen Freeholders (originally only landowners could hold office). Each Freeholder led a different department of the government. There was a County Supervisor who was a nominal, almost ceremonial, head of government. Freeholders were all elected county-wide. All the political control lay in the hands of the County Democratic Chairman.

Phyllis and Shuchter at the convention.

CHAPTER 25

Rage Against the Machine

Challenges to the County Chairman's rule by insurgents, reformers, and those who'd simply been excluded from the Chairman's patronage largesse were common. Indignant good government liberals, almost all of them from the suburbs, passed around stories of nepotism, corruption, and general incompetence. And what a drain on the public treasury this machine rule was. In addition, there was always some share of minor political power brokers who for some reason or other were on the outs with the chairman and cut out of the spoils. Black political and community leaders were either used or ignored by the Democratic Party. The only toeholds they had on power were at the municipal level in the cities with rising Black populations. So there was lots of animus to the Machine but never a substantial enough challenge to loosen the County Chairman's hold on the reins of power.

To unseat the chairman, all that was needed was a majority of District Leaders directly elected by their neighbors, precinct by precinct. With enough of them at the annual Party reorganization meeting and backing an alternate candidate, the corrupt political boss was out. Grassroots challenges to machine rule flared up. Challengers looked to oust their municipal Democratic Chair in this town or that, like the 1973 uprising that PACT participated in. But those revolts never resulted in a coup. They never succeeded in unseating the County Chairman. Harry Lerner had survived a few. With the bucket of patronage that he controlled—jobs, contracts, appointments, access to the governor and state patronage, he maintained a lot of loyal district leaders. Eventually, the powerless and desperate suburban Dems, aided by the Republicans who were *totally* ignored in this majority Democratic county, hatched a different sort of coup. They'd break the chairman's hold by changing the form of county government.

Tom Kean, a patrician Republican from suburban Essex, the Speaker of the State General Assembly, sponsored a law that allowed voters to change their county's charter. The idea was that a more modern and equitable form of government with a chief executive would also diminish the power of the County Democratic Chairman. Of course, there was no guarantee that the chairman's ticket wouldn't win all the county offices after a charter change.

In 1977, this coalition of suburban good government folks and Republicans, under the banner of the nonpartisan League of Women Voters, finally won a ballot referendum to change the county's charter. The issue passed by six thousand votes. It was the culmination of an effort begun in 1972 and the road to victory was littered with roadblocks by Democratic Party leaders to derail a change in the charter that might upset their absolute rule of county government.

The first attempt resulted in a commission authorized to review the county charter, with commission members selected by the voters. The elected commission was dominated by Regular Democratic Party loyalists, and after months of meetings, the commission voted, incredibly and against all the evidence presented, to keep the old form of county government saying it was "more efficient and cost-effective."

The latest attempt by the reformers was the submission of petitions with signatures equaling at least 15% of the registered voters. The County Clerk rejected thousands of the signatures. So Ruthi Zinn from Livingston and the Short Hills League of Women Voters, who organized the petition drive, brought court challenges to Clerk Nicholas Caputo's rejection of their signatures. With a stay from the court, Ruthi, the intrepid reformer, led volunteers during hundreds of hours of signature checking and re-checking, all made more difficult by uncooperative staff in the Clerk's office. At one point, under a court deadline, her volunteers arrived at the Hall of Records and were informed they couldn't view the records. Painters had just arrived for a "routine painting of the office." Everything was covered with drop cloths.

Eventually, the plucky suburban crusaders prevailed. They had enough valid signatures and the referendum went forward. The Machine campaigned hard and in an incredible twist of irony, their message warned voters that the Office of County Executive would have too much power.

Finally, votes were in and counted. Voters approved a charter change and created the new Office of County Executive with nine Freeholders, five of them elected by district. Republicans now had a chance of electing two representatives to the Freeholder Board.

The question of whether reform would bring an end to party boss rule in Essex would finally be decided by the voters. Maybe the powerful chairman would get his candidate elected as County Executive and nothing would have changed.

Key to breaking the hold of the Democratic Party boss was whether the anti-boss faction could coalesce around one candidate.

Phyllis and I attended more of the anti-Machine meetings. Discussion usually began with political gossip about who Boss Lerner might give his blessing to. Some seemed certain that Sheriff John Cryan had the upper hand with Lerner. Tom Giblin's name came up as a crossover candidate. There was talk that if Giblin, a Freeholder and labor leader, were anointed by Lerner, he might also win substantial votes in the suburbs and among liberals. People laughed when they heard that Sam Angelo, the County Treasurer, wanted to be County Executive.

Someone said, "Please. Yes, we'd love to run against Sam Angelo."

Someone else offered, "Lerner made him County Treasurer to shut him up."

Tom Cooke said he was talking with a close ally who was considering a run, but that no decision had been made yet so he wasn't ready to go public.

John Cryan was an Irish fixture in Newark and Essex County politics and probably had a lock on Lerner's support. Cryan emigrated as a young man from County Roscommon in Ireland. After serving in Korea, he was appointed Essex Undersheriff, and in 1960 he opened a tavern in Vailsburg, the heart of Newark's West ward. He was the Democratic Chairman of the West Ward and elected sheriff three times. An aggressive and dominant forty-nine-year-old, he was already the acknowledged boss of Irish Democratic politics in Essex County.

Freeholder Tom Giblin, at thirty-one, was itching to claim his place as the leader of the next generation of Irish pols, and the older Cryan was blocking his way, clogging up the elected office pipeline. Giblin's father was a labor leader and a Freeholder before becoming State Senator. He came from the same area of County Roscommon as Cryan. Tom had followed in Dad's footsteps. He was now a Freeholder and on the payroll of the International Union of Operating Engineers.

People speculated constantly about what Steve Adubato would do. He led a well disciplined organization based in Newark's North Ward, a top-down operation that demanded loyalty. He rewarded his friends and punished his enemies. Adubato was cagey, and without a candidate of his own, he saw no reason to engage with an anti-Lerner group at this point. Why not wait, get wooed by both sides and then choose.

In the spirit of the New Democratic Coalition, it was decided that the coalition candidate would be chosen at a wide open convention. Every Democrat who wanted to attend would get a vote. No more picking candidates in smoke filled back rooms. The organization called itself: Democrats United in Essex. The DUE convention was set for Saturday April 1st.

Endorsing a Tenant Candidate

Phyllis and I reported back to John about the decision for a wide open convention to choose the anti-Machine candidate.

John beamed. "This is made for us. One thing we do well is mobilize people for public meetings. But first we'll need to endorse a candidate."

Phyllis and I both figured that obviously we'd be endorsing Shapiro and we said so.

"Yeah, we undoubtedly will," said John. "There's nobody better on our issues, but we need a *process*. Like we do for state legislative candidates. We need to bring together tenant leaders from around the county to interview prospective candidates and make the choice of who to endorse." He looked at both of us. "Right?"

Of course he was right. We'd always been about consensus building and democratic decision making.

He continued, "Then, those same leaders will be motivated to bring their members out to the convention." John was wound up. "You know we've been talking about this Essex County Housing Coalition. Well, endorsing a countywide candidate and a substantial turnout at the convention, that'll put us on the map." As usual, John had assignments for us. "Phyllis, you need to put out the word to the tenant leaders. Pat, you organize the interview process, okay? I'll draft a candidate questionnaire and share it with the two of you." We were fired up.

Things were moving quickly. I was stunned by how caught up I was with the prospects of playing a role in picking the next County Executive. We had a liberal candidate who respected activists and grassroots movements. And we'd be doing it on our terms. Engaging grassroots leaders, bringing them into the process. This was a chance to make our mark—to march into the liberals' house and claim our rightful place. Fortunately, Phyllis felt at least as strongly as I did that we needed to show those liberals what grassroots power was all about.

That night when the house quieted to its late evening hush, I huddled in the parlor-turned-office, behind the closed pocket doors with the radio on low, reviewing what had transpired that day. Just three weeks ago I was the skeptic, not at all convinced that I wanted to get in bed with a bunch of suburbanites and muck about, maneuvering to see who the next County Executive might be. I'd never given the county government any thought. Shit, I hardly knew what it did. Besides the County College, a handful of parks, and the County Jail. And now? I was planning how to help pack the convention and get *our guy* elected.

In truth, the prospect did excite me. Win or lose we were going to show what the tenant movement could do. I marveled at how easily John, Phyllis, and I came up with what we wanted if *our guy* was elected. The answer was simple. Resources. To hire organizers. It was obvious we couldn't survive on volunteer effort alone. It was like when we made our case to the City of East Orange. Tenants were suffering. EOTA could help but we needed some dough to open and staff an office. But most of the towns in Essex didn't have that. A County Tenant Resource Center could support those grassroots leaders.

But first things first. I began to think about the convention. After our candidate screening and selection process with maybe a dozen tenant leaders from as many towns, we'd go to the press with our endorsement. Then working with all those leaders, we'd make sure we had a big enough contingent at the convention to wipe away any doubt that the tenant movement was real and knew how to flex its political muscle. I knew Phyllis would work the phones overtime to bring people out. I imagined all of us sitting together with signs, *East Orange Tenants for Shapiro, Bloomfield Tenants Organization, Orange, Irvington, West Orange, Caldwell, Verona, Belleville*. All chanting and cheering together. We'd make sure that Phyllis gave one of the seconding speeches. We'd need to talk with Shuchter. After the candidate screening.

I made a list of what we needed to do:

Draft a press release. ECHC is inviting candidates who are seeking our endorsement. (Pat and John)

> *Pick a date, time and place. We can use the Shelterforce office. (Pat)*
> *Call all the tenant leaders. (Phyllis)*
> *Draft the candidate questionnaire. (John)*
> *Circulate a draft set of questions to invited tenant leaders. (Pat, John and Phyllis)*

We got responses to our press release. Bill Brach, Peter Shapiro, and Joel Shain sought the ECHC endorsement. We scheduled them all for the same evening. About ten of us gathered in the *Shelterforce* office on Main Street, adjacent to the Legal Services Housing Unit and across the hall from EOTA. We gathered the assembled tenant leaders, though the only ones I can remember besides Phyllis and Jackie were Betty Hutchinson and Trish Comstock representing Bloomfield. We sorted through who would ask what questions. Then the first candidate arrived.

Joel Shain proudly touted his sponsorship and defense of rent control as mayor of Orange. He made sure that we all knew that he and Ronnie were friends, going back to their days in the dorms at Rutgers. Joel was in his mid-thirties now, confident, and a bit of a bragger. He gave all the right answers and he had accomplishments to back them up. Of course, he loved the idea of an Essex County Tenant Resource Center.

We asked him, "What makes you confident that you can beat the Machine in the Primary?"

"Look at me," he said, spitting out his response as if we'd taunted him. He leaned into the assembled leaders. "You all know how rough politics are in Orange. Those Italians and the Irish, they play hardball but"—he paused and leaned in further—"I became mayor. And I'm a Jew." He sat back in his chair, and in the silence that followed, we told him we'd be getting back to him once our decision was finalized.

Shapiro was next. I admired how he listened so intently as each tenant leader introduced themself. His knowledge of rent control and state tenant law was impeccable, and he showed such utter respect for the volunteer leaders around the table. I was shocked at the relaxed presence of this boyish state legislator who barely looked his twenty-five years. The tenant leaders loved him. He made it clear that he didn't want to just fund a tenant center but make sure it was built into the county government so that it would live on beyond just his time in office. He pledged to use the office of County Executive to defend and maintain rent control. John walked him to the door.

On leaving, Peter said to him, "I don't know if you know this but I paid your brother a visit to get his advice before I decided to run. He's quite a guy."

Older and more established Bill Brach was next. Some of the tenant leaders knew that we had it in for Brach even if they didn't know the details. The interview went smoothly. No argument with his record on the issues. As an East Orange Councilman, he told us he'd introduced the first rent control ordinance, sometime back after World War II, I guess, maybe the early fifties. *About when Shapiro was born*, I thought. He answered our questions well. He supported the Tenant Resource Center idea and then we brought up our gripe. Brach was the attorney for the Newark Housing Authority during the four-year public housing rent strike. When the strike was finally settled in 1974, our friend and legal services attorney Harris David, who represented the striking tenants, returned all the escrowed rent money to the tenants in violation of the signed agreement. When that happened, Brach took action to have Harris disbarred.

We couldn't imagine anything worse. And we told him so.

Brach answered calmly and seriously that yes he'd gotten "hot under the collar" and that he now regretted his actions. None of us said much after that. His look of resignation made clear that he knew he wasn't getting our endorsement. We had nothing left to say, so we thanked him for his time. He thanked us for ours and quickly departed.

Support for Shapiro was unanimous. There was no doubt in anyone's mind. For those of us like me who'd never met him, we were totally impressed. Before the meeting adjourned, we made it clear that this was our moment. We all needed to drag every person we could to that convention, set for Saturday morning April 1st at Upsala College in East Orange.

The DUE Convention

The banner above the door to the Upsala gym that sunny April morning proclaimed *Democrats United in Essex*. Phyllis and I arrived early and stood on either side of the big double doors while the convention organizers with coffee cups in one hand and lists in their other hand huddled just inside. Phyllis's chattiness telegraphed her apprehension. I knew she felt like her reputation was on the line. I probably looked cool on the outside but my stomach was clenched with the dread that maybe we'd be embarrassed by the tenant turnout. We planned to show the liberals that we were a serious political constituency.

Tenants better show up.

We'd printed a thousand flyers endorsing Shapiro. People began to show up and we could see our work was paying off. Betty and Trish brought a big contingent from Bloomfield. Tenant leaders made sure we saw how many people they'd brought out. It was thrilling. The buzz of a

Part V: Taking Our Shot (1978)

political convention was intoxicating. We passed out flyers as quickly as we could.

The gym was filling up and alive with the anticipation of a movement that would take down the Machine. David Hull, in his blazer and rep tie, pulled Phyllis and I aside. In his most political insider voice he said to us, "Look, we appreciate your help, but we already know that Peter's got this thing locked up. We need to start building unity so we need you to stop passing out that piece of lit. We want to bring Bill Brach into the fold right after the vote." David wasn't happy that our handout didn't just endorse Shapiro, it also took aim at Brach who we called *unsuited for County office because of his "hot under the collar" temperament*.

We laughed at the idea that David saw us just as members of Team Shapiro and thought he could tell us what to do. We told him no and continued to pass out flyers.

By the time the convention was called to order, there were 1,341 people registered. Phyllis and I were elated. At least 350 of them were brought out by the Essex County Housing Coalition.

Brach, Shapiro, and Jeanne Graves, a leader of the Charter Change Campaign, sought the convention's nomination. Donald Payne, the Black Freeholder from Newark, was noticeably absent. Mayor Gibson, who was known to support Payne, was outside in a tracksuit jogging on the running track. He came in to address the convention, simply saying "what an important gathering" it was. When the press interviewed him he said he was personally embarrassed that his candidate had not shown up. Mayor Tom Cooke, who supported Bill Brach, brought out a big group from the East Orange Democratic Committee.

The convention's 102 votes were allocated by town based on the previous year's Dem Primary turnout, so town delegations sat together. That meant our tenant signs were sprinkled throughout the gym. While convention rules and procedures were being dealt with from the stage, Phyllis and I wandered around talking to tenant leaders and meeting their members. Once the real meat of the convention began, we sat with the sizable EOTA group alongside Cooke's loyalists in the East Orange delegation. Phyllis was nervously studying her speech, ready to be called up on stage to second Shapiro's nomination.

When it came time, Dan Gaby came to the mic to nominate Shapiro. The tall, handsome advertising executive was revered by suburban reformers. He called upon the convention to endorse Peter Shapiro for the office of Essex County Executive and take back control of County Government from the self-dealing Machine. A clear majority roared our approval from the bleachers. Phyllis was next. I patted her on the arm as she rose to go up on stage. The tenants cheered wildly when she was introduced as Chairwoman of the Essex County Housing Coalition.

Phyllis looked tentative and her smile was tight as she waited for the cheering to die down. I knew that smile. She was nervous. I knew she'd do fine delivering the speech that Ronnie helped her write. I just hoped she didn't talk too fast and would look up occasionally from her typed pages. Just having her in this key position on stage was a massive statement about our clout. Tenant leaders erupted again, making their numbers known when she finished with, "Peter Shapiro, our new County Executive."

After more nominating speeches and the three candidates addressing us all, it was time to vote. It took a little while but then the result was announced.

Shapiro won with sixty-one of the apportioned votes. Brach had thirty-nine and Graves got only two. The bleachers erupted again. Shapiro took the stage and called upon us all to maintain our unity and defeat bossism and bring Essex County into the modern era of honest and responsive government.

Phyllis, John, and I hung around outside the gym, talking with tenant leaders about next steps to getting Shapiro elected and what it would mean to have a Tenant Resource Center. It was exhilarating. Shapiro was shaking hands with everyone in sight and came up and gave us some special recognition. Amazingly, he remembered some of the tenant leaders' names from his interview.

Dems Disunited in Essex

The Democrats United in Essex coalition didn't remain united. Leaving the convention, Tom Cooke told *Star Ledger* political reporter David Wald, "I made a commitment to Bill Brach, not Peter Shapiro." It was a week later that Cooke got the East Orange Democratic Committee to unanimously endorse Sheriff John Cryan. Mayor Gibson told Wald that he wouldn't announce his choice until after the Newark election on May 9th. Gibson was running for a third term.

I'd been at meetings with Gibson and Cooke, and they both talked about the importance of unity if we were going to take control of Essex County government. And now they were defecting? I had a lot to learn about how politics was played. My simple scenario of unified reformers versus a monolithic machine continued to unravel. Not only was the DUE coalition splintering, but fortunately the Regular Dems were in disarray. Several candidates claimed the right to the Line in the Primary. Meanwhile, Boss Lerner, who was in his seventies and spending more and more time in Florida, left everyone in suspense, creating a power vacuum.

Apparently Sheriff John Cryan, the forty-nine-year-old Irish immigrant and tavern owner, planned to run with or without Lerner's blessing. Younger Irish pols led by thirty-one-year-old union leader Tom Giblin felt it was their turn to move into leadership. Meanwhile, Gibson and Freeholder Donald Payne, who'd been a loyal supporter of The Organization, argued that the County Executive should be Black.

In spite of intense pressure from within the ranks, Lerner kept everyone guessing. Then he suddenly resigned. County Vice Chair May Maher was abruptly thrust into the boss's seat. She was rumored to favor Giblin and she hastily appointed a nominating committee, apparently to legitimize that decision. As soon as Maher's group selected Giblin, the other candidates—Cryan, Payne, County Supervisor Phillip Rotondo, and former County Treasurer Sam Angelo—all said the nominating process was rigged and announced they were running regardless of what the County Chairman decided. Suddenly, the Machine was in more disarray than the reformers.

Giblin tried in vain to solidify his backing within the party. He pressed Governor Byrne's chief of staff, hoping to get the governor's endorsement. It was thought that Byrne and Lerner had once agreed to both support Giblin, but once Lerner lost control of the process and resigned, that deal evaporated. Byrne stayed out of the race and didn't endorse anyone.

Years later, Shapiro told me of a meeting back then at the West Caldwell office of Local 825 of the International Union of Operating Engineers, where Giblin was the business manager. "I walked into the conference room and there was Giblin at the far end of the table, and along both sides were young Irish political guys—Phil Keegan, Dick

Codey and that bunch. I sat in the empty seat at the other end opposite Giblin. So Giblin tells me that I have to get out of the race because I'll end up throwing the election to Cryan. I told him I have no intention of dropping out. I'm running. Giblin throws a fit. You know he's got a terrible temper. He stands up, red faced, and picks up his end of the conference table like he's going to overturn it right on me. I start heading for the door with Giblin yelling behind me, 'You're going to give this election to Cryan!' As I got in my car, I saw Cryan driving in."

When I asked Shapiro why Giblin didn't run without the Organization's backing, he answered derisively, "Giblin didn't have the balls to run off the line. But Cryan, he's got balls."

I had the opportunity to ask Giblin why he didn't run that year. All he said was, "You've got to appreciate, Cryan was *really* popular." I took that to mean that with Shapiro in the race, suburbanites who might support Giblin would vote for Shapiro and make Giblin's path to victory impossible.

When the dust finally settled, four candidates had filed to be on the ballot for County Executive in the Democratic Primary: State Assemblyman Peter Shapiro, Sheriff John Cryan, Freeholder Donald Payne, and County Treasurer Sam Angelo.

With the Primary just two months away, Shapiro kicked his campaign into high gear. Phyllis and I were dismayed when Shuchter wasn't named Campaign Manager and instead was given the position of Field Manager. Shapiro hired Gina Glantz, fresh off of victories, for Congressman Andy Maguire and Governor Brendan Byrne. Glantz was a rising star in liberal Dem circles. We began to understand what was at stake in this high profile showdown.

Peter Shapiro with tenant leaders Lil Maurice, John and Mary Donoghue and Lilly Shateen.

CHAPTER 26

Lightning in a Bottle

Phyllis and I were in charge of getting out the vote (GOTV) among tenants for Shapiro. We met with Shuchter and insisted that unless we had a special piece of literature addressing tenant issues and highlighting Shapiro's promise to create a tenant resource center, our job of convincing uninformed tenants would be very difficult. He agreed to push to make it happen. We said we'd line up prominent tenant leaders to use their names in a list of endorsements.

Shuchter got permission for thirty thousand pieces of special "tenant lit," and I got to work writing the copy for John and Phyllis to approve. Phyllis and I distributed the tenant piece to dozens of tenant leaders, who got it out to their followers. It was an impressive operation.

It was a hard-fought and bitter race, with both sides having so much at stake. A sharp politico might have predicted the outcome based on the field of candidates—the popular Irish Sheriff, a well known Black Freeholder from Newark, an old stalwart from the Italian North Ward, and a young Jewish reformer from the suburbs. Cryan got a big share of the Machine loyalists, but Payne siphoned off most of the Black vote. Shapiro swept the suburbs, and Angelo peeled off a small group of Italians who might have supported Cryan. Shapiro emerged the victor with just 35% of the vote. Our tenant resource center dream was going to come true. We'd captured lightning in a bottle.

The *New York Times* quoted Shapiro about Donald Payne's role in the race: "We clobbered Cryan in suburban town after suburban town. Payne was so strong in urban areas and took away any margin that Cryan would have had."

The *Times* went on to say, "It was Mr. Payne's strong vote-getting ability in Mr. Cryan's home base of Newark, plus votes that Mr. Angelo was able to pull away from the regular Democratic organization candidate, that spelled the difference between victory and defeat for the Essex County Sheriff. Mr. Shapiro trounced his opponents in Millburn, Montclair, Maplewood, South Orange, West Orange and Livingston. To his surprise, he won in Nutley and Orange and did not do as badly as he had anticipated in Bloomfield and Belleville."

What an incredible turn of events. Our candidate, who promised to create the Tenant Resource Center, had just won with the help of organized tenants throughout the county. In solidly Democratic Essex County, any Democrat was expected to win easily in November, but the Democratic Machine wasn't nearly as motivated with a young reformer heading the ticket. Phyllis and I took our GOTV as seriously as in the Primary. Our tenant system was pretty organized now, and rallying tenant leaders and their followers throughout the county again was valuable. Distributing campaign lit that spoke to tenants' pocketbook concerns and then winning an election, that's how organizations get stronger and build solidarity. Phyllis and I planned to gear up late in the summer and hit the streets after Labor Day.

Once we won in November, the new tenant center could

catapult our work. We could help more tenants and support local leaders. A stronger Essex County tenant movement could help coalesce the rest of the state into a stronger tenants' movement through the NJTO and win and preserve tenant protections. Maybe with Shapiro in the County Executive seat, we could create some programs to help tenants like Jackie and her neighbors on Lenox Avenue. A stronger statewide movement could advocate a housing program that was broader than just tenants' rights.

With all that was happening across New Jersey, the statewide tenant organization should have been growing and expanding. Middle-class tenants were mostly fighting to win or strengthen or just defend rent control. Poor tenants were organizing to combat deteriorating living conditions, lack of repairs, and host of other issues. This burgeoning grassroots tenant movement was outpacing its parent organization. Every local organization was independent, but aside from having a NJTO representative come and speak when rent control was up for a vote, there was little participation in the statewide group.

NJTO's problem was its top leadership. David Baslow was the president and he wasn't the type who wanted to share the spotlight or the decision making. Marty Aranow, the charismatic businessman who founded NJTO with Ronnie at his side, had died of cancer in 1973. Marty's wife, Sylvia, took over for a couple years and then Baslow became president. To me, from a distance, the new organization president seemed knowledgeable and he actively advocated for tenants' rights around the state and in Trenton, but John and Ronnie and others like Mitch Kahn and Matt Shapiro experienced Baslow's dictatorial style.

It was sometime early in 1978 when the first rumblings of discontent surfaced in the statewide organization, which had accomplished so much. Important tenant protections had been won in the state legislature—a Just Cause Eviction statute, security deposit legislation, Truth-In Renting, and more. Rents kept rising rapidly everywhere, and the possibility of enacting rent ordinances gave birth to city- and town-wide tenant organizations across the state. Those battles brought so many tenants into the political process. NJTO could now engage these new citizen leaders in every corner of the state. Ronnie and John were on the NJTO Board of Directors and could feel that this tenant uprising, at least in New Jersey, had the beginnings of a mass movement.

Meanwhile, Dave Baslow had a different approach. Marty, the founder would have relished this opportunity to expand leadership. What Baslow relished was his role as the spokesman for New Jersey tenants and the person who state officials and legislators went to on all tenant matters. Baslow wanted the state organization to always speak with one voice—his. John and Ronnie imagined something very different. Baslow chafed when John was frequently quoted in newspapers on tenant issues as a "leader of New Jersey Tenant Organization."

The issue came to a head at a Board meeting when the irritated president presented a resolution that said something like, "Only the president could speak on behalf of NJTO, and any public comments by others had to be cleared with him."

A leadership battle seemed inevitable, but grassroots organizations are fragile creations. They depend on a level of solidarity and even camaraderie. Local leaders who were prepared to do battle with their city or town council didn't like having to choose sides in a leadership struggle within the home team. Ronnie and John spoke with board members Matt Shapiro, Leo Hammer, and Hanni Duffy about mounting a competing slate of officers at the upcoming annual meeting.

The group let Baslow know that if he didn't open up the board leadership to more local tenant leaders, then he'd be facing a formidable slate at the annual meeting. Rather than risk losing his position in the election, Baslow agreed to a compromise and an expanded slate. He would remain president and Ronnie would become Chairman of the Board. Phyllis and Joan Pransky were added to the board and so was Jim Tarella, a young tenant lawyer who was co-chair of the dynamic New Brunswick Tenants Organization.

Nearly eight hundred people attended the annual meeting held in Bergen County and without any knowledge of the brewing leadership challenge, they enthusiastically approved the leadership slate with a voice vote. Baslow could not have been happy. Ronnie and John knew that if NJTO was to grow, Baslow had to go, but that nasty battle was put off for a year.

The negotiated peace within NJTO was short lived. When FLEET, the powerful Fort Lee tenants organization, announced it was backing a couple of candidates in the upcoming municipal election and called upon NJTO to back them up, Baslow balked. He had some disagreement with one of the candidates. It was unheard of that NJTO wouldn't back its largest local organization. Then we heard that Baslow publicly criticized Fort Lee's rent law that limited annual increases to 2.5%. A public battle in the press broke out between FLEET president Matt Shapiro and Baslow, whose next move was to call for Shapiro to be dumped from the NJTO board. Shapiro called for Baslow's resignation.

Thirty NJTO board members showed up for a board meeting at Fort Lee High School. They quickly approved a resolution to back all of FLEET's election endorsements and then debated a bylaw amendment late into the night. The amendment would allow for impeaching the NJTO president in between annual elections. Baslow had a lot of support among Bergen County tenant leaders, and the impeachment amendment was defeated by a whisker.

It wasn't long before I was on the board. I proposed to our group that the growing statewide organization needed a better publication than the dry and clinical *NJTO News*, a stapled newsletter that mostly reiterated state laws. I laid out a vision for something like a local version of *Shelterforce*, a newspaper that heralded the victories of local tenant organizations, pages that brought the tenant movement alive, where people could see their own successes in print and the winning campaigns of organizations in neighboring cities and towns. I was voted onto the board and named editor of a much expanded *NJTOnews* newspaper.

I had just added another volunteer commitment but I couldn't pass up playing a valuable role in this powerful grassroots movement. I'd make it work. I immediately reached out to Steve Krinsky, who had as many volunteer jobs as I did. Just as I expected, he only hesitated slightly before agreeing to pitch in with the newspaper.

The battle over Fort Lee's 2.5% rent limit suddenly got statewide attention when a lawsuit looking to overturn it and challenging "strict" rent controls was heard by the Supreme Court. Baslow jumped in publicly, and not on the side of the tenants. He was quoted in the papers saying, "Moderate rent controls work and if they become too restrictive and tenants become too militant in their demands, the Court is not going to sit by and let private landlords be put out of business."

We were incredulous. Baslow wasn't wrong but why was he weighing in against what the Fort Lee tenants had fought for and won? Why offer up language like "landlords being put out of business" or call tenants "militant?" He could have defended the ordinance and said that if landlords can't live with 2.5% they can come before the Rent Leveling Board, open their books, and plead their case. At that point we knew that Baslow had to go. All of us in Essex, and a bunch of tenant leaders in Bergen and other counties, agreed. The annual membership meeting and election was scheduled for the following June. It was time to take over leadership. We'd probably have to run a competing slate of officers and board members.

Baslow viewed NJTO differently than we did. Ronnie, John, Joan, Phyllis, Mitch Kahn, and some of the older left-wing tenant leaders, we saw NJTO radically different from Baslow. The imperious organization president saw the landlord and tenant conflict as something to be managed by "reasoned" brokers like himself. He wanted local tenant leaders to grant him permission to speak on their behalf and represent their interests. We saw tenants fighting back against rent gouging and bad maintenance as a grassroots movement with average people stepping up into leadership. Our job as NJTO leaders was to help empower them. Encourage them to speak for themselves and on behalf of the whole movement.

Meanwhile, the Fort Lee rent ordinance was in the crosshairs. Maybe Fort Lee tenants *had* overplayed their hand. We feared municipal rent control was in jeopardy and might get overturned. In October 1978, the New Jersey Supreme Court struck down the Fort Lee law as too restrictive, but it reaffirmed the right of municipalities to regulate rent increases. But the Court offered no guidance on what a fair return on investment was. Ronnie was quoted in the papers calling the decision a victory because "it continues the right of municipalities to adopt strict rent control ordinances." The landlord tenant battle at the local level wasn't going away.

Death to the Machine

I was still relishing our amazing electoral victory when I went to visit my parents for a few days. I'd started coming back more often because my mom was stuck. My dad was in a wheelchair since his stroke and his father, Papa Moe, was now living there too. Mom was their full-time caregiver, cook, domestic help, and more.

With my dad's stroke, he'd lost his ability to talk and had taken early retirement. I felt pretty bad for him, and through some therapy and the passage of time, I'd resolved a lot of the resentment I had for the critical and judgmental way he treated me. I reasoned that he and I were simply fallout from the sixties' and seventies' *generation gap*, and I wanted for us to get past that.

I hugged my dad in his wheelchair in the family room. Because he'd lost his ability to speak, I began to make one-way conversation. Thinking he might be curious about what his oldest child was doing, I began to tell him about my latest exploits.

"So, Dad, I got involved in this political campaign and we got behind this young politician, a guy named Peter Shapiro. We defeated the entrenched Democratic Machine in the Democratic Primary. In our county, the Dems always win the November election, so he's going to be the next County Executive."

To make my point, I elaborated on the evils of the Machine and how they used patronage jobs and contracts to hold on to power and basically rip off the public and defeat any good government reform efforts. "Look, Dad, it's like Mayor Daley in Chicago. He maintained power through patronage and kept anyone interested in honest government from challenging him."

My dad had been listening to my story, interested I assumed, but he suddenly turned red-faced and shot daggers from his eyes. "No," he said, in his garbled-stricken voice. "No!"

With difficulty, he reached into his back pocket and pulled out his bulging wallet. With his one good arm and hand, he set his wallet in his lap, propped the wallet open, and pulled out a dog-eared news clipping. He unfolded it and pushed it at me with a nasty look on his face.

It was a lengthy obituary from the *Chicago Tribune* of former Mayor Richard P. Daley.

What an idiot, I thought. *How did I not make the connection? It was so obvious.*

My dad had great admiration for Chicago's Irish Democratic boss. I had just widened the gulf between us. Of course he wasn't proud of what I'd accomplished. I just reminded him that not only was I not in a traditional occupation and had moved six hundred miles away, I rejected his whole cultural heritage and had disdain for his hero.

I felt like shit.

Back in New Jersey, there was a General Election to win. A Democrat hadn't lost a countywide race in at least two decades, but Shapiro took no chances and he wanted to be sure that voters got to know him and gain some confidence that this twenty-six-year-old was capable of running their $200 million a year government.

Phyllis and I were a familiar arm of the campaign now. Shuchter reached out and we made a plan. Phyllis was at home at 209 Prospect with Joanna, her newborn. It was her job to make calls and mark up lists. I was the runner and delivered literature to tenant leaders all across the county. There wasn't any of the day-to-day urgency we felt during the Primary, but we felt like Shapiro did. The young reformer campaigned hard in every corner of the county and we moved thousands of pieces of tenant lit. We wanted tenants invested in this race. When he won they'd feel a sense of their power and an ownership stake in the new Tenant Resource Center.

I was spending time in Phyllis's apartment every day with her and her new baby. That's when I finally quit smoking. Determined not to gain weight, I began a health routine. It was the first time I ever jogged. One day, in my white U-D sweatshirt and stocking cap, I was running the streets through the neighborhood.

A Black guy across the street walking his dog yelled to me, "Hey, Rocky."

I waved and threw a few punches in the air.

He laughed.

I thought about the palooka played by Sylvester Stallone whose goal as a boxer was simple—not to be seen as a "bum." I thought about that as I continued running. I too was still being chased by a negative image.

Like Rocky, I was still trying to prove myself. I hadn't *quit* any of those things. A promising career in accounting or business. My young marriage. The religion I grew up in. I was simply involved in finding something that had greater meaning for me. I thought, *Who am I trying to prove myself to? My dad still? Or maybe just to myself.*

On election night, a bunch of us gathered with Shapiro

Part V: Taking Our Shot (1978)

campaign workers, volunteers and elected officials who supported him. The beer and wine flowed as we waited for all the returns to come in. I shook hands, hugged and slapped the backs of a bunch of the politicos who I'd met as far back as the first meetings that created the DUE convention. I felt swept up in a political insurgency. Phyllis stuck close by my side. She was becoming a powerhouse in Essex County, but she was tentative when people greeted us.

As we'd walk she'd lean close and say things like, "I can tell they really don't respect us, like when they say 'Well look who's here. It's the tenant people.' I know they don't think we belong here."

"Phyllis," I'd say, "maybe so, but we *do* belong here. We delivered a lot. Starting with our amazing turnout at the DUE convention."

We waited for election returns but there wasn't really any doubt about the outcome. The goal was a decisive victory. Shapiro handily beat the Republican, Robert Notte, with over 60% of the vote. The victory was sweet.

I immediately wondered what awaited him when he walked into the musty old Hall of Records and tried to wrestle control of County Government after decades of Machine rule. The day-to-day work of Essex County government was the domain of people who owed their jobs to the Regular Democratic Organization, not to Peter Shapiro.

Shapiro went off with his family on a ski trip and while he was away he mapped out a reorganization of county government into eight major departments. I immediately called Shuchter to ask where the Tenant Resource Center was.

"Don't worry," he said, "it's in the Division of Consumer

Services, within the Department of Citizen Services. It's in a good place. I think Becky Doggett will be heading Citizen Services." That was a bit of unsuspected news.

Wow, that's really a bold move. Shapiro appointing a community organizer to head up this department that includes the massive County Welfare Department. She'll be a supporter of tenant organizing.

While we were connecting nationally with local tenant and housing groups, an unheralded group of New Left crusaders were continuing to build a citizen/labor political alliance, trying to unite average Americans and labor unions in a political coalition to do battle with the forces of rising corporate power. Heather Booth from Chicago, founder of the Midwest Academy school for organizers, was one of those early leaders. The young teacher of organizers and civil rights veteran believed that efforts around energy politics "would provide the chance to come together across the divisions which had torn apart so many groups in the 1960s. This was the chance to rebuild a sense of who we are as *Americans*, as a whole people." With rapidly rising gasoline and heating prices, Big Oil was the target.

In April of 1978, Booth and William Winpisinger, president of the Machinists Union, and William Hutton of the National Council of Senior Citizens founded the Citizen Labor Energy Coalition (CLEC) to fight to control rising energy prices. They brought together more than seventy citizen and community groups, labor unions, senior citizen groups, farm organizations, and low-income organizing projects to form CLEC. They were doing nationally what we hoped for in New Jersey.

CHAPTER 27

The Fight's Not Over

Main Street was looking more and more dreary. It was July 1978 when the Housing Authority's stranglehold on the Brick Church project was finally broken. Tom Cooke, the new mayor, was granted power over the development and sale of the Urban Renewal sites. The Housing Authority retained the power of acquisition, demolition, and relocation. The Authority's executive director was clearly holding on to the federal funding and all that staff while dodging the headaches of development where the Authority had already exhibited its total incompetence. The city had a new, seemingly impressive and business-like mayor, and he now had control over the downtown's future. The city badly needed to feel optimistic again. Most people were willing to give Tom Cooke a shot at fixing the downtown.

That's not how we felt about Cooke. We saw him as slick rather than impressive, a guy who preferred to talk about *slum tenants* rather than *slumlords*. He might be business-like but we didn't like the business he was up to.

The Chamber of Commerce weighed in, anxious to hold Cooke accountable. The Chamber challenged him to specify a timetable for naming a developer.

No sooner had Cooke gotten the power over urban renewal sites that he announced a six month agreement with a Los Angeles-based developer named Ericson to determine the best possible uses for the Brick Church site and whether an enclosed shopping mall was feasible. Cooke claimed the entire amount of proposed tax ratables for the redevelopment was $420 million, an improbably large sum, while claiming the city had lost $50 million in ratables over the last five to six years.

Within a couple months, Cooke and Ericson announced plans for a $70 million shopping, office, and hotel complex, way short of the $420 million talked about just months before. Ericson said construction would start in April 1979 and the complex would open by July 1980. The ambitious project envisioned a three-hundred-room hotel and convention center, an office tower, two apartment buildings, and two department stores. Council president Bob Moran backed up their claim, "I've studied the plans and I think they'll get their approvals very soon." Hope was in the air again. I was still dubious but it seemed that East Orange, ever hopeful and desperate for a boost, was prepared to trust its new mayor and his dynamic West Coast developer.

Raising Capital for Lenox Avenue

The tenants at Lenox Avenue weren't quite as bullish, but Marty didn't think that a quarter million dollars to save a dozen low-income apartments was an insurmountable sum to raise. I couldn't believe it but Marty was finding a way forward for the Lenox Avenue tenants. A support system for affordable housing in urban neighborhoods didn't exist, even for projects as inspiring as the Lenox Ave co-op. Sal Santinello had a plan and he introduced Marty to the complex world of tax shelters and paper ownership. With the right ownership structure on paper, the project could attract capital to rescue 66-68 Lenox by sharing tax benefits with its paper owners. What began as a simple concept of cooperative tenant ownership was morphing into a legal abstraction called a Limited Partnership.

Twelve low-income tenants were about to become partners with ten high-bracket taxpayers, all for the purpose of attracting an additional forty thousand to help pay for the renovation. The investors put up the cash in exchange for the depreciation deduction on their federal income taxes. Welcome to the world of tax shelters.

I majored in accounting; I knew about accelerated depreciation, but I thought you had to own the asset to take the deduction. But buying only the depreciation deduction as a tax shelter? I didn't recall that. Maybe the white shoe lawyers who made their living helping the wealthy avoid paying taxes hadn't invented it when I was in college. Stretching and contorting federal tax law made it all legal.

Just the term *tax shelter* set me off. All I could think of was that wealthy people were unwilling to pay their fair share of taxes and the rest of us working stiffs picked up the tab. Why didn't the government just help out low-income tenants?

The legal mirage of the Limited Partnership was only matched by the complexity of the *capital stack,* a new term to me. The potpourri of financing sources Marty and Sal cooked up was a Wall Streeter's wet dream—but without the extra zeros. There was a loan from Lincoln Bank, a second bank loan, the Department of Community Affairs grant, additional grant funds from the City of East Orange, a small grant from the Prudential Foundation, ten units of syndicated equity (the tax shelters), and a donation from the Ethical Culture Society. It was dizzying. All to raise the grand sum of $250,000.

Funding sources were starting to fall into place. The

same day that Sal got the good news that the DCA grant was approved, he got a second call that was so distressing that it looked like the project was doomed.

There was a fire on one side of the building. Six of the families were now homeless. The building would have to limp forward with rent from the remaining six tenants while Sal and Marty tried to secure the rest of the financing.

Main Street Limbo

Over on Main Street, it was finally time to start construction at Brick Church, at least based on what Ericson, the developer, said seven months earlier. Instead he announced a delay. He said it was "because of the demographic studies." We couldn't help but wonder. We suspected that the studies didn't support the oversized dream that he and the mayor had so proudly touted a year earlier, but Ericson added, "I am working with three major department stores and hope to land two who will take two hundred thousand square feet each." Those words rang so hollow. We'd heard them before. The term "working with" was empty and vague. This latest iteration was starting to feel all too familiar. We'd all seen this movie—and we didn't like how it ended.

The Urban Renewal project wasn't the only effort stuck in limbo. EOTA had made no progress in the last two years on two of its important initiatives—The Emergency Repair Ordinance and Landlord Security Deposit that was first proposed by EOTA in 1974. It was August 1979 when EOTA called a city-wide tenant meeting at Munn Avenue Presbyterian Church to discuss a campaign to pass the stalled Emergency Repair Ordinance. The ordinance was held captive in the Law Department for months, allegedly being studied. Tenants believed city leaders were just stalling.

The next month, dozens of tenants were again at a City

Council meeting, calling for action on a law to mandate immediate repairs be made by the city when landlords failed to make repairs when a specified emergency exists. And to back it up, they wanted a Landlord Security Deposit to be held by the city. Lorraine Lavender, one of the new strong Black leaders and EOTA Vice President went to the mic.

"Every winter we get a flood of complaints of no heat, no hot water, and problems affecting life and safety. This is a crisis situation and can't be delayed any longer."

Theodore Murnick of the East Orange Property Owners Association, the landlord lobby, spoke next. "Landlords are not making money and if you take away more money, East Orange will become a less attractive place to do business." If he was truthful, he'd have said that landlords had *already* lost interest in East Orange.

In October, tenants and landlords spoke at the Public Session for and against the Emergency Repair Ordinance that was to be introduced that evening. Later in the meeting, the ordinance was introduced on First Reading and immediately went down to defeat.

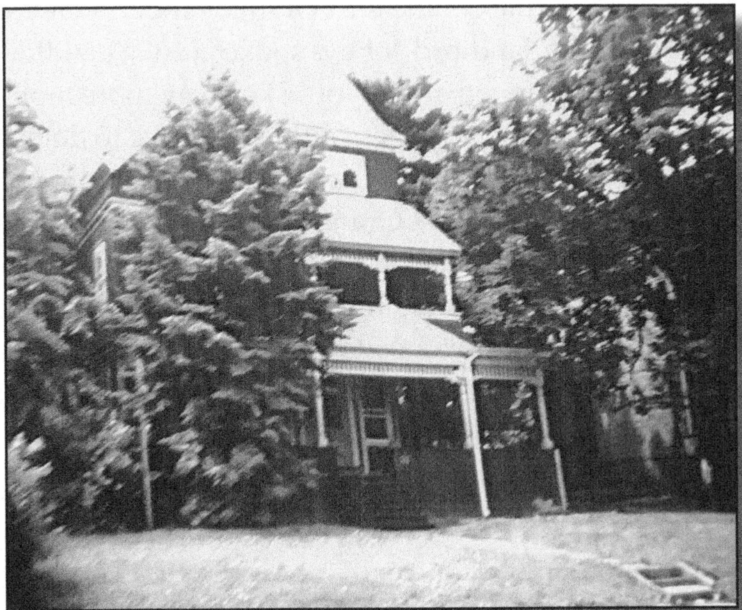

PART VI

Unfinished Business

1979

Phyllis with East Orange tenant leaders
Sam Webb and Jackie Cooke.

The decade was coming to an end, and the stubborn economy remained the foremost issue, and now American world dominance was in question. Global issues were shaping what was happening at home.

Western influence in the Mideast spawned a revolution in Iran that overthrew the US-backed Shah and declared an Islamic Republic. An exiled cleric Ruholla Khomeini became Supreme Leader and he expelled all foreign oil companies and nationalized Iran's entire oil sector. The disruption that followed reduced Iranian oil production by 90% and created a global oil shortage.

Suddenly, the most important issue was energy independence and the development of alternative energy sources. President Carter had solar panels installed on the White House.

A nuclear reactor at the Three Mile Island nuclear power plant in Pennsylvania experienced a partial meltdown after just four months of operation. There was no widespread release of radiation but a lot of people were freaked out about the safety of nuclear power. It looked like nuclear power might be off the table as an alternative to coal, gas, and oil.

Inflation was eroding purchasing power. Wages doubled during the seventies to keep up, but consumer prices rose by 112%. The middle class was losing ground for the first time since the Depression.

To combat inflation, the Federal Reserve continued to raise interest rates, and by the end of 1979, a thirty-year fixed-rate mortgage was 12.9%. People who already owned a house saw their home values rise by 180% in the decade, but new homebuyers were out of luck. Home prices were rising faster than incomes, and mortgage interest rates were hopelessly high.

Hoping to unlock a stagnant economy and increase competition and lower prices, Carter began deregulating the airlines and the trucking industry. Unfortunately, the trade off was job losses and some instability in those sectors.

Prolonged high inflation and a stagnant economy caused a lot of Americans to lose faith that the government could help them. This prompted Carter to have a heartfelt talk with the nation. He said that America was suffering a "crisis of confidence" and that a national "malaise" had set in.

Gender equality seemed inevitable, but when the 1979 deadline for ratifying the Equal Rights Amendment approached, only thirty-five states had ratified it. Three short of adoption. Congress extended the deadline three more years.

America's cultural clash spawned some crazy stuff. At Comiskey Park in Chicago, Disco Demolition Night resulted in a stadium full of baseball fans rioting between games of an evening double header. It was seen as a reaction to the racial and gay origins of disco. The Vietnam War still hung over the American consciousness when the film *Apocalypse Now* captured the psychological turmoil of the Vietnam War.

On the electoral front, Barry Commoner and Ralph Nader and some philanthropists launched the Citizens Party, stating that the two political parties "have abandoned even the discussion of the major issue of the day—who governs the economic interests of this country."

In November of '79, Ronald Reagan announced his campaign for president. That same month, Iranian students stormed the U.S. Embassy and took fifty-two American diplomats hostage. Jerry Falwell named his conservative political action group the Moral Majority. It was an effort to unify a broad swath of conservative Christians under one activist banner that suggested widespread societal agreement on conservative values.

By the end of 1979, 21% of new cars sold in the U.S. were made in Japan. A new term was showing up in the press to describe the manufacturing decline and job losses in the Northeast and Midwest—the Rust Belt.

SHELTERFORCE

Vol 2 No. 3   A NATIONAL HOUSING PUBLICATION   Winter, 1977

Rent Control
—Across the country rent control is a major issue with the battle line clearly drawn.

Judges And The Law
—Tenants continue to win important legal reforms only to find that judges continue to take the law into their own hands.

Housing In Italy
—The Italian experience shows that urban renewal need not mean wholesale destruction.

CHAPTER 28

A National Tenants Union

Shelterforce content was meatier than ever. One major analysis piece by Joan, John, and Ronnie was built off of our fight with a local Judge named Albano. It was titled "Ignorance of the Law is No Excuse" and it examined cases from around the country where judges were routinely ignoring legal protections for tenants. Ronnie and Kathy Aria, who worked as Joel Shain's administrative assistant, wrote a series on "Using the Media." We continued to cover major tenant and urban renewal conflicts like the poor tenants at the International Hotel in San Francisco. We began to analyze the growth of CDCs, community development corporations that were rehabbing and developing housing, and raised the issue of how community organizing could get compromised when a group also did community development. We covered the new statewide housing coalition in California, CHAIN, and we connected with Carole Norris, the group's dynamic first executive director. We began profiling a citywide tenant organization in each issue. We began with the Seattle Tenants Union, then Met Council in New York and then Tenant Action Group in Philly.

Almost four years of publishing created close relationships with dozens of tenant groups around the country. We could feel the racing heartbeat of a populist uprising, a revolt over rising rents and declining housing conditions. John said "a *sleeping giant* was awakening," and that the tenant movement would continue to grow and do battle with the moneyed interests that profited from tenants' plight. He lent me a book titled *Democratic Promise: The Populist Moment in America*. I couldn't put it down. I raced through the dense pages about the agrarian rebellion of the late 1800s against exploitation by the railroads and the banks. How the farmers created cooperatives and how a movement with a vision of economic democracy grew into the Populist Party and became a national force. Maybe our ascendent movement would galvanize a *populist moment*.

All of this connecting with grassroots organizers and their local campaigns got us thinking about how we could have a bigger presence nationally, and the concept of a united national voice began to take shape.

We knew that a solution to America's housing needs was ultimately decided at the federal level. Tenants needed a voice on federal housing policy. We harbored thoughts of a national tenants organization. We could publish *Shelterforce* from East Orange, New Jersey, but a national organization would need to be in DC. It would need staff and a decent budget. In 1978, John and Woody took the lead and we kicked off serious discussion with some of the best organized tenant groups from around the country: Met Council in New York City, Tenant Action Group in Philadelphia, California Housing and Information Network, Texas Tenants Union, United Tenant Organization in Topeka, and two groups in Massachusetts. There was strong

Part VI: Unfinished Business (1979)

interest in a national organization. Woody volunteered to coordinate things and organize a national meeting.

In the pages of *Shelterforce*, we wrote about all the local rent control battles. There was some form of state or local rent control in nine states and the District of Columbia, and seventeen other states had rent control proposals under consideration.

It was 1979 when word went out and nearly a hundred of the best tenant leaders from eighteen states met for an entire weekend at Independence High School. The National Committee for Rent Controls was born. John addressed the charged up group and reminded us all that our local work was a *movement*.

"Our budding tenants movement is like the early stages of the women's movement and the civil rights movement and the labor movement, deepening tenants' consciousness." He said, "Tenants are beginning to think of themselves as members of a group, with common problems."

We got a two-thousand-dollar grant to pay Woody as a coordinator, and the following year at a follow up conference in Cleveland, the National Tenants Union was born. No sooner had we convened our fledgling national group when we were immediately put on the defensive when the landlord, banking, and real estate lobby got legislation introduced to bar federal housing subsidies to cities and states with rent controls. The populist battle was engaged. The *sleeping giant* needed to get on its feet and fight back. Nothing galvanized landlord opposition like rent control.

The anti-rent control forces were organized, but they had a one-size-fits-all approach. One time, a West Orange organization, I think it was the Chamber, asked me to debate a realtor at a forum about rent control. I expected the average realtor would have no intimate understanding of how rent leveling actually worked, whereas I knew the subject inside and out. I'd heard all the arguments against rent control and I knew how to counter them. Nonetheless, I was a little on edge when I walked into the Elks hall. I shook hands and chatted with as many in the crowd of about sixty as I could. When I got up front, I saw the movie screen. The realtor went first. I was right. He was pretty clueless about the details. He let his audio-visual presentation do all the talking. It was prepared by the National Association of Realtors. When I saw the slick title slide: *The Truth About Rent Control*, I pulled out my notes and started to study them.

The first slide was a picture of abandoned apartment buildings in the South Bronx. The caption read: "This is what Rent Control produces." Each new slide was another dire prediction or a gross overstatement. The audience that was made up of mostly retirement-age tenants just scratched their heads. This was West Orange, a stable middle-class suburb. When I spoke, I ignored the arguments made by the realtor's hyperbolic slide show, except for a few sarcastic cracks that I couldn't resist, and simply told the folks how West Orange's rent leveling law works. During the Q and A, all the audience questions came to me. The moderator lobbed the realtor a few soft balls, but he didn't hit 'em out of the park. I hung around and chatted with some of the tenants. I asked them all if they paid dues to New Jersey Tenants Organization and reminded them that all the rights they had as tenants came from the battles waged by the state organization.

CHAPTER 29

All Things Must Pass

After Phyllis and Stu moved out, I began thinking that we were approaching the end of our communal experiment. But I didn't want to give it up. Maybe there was a way to keep us together.

Then Mary and Woody split up, though for a while they remained in the house. Eventually, Woody moved to West Orange. Mary was attending Essex Community College, where she met history professor Gene Lieber and their relationship began heating up. I began looking in earnest for the next collective and cooperative experiment.

I knew my next place wouldn't be in East Orange. Mary's boys had been the only White kids in the local public school and were now at the Ironbound Community School. We all wanted to live in a racially integrated town but it seemed that in a few years, that definition might not apply to East Orange.

I prowled around Ironbound and spotted a handsome red-brick, vacant factory building with a for-sale sign. It was on McWhorter Street just blocks from Newark Penn station. I called the number on the sign and arranged a tour. Oh man! I loved this place. And it was cheap. It was three stories, all brick, built in the 1800s. The corner where it sat was marked by a four-story tower. It was built around a courtyard where delivery vehicles would come and go. It was perfect for cooperative living. Separate living spaces. Some shared space also. A shared courtyard. And it was close to Simon and Michael's school. I figured Woody would want to join us. Maybe if I offered part of the corner space to John as a separate condominium, he'd be interested.

That could be the next phase—loft living, separate but with some common spaces, cooperative ownership, affordable, in a mixed ethnic neighborhood. And this would be my next building project.

But this project was big. I needed some expert advice. The father of Steve's friend Angela was a builder. So Angela and white-haired Angelo Cali tramped through the building with me.

Angelo was encouraging, "It's a solid old building. It'll make great housing. There're plenty of windows, high ceilings. It'll make a nice renovation."

Larry Bogdanow loved the project and prepared some quick floor plans and unit layouts. I consulted a guy who'd done some factory conversions in Hoboken. "Don't count on doing it for less than thirty- to thirty-five-dollars-a-foot," he said. "Renovation's full of surprises." I was sure I could get in under thirty.

Mary was excited. John was noncommittal. I began to crunch some numbers. The building was huge, at least twenty-five thousand square feet. *If my Hoboken friend is right, the renovation will cost $750,000. Am I out of my mind? Even if I net $10,000 on the sale of Chestnut Street, where am I going to raise that kind of dough?* I had no credit, no backers, no experience as a developer.

It was a hard truth. I couldn't just *will* this project into

Part VI: Unfinished Business (1979)

existence. Cooperative, affordable housing was a wonderful vision, and if loan money were available, maybe I would have succeeded. I rolled up Larry's floor plans and stashed them. I didn't have a Plan B. It would be another twenty years before I renovated my first factory.

Some months later, the group began to disperse. Mary and Gene would soon be married and buy a house in Montclair, where Simon and Michael would attend the Montclair public schools. John was getting married and they bought a house in Montclair too.

I rented the third-floor apartment to Walter Hetzel. He was a bit of a recluse, and soon it was just me occupying the lower two floors. The house felt enormous. I sorely missed the energy, the family and the community that once filled it. I resisted the idea that an era was over, and I wished against hope there was a way to keep it going. But the moment that was 31 Chestnut Street was likely drawing to a close.

Joanne Young had finally had it with typing legal letters, answering phones, and retyping legal briefs. She decided to take the leap and move to the East Village and become part of the New York art scene. When I saw her, she had a job tending an art gallery, greeting people who came in the door, ready to answer questions about the art and the artists whose work hung on the fresh white walls. Her look had changed, like she belonged there and she was happy.

"The pay sucks," she said, "but I'm not stuck behind an IBM Selectric in New Jersey. I'm where I need to be."

I could tell by her look, her attitude, and even her body language that she was right. I was happy for her.

Ronnie was around less. He had been sick, some respiratory thing. He seemed to get better but then he was sick again. It seemed to be a lung infection. Doctors couldn't diagnose it accurately, so they didn't know how to treat it. But I saw him a lot less. He no longer worked in Orange and he and Joanne were tucked away up in Ringwood. My close friend was getting ready to teach part-time at University of Bridgeport, so he'd be commuting at least twice a week. I missed him.

Our work was expanding on all fronts without our leader. We were on fire. Four of us—John, Joan, Phyllis and I—were now on the NJTO Board. We were laying plans for expanding the state organization's leadership base, especially in urban areas, starting with Newark and the Oranges. *Shelterforce* was growing. Our amateur production team was aided greatly by Steve Krinsky and the talented Chip Cliff who had graphic art and layout skills. They both helped me with *NJTOnews*. As busy as we were, pretty soon we'd have a county tenant resource center to create. But then we'd have paid staff to support our work in Essex. I felt like our team was entering a new era, in that same way I felt that our vision for America was ascendent. Despite a conservative swing nationally, I saw our movement becoming the dominant political and cultural force. It would take time, but to me that seemed inevitable.

I thought we were emblematic of what was brewing around the country. The youth movement had been galvanized by the War and the draft and had now matured and expanded its reach. We were the youthful energy that would rescue cities and fight for justice on pocketbook issues, not just housing. Young civil rights activists like Becky Doggett were staking a claim in urban neighborhoods. Look at the community/labor coalitions organized by people our age to fight Big Oil. Same with the environmental movement and the women's movement. We were witnessing big cultural changes in how minorities and women were being treated. Educational institutions were opening up. We were changing consciousness. With a vision like that, how could we not be the wave of the future?

I was aware of the growing conservative backlash. That was inevitable, I thought, and it was generational. I figured Americans wouldn't stand for the wealthy and big corporations becoming any more powerful. They knew that concentration of power like that flew in the face of everything that was American. My experience of life in Detroit where miles and miles of neighborhoods were home to thriving working-class and middle-class people—that's what people wanted. People of all races.

Meanwhile, it was hard to deny that in 1979, the nation was in a state of disequilibrium. The economy sucked. We had high inflation with soaring interest rates *and* high unemployment. This previously unknown combination called *stagflation* meant that we were all suffering economically. Lots of people were despondent and angry. Policies like busing and affirmative action were met with a blue collar rebellion. Watergate and revelations about CIA and FBI abuses at home and abroad undermined everyone's faith in the government and its institutions. Trust in government was at an all-time low. Nobody was happy with the current state of affairs.

It was time to draw people together, project a strong vision of what we'd been fighting for—a just economy and a socially equal and prosperous society. But we had Jimmy Carter in the White House and we were beyond dismayed when he decided to address the American people about the nation's "moral and spiritual crisis." That was Carter. The deeply religious father figure.

There he was on national TV at a time of deep public anxiety to talk about what's "wrong with America," and he beamed out to Americans across the country, "I want to talk to you right now about a fundamental threat to American democracy." He declared that America suffered a "crisis of confidence." He went on, "It is a crisis that strikes at the very heart and soul and spirit of our national will. We can see this crisis in the growing doubt about the meaning of our own lives and in the loss of a unity of purpose for our Nation. The erosion of our confidence in the future is threatening to destroy the social and the political fabric of America." He talked about the "the growing doubt about the meaning of our own lives and in the loss of a unity of purpose for our Nation."

Carter wasn't wrong that Americans were divided and that we weren't feeling a unified national purpose. Things had changed fast during the sixties and the seventies. A lot of people were having a hard time adjusting, and their anxiety was being stoked into anger by far-right activists and politicians. But a fatherly fireside chat wasn't going to soothe Americans. Didn't Carter know that Ronald Reagan and the Far Right and now the evangelical Christians were looking to take him down in 1980? And that he was providing them with the ammunition?

The Right had the balls for a fight for the *soul of the nation*, while we had a moralizing father figure telling us the hard truths he thought we needed to hear. The election was a year and a half away. We needed Carter to go on the offensive and fight for everyday average Americans. Maybe a different Democrat would emerge and beat Carter for the nomination. Then beat back the Right's last desperate reactionary gasp. Clear the way for our vision of a better society.

CHAPTER 30

Unfinished Business

Peter Shapiro took office as the first Essex County Executive on January 1, 1979 and moved into the fifth floor of the County Hall of Records, an aging hulk from the last century, in downtown Newark. County employees, who seemed to have been there since the building first opened, worked from 9am to 4pm with an hour off for lunch, and they all moved slowly through the mausoleum-like structure, viewing all the Shapiro people with suspicion, wondering how their comfortable existence might change as a result of regime change.

By the end of January, Phyllis figured Shapiro had been in office long enough, so she started hounding Shuchter about when the new County Executive was going to establish the Tenant Resource Center. Shuchter was in charge of Constituent Affairs and was housed with the rest of the executive staff stretching along the fifth floor from Shapiro's spacious corner office. Shuchter, perhaps overacting a little, was incredulous in the face of Phyllis's demand.

"Do you have any idea what we're up against at the Hall of Records? The place is full of Civil Service folks who all owe their jobs to our political enemies. They hate us. They want to see us *fail*. They treat us like *foreign occupiers*. Peter's doing everything he can to assert himself. He hasn't had a moment to even think about the Tenant Resource Center. Give us some time. He hasn't forgotten about you and you certainly know I haven't."

To me, that all made sense but not to Phyllis, who said, "We did all that work to get him elected and we're getting ignored. We're treated like people who are just begging for a job because we worked on the campaign." So she pestered Shuchter every week. He'd listen patiently and try to reassure her. She was not the only person hounding Shuchter post-election. Everybody who'd been shut out by the old Machine wanted in. Shuchter was the gatekeeper.

John and Phyllis and I met a couple times to talk about what the Tenant Resource Center would be like. Who should get hired on staff. We met with tenant leaders who'd worked to get out the vote and assured them that we were in touch with Shapiro, and we repeated some of the same stuff that Shuchter said.

One day, John proclaimed to Phyllis, just flat out, as he often did, "Pat should be the director." He looked at me. "You should definitely do it. There's nobody better for the job."

I liked the idea and before I could say anything, he continued, "We should meet with Shapiro and tell him we know how busy everyone is down there, that we want him to hire Pat to set up the Center." Maybe Phyllis thought that she should be the director, I don't know, but she agreed.

"I'll call Shuchter and get a meeting."

Peter Shapiro seemed remarkably relaxed in his corner office on the top floor. He welcomed us to his spacious office, showed us the view looking west across Newark to the suburbs beyond, and told a few war stories about how he was slowly taming the angry hordes.

Then he said, looking straight at Phyllis with his sly

smirk of a smile, "Peter tells me that you guys think I forgot about the Tenant Resource Center."

Phyllis started backtracking and looked down at her notes. "Thank you for meeting with us." Then she relaxed a little. "No we didn't think you *forgot*, it's just that we promised people you'd do this thing for tenants in the county."

"And I will," said Shapiro. "But I honestly haven't had a free minute. It's a battle zone down here. They're coming at me from all sides. I really haven't had time to even think about it." Shapiro did a little more reassuring, commenting on how valuable our support had been, when John intervened.

"Peter, we get it. Totally. So we have an idea. Why don't you hire Pat and he'll come in and set it all up."

Shapiro cocked his head, as if thinking about it, then looked at me. I nodded my agreement.

Shuchter began to offer some cover for Shapiro with a statement about having to find room in the county budget at this time of year, when Shapiro broke in, "Peter we could bring Pat on our staff and once we've identified all the funding for the Center he'll be paid out of those funds. We've got room for him up here. Maybe he'll share *your* office."

That was it. Shapiro asked me what I thought and we noodled a bit about funding sources like Community Development Block Grant funds and then he said, "What about starting June first?"

I said I'd love to.

He stood up, signaling the meeting was over. "Let me get back to saving the kingdom we took over. Pat and Peter can work out the details."

We shook hands all around.

Shapiro winked at John and me. "I haven't even played any tennis. That's how bad it is."

In six weeks I was going to become a government employee. Steady salary. Benefits. Paid vacation. As we walked down the hall, I asked Shuchter, "So what's my job pay?"

Shuchter looked up and scrunched his face. "Fifteen or sixteen probably. I have to check with Gina. I'll ask for sixteen, okay?"

"Sure," I said. "Thanks." My life would be changing fast.

Shapiro's hiring choices were a mixed bag. The suburban liberals wanted him to clean house. The county workforce was packed with Machine loyalists whose political allegiance wasn't to the newly elected county executive. But Shapiro needed to keep peace if he was going to move county government into the twentieth century. His choices for leadership posts were strategic. Tim Hull conducted a national search and recruited Dan Bogan, a tall, handsome Black man with a commanding presence. Bogan had been City Administrator of Berkeley, California. For many of the in-house and administrative posts like Purchasing and the Personnel Department, the unwelcome young reformer left the old line people in place. For public-facing positions and areas where he wanted to make big changes, Shapiro recruited nationally or brought in his own loyalists who he could count on to both work hard and make his government run efficiently and effectively. I wasn't the only hire from the grassroots movement. Becky Doggett the dynamic founder of Tri City Peoples Corporation was hired to head the Department of Citizen Services, overseeing the welfare department and the new Division of Community Action, which was headed by another community activist hire, Catherine Willis.

CHAPTER 31

Really Shitty News

In early May of '79 Ronnie was hospitalized. His chest thing was now some sort of infection. I went to see him in the hospital. In his stark and lifeless room, I found Rae and Manny, John and Joanne. I got weak smiles from everyone. No banter. Everyone was subdued and serious. I thought I'd probably interrupted a family-only meeting.

"Pat!" Ronnie called out hoarsely when he spotted me. His eyes lit up and he flashed me that quick smile. The look and smile that always to me, meant, "My brother, my friend, my partner, I'm so happy to see you." It warmed me as it had hundreds of times before.

He made some cracks about being in the hospital and complained about everyone hovering over him being all so serious.

But then he said, "They're telling me I have cancer."

For the first time, he'd said the word *cancer*. My mind went blank. For an instant I couldn't catch my breath. When he said *cancer* I heard: *death sentence*. My eyes started to tear up. I couldn't say the word out loud. I wanted to cry and scream. I didn't look at anyone else.

I stumbled through some unmemorable conversation with Ronnie and then I told him I was on my way to Detroit to meet my first nephew, Marie's son Brian. I insisted that he be home and out of the hospital by the time I got back. I think he suspected this might be our last time together. I couldn't face leaving my best friend, but Marie and John expected me in Detroit, and I strangely felt like an intruder with his already grieving family crowded around. On my way out the door, I stopped and waved. He must have sensed my hesitation. He wouldn't acknowledge my trepidation. He flashed me that big smile and waved me off.

It was a week later. I was in Detroit at my parents when I got a call from Marsha. Without even a hello she yelled, "HERE'S SOME REALLY SHITTY FUCKING NEWS. Ronnie died."

My heart sank. In the back of my brain I knew this might happen, but I'd kept myself from even thinking that *maybe* it could. It was the farthest thing from my mind, that my closest friend, the person who I *knew* would always be there, was gone! Marsha wanted to talk, she needed to. But I couldn't. I had nothing to say. I told her I'd come back tomorrow or the next day. And then I hung up.

Over the last year, Ronnie and I had spent a lot less time together. He and Joanne bought that cool lake cabin up in Ringwood. It was idyllic. Like a vacation place, though Ronnie kept his Fort Lee third-floor garret under the George Washington Bridge as his law office.

Even though we saw each other less, to me he was always there, always my partner. Then suddenly he wasn't. How would I go on without his friendship, his guidance, his love? Of course I had a whole big community of friends and comrades, but no one was like Ronnie to me. He was more than a best friend, more like an older brother, someone who took me under his wing. He encouraged me to follow my dreams. Buy that big house, if that's what I wanted to do.

He taught me stuff. Like how to get around in places like Central America where we didn't speak the language and how to find cheap places to stay. And not to drink the water.

And he let me know in a hundred ways that he admired my passion for my work and for renovating the house and learning all those construction skills. He loved that I created a home for people, especially Mary and the boys, and he let me know it.

One Halloween he showed up at a costume party wearing a red flannel shirt and sporting an Irish working man's cap with a pencil behind his ear. He showed me the pocket knife in his pocket and the toothpick behind the other ear, and he was carrying a rectangular piece of cardboard. Joanne had drafted an exact replica of my business card.

He was poking fun at my carefully curated identity, but I was flattered. He took time to capture every detail. My smile turned to a laugh. He had nailed it and I told him so.

It was unthinkable, going ahead without Ronnie. We had so much more to do. There was so much uncharted territory ahead. We needed our sage, our guide. It was a lesson about impermanence. Nothing is guaranteed. Tom Jackson, my other close friend and mentor, I hadn't seen or heard from him in at least seven years. Now Ronnie was gone. I felt more alone than I'd ever felt.

A few hundred people gathered at Ronnie's memorial service at a Jewish funeral home on busy Route 4 in Paramus. It was a plain and simple setting, nothing like a Catholic funeral in a church. I couldn't imagine what John and Joanne must be feeling and his parents, Manny and Rae. The rabbi stood alongside Ronnie's plain pine box and talked about what a moral and committed person our dear friend was, saying that the Talmud tells us that in every generation there exist thirty-six righteous people whose role in life is to justify the purpose of humanity in the eyes of God. He went on to say that their existence is unknown except to God. The rabbi knew that was how we saw this special guy who we admired so much, who was a friend and role model to all of us.

After the service, a group of us gathered at Joan's house and drowned our sorrows and toasted Ronnie and shared stories about this amazing guy who had left such a big hole in our lives and our hearts.

CHAPTER 32

Tenant Resource Center and a Leadership Battle

On the first of June, I reported for work on the fifth floor of the Hall of Records. I had one responsibility: Create the new Essex County Tenant Resource Center. I'd already prepared a budget that included a staff of five, most of us, full-time organizers. Now I needed to make sure I corralled enough county resources to pay all those salaries. I hadn't cleared it with Shapiro yet.

I found my desk in a group of offices on the fifth floor and got to work. I knew I'd be competing for funds, and Shapiro was determined to create a host of new services but keep the tax rate down. If I ran into trouble, I'd call Phyllis. My budget was ambitious. We needed an office and a team of organizers. I built my budget around five positions—me as director, an administrative assistant, and three organizers. Shapiro approved my budget with funds from the county's federal Community Development Block Grant and from the regular county budget and gave me complete freedom in my hiring choices.

I had a few personnel choices in mind and ran them by John and Phyllis. Jackie Cooke was my first choice. She was streetwise and by now very experienced. East Orange would get lots of help with Jackie on staff. I knew John Donoghue, an older working-class Irishman who led the Irvington Tenants Organization. John was streetwise as well with an innate class militancy, and he traveled in different circles from Jackie or me or Phyllis. John and Phyllis liked both those choices, and one of them suggested the fiery new leader of the Montclair Tenants Organization for the third position. For my administrative assistant, I hired Chip Cliffe who worked with us on *Shelterforce*. Chip had a wide range of valuable skills. We had our staff and I started searching for a storefront office. John Donoghue was flabbergasted that I offered him a job in the Shapiro administration. He had supported Cryan for county executive. One day, Shapiro buzzed my desk and asked me to come down to his office.

"Hey, I just had this idea. Why don't I name the Tenant Resource Center after Ron Atlas."

The Leadership Battle

The NJTO annual meeting and board election was scheduled for June at the Rutgers New Brunswick campus. Steve and I produced a special four-page issue of *NJTOnews* with long pieces about the two competing slates. The day before the Annual Membership Meeting, we drove over to Harrop Press on Route 22 to pick up the 1,500 copies. When we got there, the manager told us that the paper had been picked up two days earlier by the organization's president. We used the manager's phone but couldn't get a hold of Baslow. Our minds spun as we speculated what he was up to. Would he alter the paper? Would Slate B's platform and candidate list be deleted? We'd find out the next day. In the meantime, we needed to continue recruiting for the showdown in New Brunswick.

Part VI: Unfinished Business (1979)

I had just started my new job at the Hall of Records and was consulting regularly with Shuchter about our upcoming election. The experienced political operative and paid member of Irvington Tenants Organization jumped in and treated the NJTO election like any electoral battle he'd been in. He helped me recruit some campaign loyalists, making sure they had up-to-date NJTO memberships and he volunteered to act as floor manager at the annual meeting.

Steve and I carpooled to New Brunswick early with a couple of recruits, speculating about what we'd find when we arrived. Baslow and a few volunteers were waiting, copies of the *NJTOnews* in hand, to greet arriving tenants. I snatched a copy from his hand. There it was. The newspaper had doubled in length with a four-page insert of photos and articles extolling Baslow's work on behalf of New Jersey's tenants. I leveled some curses at Baslow and decided my time was better spent talking with the tenant leaders I recognized and encouraging support for Slate B.

Buses arrived from all corners of the state, with the biggest single contingent from Fort Lee. The meeting would be raucous and the vote would likely be close. I sure wished Ronnie was there and was still board chairman. He'd know how to handle this.

Shuchter was our floor manager. He instructed us to be communicating with all the leaders on our slate and others who were with us. He asked us to identify which leaders supported Baslow, who we might want to add to the board if our slate won, and to let them know we would definitely consider that. If they were willing to switch their support, we should promise them a spot on the new board. We fanned out, looking to drum up support.

Shuchter had specific instructions about cheering and booing, and he wanted us to communicate that to our leaders. Cheer like hell when Phyllis was nominated and when she spoke. Only boo if they saw us booing, which meant that Baslow was lying.

The total number of voting tenant members in attendance was over eight hundred. Like most meetings like this, a lot of time was spent dealing with procedural stuff, like the voting rules. Everyone knew we were all there for one purpose. Baslow was nominated and then Phyllis and they gave their five minute speeches. There was plenty of cheering and we did some groaning when Baslow grossly overstated his accomplishments. Then the ballots were collected and the count was overseen by a couple people representing each slate. Baslow was defeated but not by a wide margin. Our Slate B had triumphed and we all erupted in applause, screaming and stomping our feet in the bleachers. Phyllis took the stage as the new president.

She promised a new wide open and stronger NJTO, and then she introduced the newly elected officers. Matt Shapiro from Fort Lee was First Vice President. John was Legal Counsel and Second VP. Hanni Duffy from Teaneck was Treasurer, and Betty Hutchinson from Bloomfield was Secretary. Joan was Vice President-Legal and Jim Tarella from New Brunswick was the VP for Organizing. Lorraine Lavender from East Orange was VP-Urban. Connie Pascale from Toms River was VP-Legislation, and the VP-Fundraising was Arlene O'Prandy from Cliffside Park.

After hugging Joan and John, Joanne and Lorraine, I sought out tenant leaders who I knew were on Baslow's slate and reassured them that we needed them to be part of NJTO leadership.

Post-election we should have been spending our energy

Part VI: Unfinished Business (1979)

reuniting local leaders, but Baslow was still fighting. Dislodging the deposed leader from the NJTO office was tougher than beating him at the ballot box. Most of the NJTO office space was subleased to an organization called Tenant Research and Education Organization (TREDO), a tax-exempt nonprofit that had secured funding from Bergen County and Baslow controlled TREDO. Fortunately, earlier in the year, Ronnie and Mitch had convinced the Freeholders to redesignate the money to Bergen County Housing Coalition, led by Mitch. It was a couple months of wrangling, some of it reported in the press, but in the end TREDO lost its funding and we could go about building a bigger, more dynamic NJTO.

The organization had new life and militancy under Phyllis's leadership. Monthly board meetings were wide open—exciting discussions about state legislative strategies, political endorsements, and how to strengthen the NJTO member organizations at the grassroots. She empowered local leaders from every corner of the state. Bonnie Shapiro, the Fort Lee tenant leader, held down the office every day and counseled tenants by phone, always insisting they pay their NJTO dues.

We had taken our local organizing statewide and were bringing the state organization back full circle to its earliest days when Marty Aranow with Ronnie at his side waged the first rent control battle in 1972 in Fort Lee. That pair of tenant crusaders then took the organization to other communities. Marty, from a high rise, upper income apartment building was the more public face. Ronnie had brought his keen legal and strategic navigation to the task of reaching and empowering new leaders.

We were taking over leadership of the NJTO, but Phyllis was still president of EOTA. Fortunately, the EOTA bench was pretty strong and well established with a wide range of additional leaders. Supporting Black tenant leaders who organized their buildings was always a priority for us, especially Phyllis, but in East Orange, Black leaders needed to *lead* the citywide organization, and that was happening. Lorraine Lavender, EOTA vice president and now a VP of NJTO, would soon be the next EOTA president.

Back on Chestnut Street, I was getting resigned to the idea that an era had ended. John, Phyllis, and Mary all had kids and a spouse and had moved on. I couldn't move on yet. I had to finish the house and then sell it.

Judy and I went up to the Catskills for a weekend in the late fall. The house was empty. When I returned that cold Sunday evening, I unlocked the front door and was hit by air that was as cold as outside. *Damn, the heat's been off.* For more than a day, I guessed. Then I heard the dripping. I rushed into the parlor. Water was coming out of the radiator air vent and water dripped from the ceiling above. Probably from the air vent of the radiator in my bedroom above. I ran upstairs. It didn't take long to figure out what was happening. The boiler was off but the automatic feeder was still delivering water to the system. It had filled up the pipes and radiators on all three floors and the only place for the water to escape was through the air vents on the back end of each radiator.

Shit! How'm I gonna drain the system? I ran to the basement and shut off the water feeder. On the side of the boiler there was a faucet. *That will empty the system but the water will just flood the basement.* Luckily there was a toilet on the other side of the basement. *Maybe I can just run a hose from the boiler to the toilet.* So I ran to the garage.

I threaded the hose onto the faucet on the boiler and stuck the other end into the toilet and opened the faucet.

Part VI: Unfinished Business (1979)

It worked. *What if I'd been gone for a week? With water leaking on three floors, the vacant house would have been destroyed.* What an end to my renovation project. Five years of work would've been gone in just a few days.

Victory!! Joanne Atlas, John Atlas, Lorraine Lavender, and Joan Pransky.

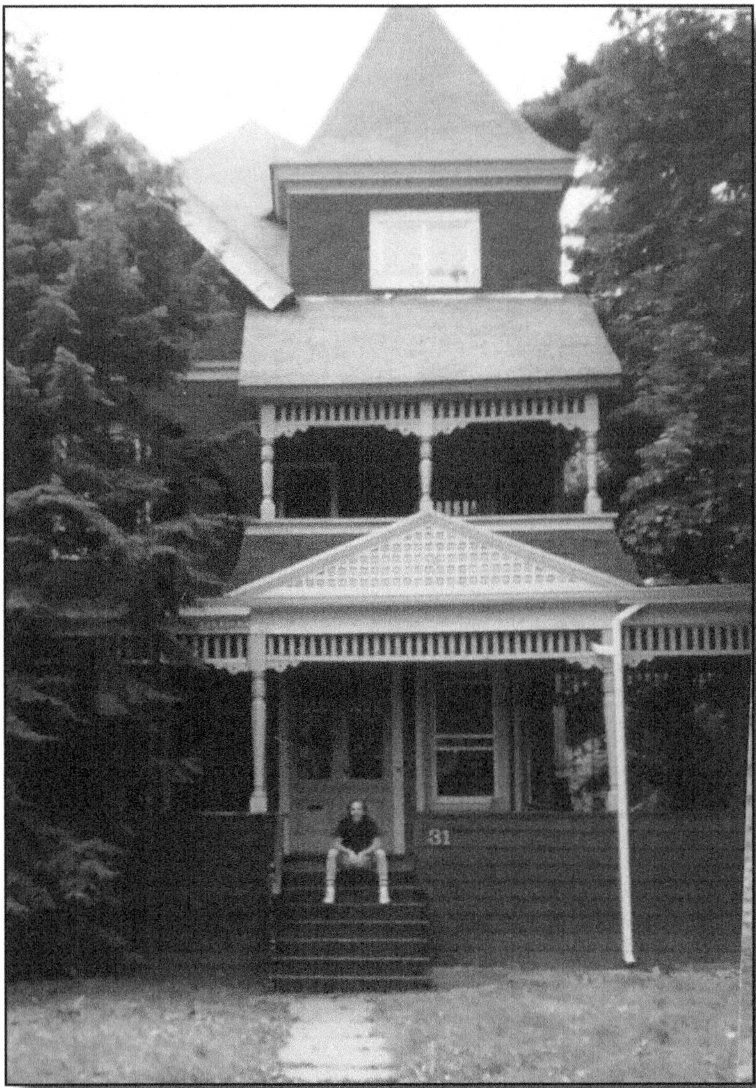
31

CHAPTER 33

Goodbye, 31 Chestnut

The seventies were an elongated moment that was now becoming history. *Shelterforce* reflected that. We'd been publishing the newspaper for over four years and the operation was still all-volunteer. Subscriptions and donations covered our costs, including office rent on Main Street. In a break with our anti-hierarchy culture, we named Woody our first editor. And, for reasons no one can recall, we stopped calling ourselves a Collective. The masthead now included a list of our names followed by a list of Friends. It would be sometime in the eighties before we'd have enough outside funding to pay Woody a part-time salary.

Our group had grown. We'd built two strong grassroots organizations. *Shelterforce* was reaching all the important activist groups in cities across the country.

We had influenced a major election and now controlled a lot more organizing resources. We took the reins of the statewide tenants organization with hundreds of affiliates and tens of thousands of members. Phyllis was president. John and Joan were two of the vice presidents. There was so much potential for growing this movement. And so much to do.

I had earned my PhD in renovation skills and was

ramping up the Tenant Resource Center with a staff of organizers. And I was editor of the *NJTOnews*. But I was still looking to find my groove. Saving old buildings and neighborhoods was now in my blood. Demanding rights wasn't enough. I wanted to create things, make things. Houses, neighborhoods, schools, businesses, all kinds of things—a better society.

It was going to be hard to leave the house. It was even harder to leave behind the communal dream. I completed the last bits of the renovation. It was now the nicest house on the block. The idea of getting rid of my creation seemed impossible, but without Mary and the boys and Woody and John, Phyllis and Stu… And with Ronnie gone, what was left? I no longer wandered through, stopping to admire the rich vintage details, because when I did it was always with a sense of longing, as if the dream house had slipped through my fingers and was no longer mine. I saw my handiwork of course and thought of how I had rescued it and honored the toil and skills of the original craftsmen. But without our group sitting around in those rooms or gathered around the dining room table, or descending the stairs running our hands along the well worn chestnut railings, or yelling "see ya later" as we passed through the carved front doors with their beveled glass, the house felt hollow.

I had brought together two halves and made a beautiful whole—a carefully restored Victorian-era house and a lively and loving group that gave it life. And now, except for me rattling around alone and quiet Walter on the third floor, the wonderful house seemed more than just empty.

It was twilight when I walked from room to room. I stopped and looked into the boys' bedroom and smiled when I thought about the bunk bed with a desk and dresser beneath that I'd built for Simon.

Part VI: Unfinished Business (1979)

I missed Mary. Her empty front bedroom with its private porch seemed bleak. All the greenery was gone—the potted plants, the climbing vines, the ficus tree in its terracotta pot. And the rabbit who lived in a cage on the porch. Of all the people who'd lived there, Mary brought the most of what the house needed. It was easy to be like a family with Mary at the center. Her two young boys added a lot. I missed Simon and Michael.

I went to the fridge that was no longer in the butler's pantry. It was now in the restored kitchen. I grabbed a beer and popped the tab. I stopped to admire the sixties stove top that I picked up from Tom Connell's parents when they remodeled their kitchen. The modern looking stove top was tucked into the original brick fireplace. I chuckled at the coincidence that I'd covered the counter with floor tiles salvaged from a church in Ironbound and edged it with a carved oak molding from that demolished church in the Urban Renewal area. Even church buildings in the inner city were being abandoned. Nothing was sacred.

I always knew the day would come when it was time to sell. I'd decided to go to a movie that night, even though I couldn't find anyone who wanted to see this latest over-the-top action flick that Kevin Kiernan told me about. It was called *Mad Max*. Kevin was an addict for pop culture, stuff that most of us turned our backs on and found too shallow.

He told me, "You'll love it. It takes place in the future following a nuclear war. There's no gasoline, so marauding gangs in souped up vehicles go around heisting gas depots and other shit. The action is crazy. It's a whole new level as far as action flicks go."

I never went to movies alone, but that night I bought my popcorn supper on the way in and found a seat not too far back from the big screen. Kevin was right. It was over the top with fast-paced action and violence. It was set in the near future after a major eco-disaster. Modern day pirates roamed the landscape in oversized death machines cobbled together from salvaged parts, looking for the limited supplies of gasoline left on the earth. It was a foretelling of the apocalypse that would result from our degradation of the earth and destruction of the environment. As absurd as that all seemed, it suited my mood.

My life wasn't post-apocalyptic, but I was feeling the end of the idyllic life I'd created. A solitary existence had never been my choice. In fact, I was at loose ends without people around me. I was plenty busy every weekday, and Judy and I spent most Friday and Saturday nights together. I still had lots of evening meetings and generally got together with Steve Krinsky for dinner at our favorite tavern in Bloomfield once a week.

When I cleaned out the last of my "treasures" from the garage and gave away my '51 Dodge pickup to a friend of Larry Looker's, the decade was officially over. It wasn't easy to walk away from my creation—the oversized derelict from another century that now had a new lease on life—and assign to the history books the amazing incubator that the house had been for all of us and our organizing work. But the potential of a well-staffed Tenant Resource Center and an invigorated NJTO had already filled my head and flooded my imagination.

I often think about the value of having a physical center where ideas and dreams take shape and are held. The Victorian house on Chestnut Street was the hatchery where a vision evolved and where the people evolving it communed—to plan and work, to discuss and argue, to kick back and celebrate. But we outgrew that place. We were no longer just local and devoted to those two loveable siblings, East Orange and Orange. We had an office on Bloomfield Avenue in Montclair and one twenty miles north in Fort Lee, the birthplace of New Jersey's tenant movement. At *Shelterforce,* from our office on Main Street East Orange, we had initiated the National Tenants Union. The reach of our small group was so much greater now. So were our responsibilities.

I listed the house for sale, and a few weeks later a woman with eight kids and an FHA loan, who worked at East Orange General Hospital two blocks away, saw it. The next day she offered the asking price—thirty-five thousand. She loved the house and her family would fill every inch.

I paid off the mortgages, and now that I had a "real" job I went shopping for a new car, one that suited my station in county government.

Detroit automakers were feeling the onslaught of reliable, affordable, front-wheel-drive Japanese imports, so they launched their X-car models. Feeling loyal to my Motor City roots, I bought a front-wheel drive Chevy Citation. Back in the day, my dad railed against the Ford workers who parked their Chevys in the lot at the Ford Rouge plant. GM was Ford's biggest competitor. Now it was the Japanese plus all those little Volkswagens.

I moved across town to share a big house owned by Stu Ball and Sara Mastellone. Craig Livingston and Linda Larkin lived there at the time. Stu and Sara's was the perfect landing spot. We all shared the shopping, cooking, and cleaning and made sure not to miss the weekly episode of *M.A.S.H.* on TV. They appreciated a housemate who loved to cook Chinese food and could handle house repairs. Soon we had another housemate, baby Kristina, who I loved most of all.

That year when the 1980 census was taken, East Orange's Black population had increased to 84% from 53% ten years earlier. The total population decreased by 7%, the result of apartment abandonment, I guess. That was a dismal sign in a city that was 75% tenant. In Orange, the Black population was now 66%, up from 36% in ten years.

• • •

We'd made a commitment to Orange and East Orange, but our horizons were broadening. Phyllis was still president of EOTA, but she now had statewide responsibilities and big ambitions as president of NJTO. She was determined to make it into the most powerful statewide tenant organization in the country. I was still living in East Orange and heading up the Tenant Resource Center. We provided help to EOTA. That job mainly fell to Jackie, who worked under me. I was working with an expanding group of tenant leaders and organizations across the county, but I still had a deep love for the Oranges and was determined to stick around.

Joan Pransky was in demand as the foremost tenant attorney in the state. She was already training young lawyers at the Rutgers Urban Legal Clinic and taking on precedent-setting cases. Her love for powerless tenants and her disgust over greedy landlords and real estate developers would fuel her passion for decades.

John remained a *Shelterforce* author and was becoming a national voice for the tenants movement and our brand of left-wing activism. He became the executive director of Passaic County Legal Aid in Paterson and remained an NJTO vice president. Despite these achievements, he was still chafing under the realization of how powerless we *really* were, and he began discussions with other single-issue groups, making plans for that multi-issue statewide coalition.

Meanwhile, Mary Tasker was getting settled in multi-racial and cosmopolitan Montclair and continued her college education while Simon and Michael continued theirs in the academically strong and integrated Montclair schools. Woody worked for EOTA, was the *Shelterforce* editor, and the coordinator for the National Tenants Union.

Ronnie's death left a big hole in all of our hearts. I wish he could have seen the results of what he set in motion and guide us through the next chapter. Nonetheless, the work we shared in that big house, the love that bound us, would all live on. Of that I felt certain.

(201) 744-4042

PATRICK MORRISSY
HOUSING SERVICES COORDINATOR

RONALD B. ATLAS TENANT RESOURCE CENTER
358 BLOOMFIELD AVENUE
MONTCLAIR, NEW JERSEY 07042

I loved campaigning.

The Next Few Years...

On May 22, 1980, County Executive Peter Shapiro dedicated the storefront office with a staff of five to Ronnie's memory, officially naming it the Essex County Ronald. B. Atlas Tenant Resource Center.

After six years in county government, running the Tenant Resource Center, I took a leap and mounted a grassroots campaign for a seat in the state General Assembly representing Orange, East Orange, West Orange, and South Orange. I enjoyed campaigning, and my campaign generated a lot of enthusiasm - from the poor tenants in East Orange to the liberals in South Orange. Michael Harrington spoke at one of my fundraisers. But I got defeated in the Democratic Primary in this solid Democratic district.

Losing was tough, but I tapped into the energy from my campaign to create a community development corporation called HANDS, led by a group of clergy and community leaders. Our goal was not modest—to help save the neighborhoods of Orange and East Orange. I had truly found my groove and spent the rest of my career running HANDS. We stabilized neighborhoods, rehabbing and building more than two hundred homes for sale to families who were otherwise priced out of the homebuying market. By ridding some of the toughest neighborhoods of problem properties and fostering homeownership, we created neighborhood stability, which is what HANDS became known for. Then we redeveloped contaminated industrial sites as affordable housing and as commercial space for small businesses.

NJTO — Phyllis, John, and Joan Pransky led a strong board of tenant leaders from around the state who together grew the membership and the influence of the NJTO. Within a couple years, NJTO became the most powerful statewide tenant organization in the country. I continued as *NJTOnews* editor, along with Steve Krinsky.

Statewide Progressive Coalition — In 1981, John Atlas brought together single-issue organizations—tenants, civil rights, labor, women, environmentalists, seniors—to form NJ Public Interest Political Action Committee. The following year, we were all co-founders of New Jersey Citizen Action (NJCA), which grew into a powerful coalition of over eighty organizations. When Phyllis retired as NJCA's executive director in 2023, the coalition had an annual budget of over $3 million and an impressive track record of political victories on behalf of poor and working people.

66-68 Lenox Avenue — The six remaining families and three of the families displaced by the fire formed a cooperative and acquired the building from the city for $7,500. Marty and Sal pulled together the rest of the financing and the six fire-damaged apartments were renovated first. By 1981, the co-op was fully occupied. Marty, Joan, and Jackie continued to manage it.

Shelterforce — The publication that started in the parlor of 31 Chestnut is still published today. It's known as the *Original Voice of Community Development*. During the eighties, we reported on two important figures, one we idolized, the other we demonized: Bernie Sanders, mayor of Burlington Vermont was our favorite elected official, and our dirty dog whipping boy was Donald Trump, with real estate holdings in New York and New Jersey.

The National Tenants Union — NTU continued for a few years to bring together tenant leaders from around the country and held annual conferences in DC, Santa Monica, New York, and Detroit. But tenant rights' work was inherently local and governed by state law, and NTU never gained enough traction to be a force at the national level.

Peter Shapiro — The young County Executive won re-election in 1982 and then won the Democratic Primary for governor in 1985 but lost that November to the popular liberal Republican incumbent Tom Kean. Exit polling indicated he'd likely be the next governor. But Shapiro was defeated for a third term as County Executive in 1986, when the Republican party gave their ballot line over to Nick Amato, a Democrat, and the old Democratic Machine organized to elect Amato and take back control of Essex County government. Shapiro's political career was over.

Sheriff John Cryan — The popular Irish Sheriff and Harry Lerner were indicted on corruption charges when the FBI found large amounts of cash in Cryan's office safe. Cryan lost his re-election bid in 1979. In 1980, due to defects in the way the charges had been drawn, the case against Cryan and Lerner was dismissed.

Judge Albano — In 1980, after seven years on the bench, the anti-tenant jurist was due to be permanently appointed and we lobbied the governor. Governor Byrne let Albano's term expire. We believe it was our public action and Pat Thornton's official complaint against Albano that brought him down.

Brick Church Urban Renewal Project — In 1980, the City Council voided the contract with Ericson, Mayor Cooke's chosen developer when it was revealed that the developer was $10 million in debt and had no liquid assets. In the next few years, one ambitious plan after another was unveiled—with hotels, convention centers, office towers, and department stores. Developers came and went. Finally in 1987, twenty years after the federal funds were awarded, a fifty-thousand square foot Shop-Rite supermarket was built along with a low-cost clothing retailer, two services badly needed by East Orange's residents. News articles still mentioned later phases that would include the hotel and convention center, even a heliport.

Peter Shuchter — After working as Shapiro's head of Constituent Affairs for eight years, Shuchter became the Political Director of New Jersey Citizen Action.

Marsha Ferber — After leaving the Mudd Farm, Marsha owned a communal house in Morgantown that she named Earth House and a bar/music venue called The Underground Railroad. The bar was a destination for indie bands from all over. Marsha's ventures were underwritten by her substantial marijuana business. In 1988, Marsha disappeared and was never heard from.

Liz McAlister — Sister Liz served jail time from 2018 to 2020 for her nuclear weapons civil disobedience at a Georgia nuclear weapons naval base. She spent more than four years of her life behind bars for acts of civil resistance against war and nuclear proliferation.

Bill Brach — The liberal stalwart we publicly criticized in the seventies became an ally and a friend. Bill and I teamed up to do housing advocacy, and he helped John and I raise funds for *Shelterforce*.

California Rent Control — In 1980, the California real estate industry sponsored a statewide ballot Initiative to ban local rent control laws. The tenants' movement led by CHAIN formed a coalition of labor unions, senior citizen groups, and community organizations and defeated the measure, getting 59% of the vote. The tenants were outspent by the real estate industry 3:1 but the tenants were able to combat the real estate industry spending on TV ads by taking advantage of free air-time under the Fairness Doctrine, which mandated equal time to both sides in political advertising.

Community Reinvestment — The federal law that required banks to make loans in areas where they took deposits had little meaning until banks started merging across state lines in 1986. John, Phyllis, and I represented Citizen Action in coalition with community groups to force banks to the negotiating table and sign Community Reinvestment Agreements that pledged low-cost loans to buyers in low-income communities and loans to nonprofit community developers.

Receivership — I wanted the county to help buildings like Jackie Cooke's. Bob Westreich, an attorney on the County Counsel's staff, suggested we develop a Housing Receivership Program. Shapiro supported our idea and gave us the go-ahead to ask the state Department of Community Affairs (DCA) to provide $175,000 in operating funds. Governor Kean's Commissioner of DCA was John Renna, a major landlord from Essex County, and he immediately rejected our proposal. Shapiro went to bat for us and convinced Renna to fund us.

Democratic Party —The loudest voices inside and just outside the Democratic Party were those championing civil rights, save the earth, equal rights for women and the gay community. Affordable housing, better wages, safer working conditions—issues that struck at working peoples' pocketbooks—those voices weren't being heard as clearly. The Democratic Party was changing.

My wonderful family, 1994.

Acknowledgements

This work began as a group discussion about the past with friends and comrades who I've known for fifty years—John Atlas, Joan and Marty Bierbaum, Phyllis Salowe-Kaye, Joan Pransky, and Mary Tasker. I hope I've done them proud with my version of our combined story.

Pat Curry has been my writing partner and my close Colorado friend since before I started this project. Together, we embarked on a journey to become writers, and he's read nearly every word I've written in the last five years. I am deeply grateful for his help, his insightful critique and his generosity.

The incomparable Catherine Willis graciously organized a long luncheon that included some elected officials from the old days—Tom Giblin, Bill Holt, Harold Karns, Claude Craig, and Mark Scotland.

I wish I could have spent more time with Marty Bierbaum, Peter Shapiro, and Norm Fruchter, who were so helpful, and all passed away during the writing of this book.

To my wife, Jeanie, who not only patiently tolerated a novice writer parked at the dining room table but encouraged him to tell his story. I love you, Jeanie.

To our three kids—Campbell, Claire, and Tim, who read early drafts and gave me such valuable advice and suggestions—this book is for you. And for my "niece," Michaela Copeland.

I loved working with Kayla Henley, my insightful editor who gave sound direction to my wandering narrative and cleaned up my sloppy writing.

To all of you who spent time with me and dug back into your memories, I am so grateful. Jeff Armistead, Joanne Atlas, Linda Barucky, my sister Marie Biondo, Steve Block, Michael Bodaken, Heather Booth, Ruthi Byrne, Michelle Cahill, Joe DellaFave, Becky Doggett, Barbara Hauke, Karen Hiller, Mitch Kahn, Steve Krinsky, Dick and Lois LaFond, Gracie Mansion, Marianne Nelson, Carole Norris, Marty Parker, Mike Rawson, my cousin Maureen Reed, Esther Ross, Mark Seglin, Joel Shain, Matt Shapiro, Eric Sherzer, Diane Sterner, Mary Tasker, James Tarella, Steve Tomczyk, Michael Whitty, Woody Widrow, Jackie Yustein.

Carbondale Writers Group, Anya Yuchyshyn and Denise Moss critiqued and encouraged me. I learned plenty from the Aspen Writers Network.

The cover photo was taken by Freda Jaffe fifty years ago.

The staff at East Orange Library and Newark Public Library were so helpful, as were Andre Virgil and Justin Brown in East Orange City Hall and Rudolph Drakeford, the head of the Historical Society of East Orange.

Selected Bibliography

Atlas, John. *Seeds of Change: The Story of ACORN, America's Most Controversial Antipoverty Community Organizing Group*. Nashville, Tennessee: Vanderbilt University Press, 2010.

Atlas, John. "The Rise and Fall of The National Tenants Union." *Shelterforce*, November 22, 2022.

Baar, Kenneth K. "Rent Control in the 1970's: The Case of the New Jersey Tenants' Movement." *Hastings Law Journal* 28, no. 3 (1977).

Boyte, Harry, Heather Booth, and Steve Max. *Citizen Action and the New American Populism*. Philadelphia, Pennsylvania: Temple University Press, 1986.

Curvin, Robert. *Inside Newark: Decline, Rebellion, and the Search for Transformation*. New Brunswick, New Jersey: Rutgers University Press, 2014.

Goodwyn, Lawrence. *Democratic Promise: The Populist Movement in America*. Oxford, England: Oxford University Press, 1976.

Leonhardt, David. *Ours Was the Shining Future: The Story of the American Dream*. New York, Random House, 2023

Rogers, Mary Beth. *Cold Anger: A Story of Faith and Power Politics*. Denton, Texas: University of North Texas Press, 1990.

Thompson, Ernest, and Mindy Thompson Fullilove. *Homeboy Came to Orange: A Story of People's Power*. Newark, New Jersey: Bridgebuilder Press, 1976.

About the Author

Patrick Morrissy is retired from a forty-six-year career in community development, working to stabilize and revitalize urban neighborhoods. He now lives in Carbondale, Colorado with his wife Jean Campbell, where he's still working politically to reclaim America for working people who've been left behind by an economy governed by the rich and powerful.

Made in the USA
Middletown, DE
18 April 2025